ABSTRACTS
of
NEW HANOVER COUNTY
NORTH CAROLINA
DEEDS

- 1789-1793 -

(Volume #4)

Compiled by:
Dr. A.B. Pruitt

Southern Historical Press, Inc.
Greenville, South Carolina

This volume was reproduced
from a personal copy located in
the Publishers private library

Please direct all correspondence and book orders to:
www.southernhistoricalpress.com
or
SOUTHERN HISTORICAL PRESS, Inc.
1071 Park West Blvd.
Greenville, SC   29611

Southernhistoricalpress@gmail.com

Introduction

This book contains abstracts of deeds in New Hanover County, NC, deed books I & K.   Book I (1789-1791) and book K (1791-1793) are on microfilm roll C070.40004 in the North Carolina Archives. All these books are recopied from the original books.   On film after the first copy of book I is a transcript made between Jul. 3 & Aug. 13, 1851.   The grantor & grantee indexes mention the page numbers in the transcription and those page numbers are mentioned first at the end of each abstract followed by a second page number [in brackets] which is the page number in the first copy of book I.   All but 3 or 4 deeds are in the same order in each copy.

New Hanover County was formed in 1729 from Craven County. All or part of the following counties were formed from New Hanover County: Onslow in 1734, Bladen in 1734, Duplin in 1750, Brunswick in 1764, and Pender in 1875.   In addition, parts of New Hanover County were annexed to Brunswick and Sampson Counties between 1788 and 1872.   Among early records in New Hanover County which have bee published are: court minutes 1738-1769 and 1771-1800 by Alexander McD. Walker; land grants, wills, 1850 census, & deed books A & B by Mae B Graves; Wilmington newspapers 1765-1775 and 1788-1816 by Raymond P Fouts; early Wilmington and early New Hanover County records by Elizabeth F McKoy; Wilmington town book by Donald R Lennon and Ida B Kellam; 1830, 1860, 1880, & 1890 census, taxes for 1815, 1835, 1836, 1845, 1885, & 1890, & marriage licenses by Delmas D Haskett; newspapers (4 volumes) by Helen M Sammons; newspapers (9 volumes), cemetery records (8 volumes), & church records (3 volumes) available through the Old New Hanover Genealogical Society; deed books C-H by A B Pruitt.

Please note: a marriage agreements are in book I p. 31 & 49 and book K p. 40, 152, & 455; land in Bladen County is in book I p. 6 & 213 and book K p. 36 & 254; land in Brunswick County is in book I p. 208, 282, 283, & 330 and book K p. 8, 11, 87, & 118; land in Cumberland County is in book K p. 133; lot in town of Brunswick is in book K p. 85; lot in Fayetteville is in book I p. 343 & 346; land in Onslow County is in book I p. 306 & 307; freeing a slave is in book I p. 173, 271, 323, & 324; description of house being built is in book I p. 264; sale of land for light house on Bald (or Smith) Head Island is in book I p. 262; sale of the distillery land is in book K p. 63 & 223; a marriage in New Hampshire is mentioned in book K p. 77; land warrant in Tennessee is in book K p. 112; a very long power of attorney is in book K p. 258; a tar house in Wilmington is in book K p. 289; sale of a "pew lot" in church is in book K p. 370; confiscated land is mentioned in items 2420, 2422, 2426, 2427, 2877, 2929, & 2958.

Following is the format of the abstracts in this book:
1. A number is assigned to each deed.   This number is used in the index of this book.   Following this number and in parenthesis is the number of

the deed which appears in the deed book.
2. Following these numbers is the date, when mentioned in the deed.
3. Next is the name (or names) of the grantor (seller) followed by his county of residence, when indicated. The county in is North Carolina unless noted otherwise.
4. Following the word "to" is the name (or names) of grantee (or buyer) followed by his county of residence, when indicated <u>and</u> when it differs from the residence of the grantor. The word "same" indicates the grantee's residence is the same as the grantor's.
5. Following a semicolon and the work "for" is the amount of the "consideration" in dollars, pounds, Spanish dollars, English pounds sterling, etc. Deeds of gift don't mention the exchange of money; for these deeds after "for" are words such as "love and affection".
6. Following the word "sold" or "mortgaged" is the amount of land. For deeds of gift "gave" replaces "sold". When the amount of land isn't indicated in the deed, "omitted" appears in the abstract unless the land area could be simply calculated from the metes and bounds.
7. The water course--creek, river, fork, branch, etc--is mentioned next. In the deeds "on" the creek usually means the land actually abuts the creek. But "on the waters" of the creek may indicate the land is near but not on the creek. All the land is in New Hanover County unless noted otherwise.
8. Following a semicolon and the word "border" are the names of adjoining land holders, buildings, or unusual natural features mentioned in the metes and bounds. Also mentioned are such things as improvements, barns, mills, etc, when they are mentioned in the deed.
9. Next is the title chain, when given, beginning with the grant and continuing (when possible) to the grantor of the deed.
10. Following "(signed)" is the spelling or mark made by the grantor(s). Unusual marks are added by hand. Please note the "signature" in the deed book is really a copy (made by a clerk) of the original signature on the original deed. Also note: an "X" written at an angle may look like a "+" in the book; so these two marks may be the same mark.
11. Following "witness" are the names of the witnesses to the sale. The word "jurat" follows the witness who proved the deed in court; "acknowledged" indicates the grantor proved the deed in court, & "recorded indicates the clerk didn't indicate who proved the deed.

      The map which follows this introduction is included to help the reader locate the waterways mentioned most frequently in the index. The creek locations are not meant to be exact. More complete and accurate maps of the counties can b obtained from the North Carolina Department of Transportation (highway maps), Department of Water Resources (maps grouped by major river basins), a book of county maps (from Puetz place, Lyndon Station, WI), or a book of county maps (from DeLorme, Box 298-6900, Freeport, ME 04032). Following the county map are maps for Wilmington and Brunswick. Some lots in Wilmington may have originally included an entire city block. But the blocks were subdivided at least by the 1760s into to five or six lots as shown on plat by R Harley in 1786.   Sometimes lot numbers North of Market Street were followed by "A"; lot numbers South of Market Street were sometimes followed by "B". The lot numbers weren't always mentioned in deeds.   Lots were 330 feet {East to West} and 66 feet (North to South) except for lots 56-60 on Orange Street which were 33 feet wide; Market & Third Streets were 99 feet wide, and other streets were 66 feet wide.   In 1785 a plat was made which added Surry Street.   There was a major revision of lot numbering in 1855 as shown on a plat in 1856 by L C Turner.   More details about the lot owners in Wilmington are found in Mrs. McKoy's book on Early Wilmington.   Only one plat was recorded in the book.   Following plat of Wilmington is a plat for the town of South Washington.

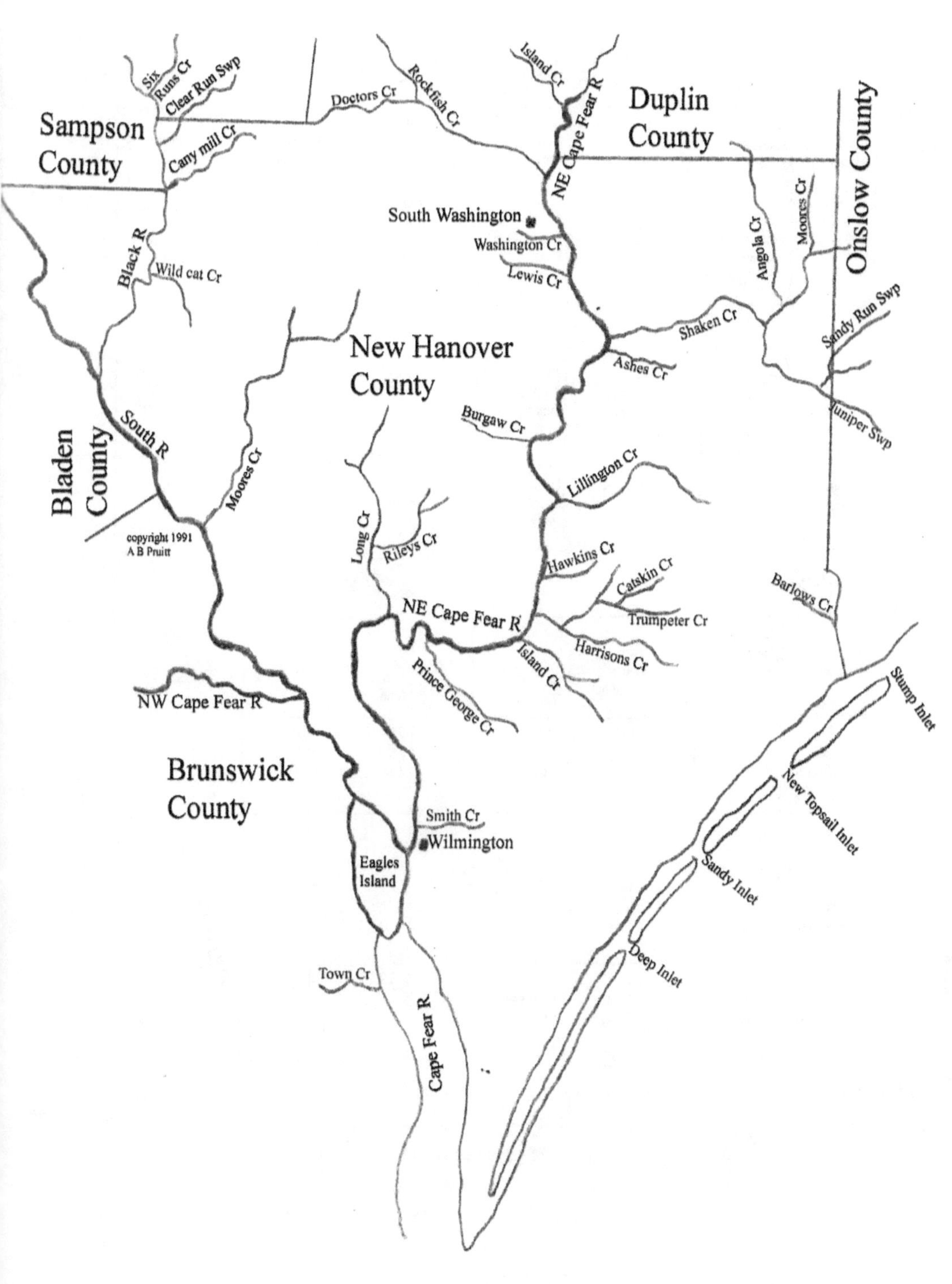

Sampson County
Duplin County
Onslow County
Bladen County
New Hanover County
Brunswick County
Six Runs Cr
Clear Run Swp
Cany mill Cr
Doctors Cr
Rockfish Cr
Island Cr
NE Cape Fear R
South Washington
Washington Cr
Lewis Cr
Moores Cr
Angola Cr
Black R
Wild cat Cr
Shaken Cr
Sandy Run Swp
Ashes Cr
South R
Burgaw Cr
Juniper Swp
Moores Cr
Lillington Cr
copyright 1991
A B Pruitt
Long Cr
Rileys Cr
Hawkins Cr
Catskin Cr
Trumpeter Cr
Barlows Cr
NE Cape Fear R
Island Cr
Harrisons Cr
Prince George Cr
Stump Inlet
NW Cape Fear R
New Topsail Inlet
Smith Cr
Sandy Inlet
Wilmington
Eagles Island
Deep Inlet
Town Cr
Cape Fear R

South Washington

N

Cape Fear River

Front Street

Second Street

Third Street

Fourth Street

Fifth (or Back) Street

Red Cross Street

Walnut Street

Mulberry Street

Chesnut Street

Princess Street

Market Street

Dock Street

northern part of Wilmington

A = Town hall; B = Episcopal church; C = Court house; D - Academy; E = St. John's Church; G = Methodist church; I = Market; K = Jail; L = Custom house; M = Cape Fear Bank; N = State Bank; lLots 66 feet by 330 feet. Market and Third Streets 99 feet wide, all other streets 66 feet wide.

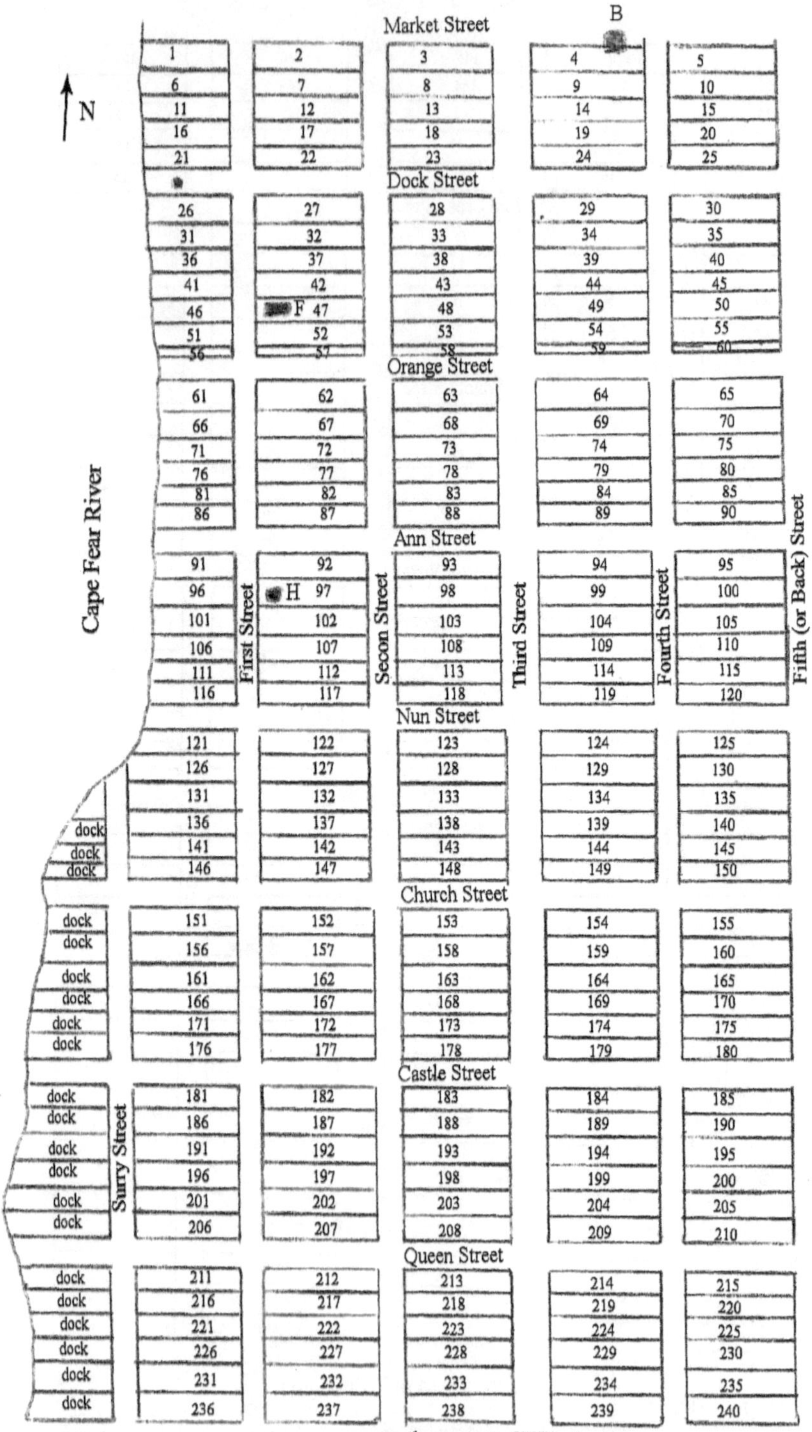

southern part of Wilmington

B = Episcopal church; F = Presbyterian church; H = Baptist church; lots 66 by 330 feet; Market & Third Streets 99 feet wide, other streets 66 feet wide

Book I

2344. Oct. 13, 1788 William Blount & wife Mary (Greenville, NC) to Alexander Hostler (Wilmington, NC); for £250 sold part of a lot [no number] in Wilmington on S side of Dock Street; border: begins at E corner of lot sold by Samuel Marshall & wife Mary to Mary Grainger on Dock Street, runs 50 feet on Dock Street, & 66 feet "at angles" with Dock Street to Mr. Maclain's lot. (signed) Wm Blount & Mary Blount; (witness) Rd Blackledge & Tho Blount; wit. oath Nov. 26, 1788 by Richd Blackledge before Sam Ashe, JSC; Jan. 13, 1789 recorded; book I p. 1 [1].

2345. Oct. 13, 1788 Mary Grainger (Greenville, Pitt Co, NC) to Alexander Hostler (Wilmington, New Hanover Co); for £400 sold part of lot [no number] in Wilmington on S side of Dock Street; border: begins at E corner of lot owned by estate of Mrs. Alice Marsden deceased, runs 30 feet on Dock Street, & 66 feet back. (signed) Mary Grainger; (witness) Rd Blackledge & Tho Blount; [note at end indicates Hostler paid Mary £400]; wit. oath Nov. 6, 1788 by Richard Blackledge before Sam Ashe, JSC; Jan. 13, 1789 recorded; book I p. 2 [2].

2346. Nov. 6, 1778 Charles Hollinsworth, planter (New Hanover Co) to Norman Harrison Chevers & David Forbes, merchants (Wilmington, NC); for £750 NC money sold 2 tracts: (a) 390 ac on New Topsail Sound; border: begins at John Simpson's corner stake "in" the sound; part of 500 ac granted May 4, 1728 by Lords Proprietor to Richard Nixon who willed it Mar. 5, 1745/6 to his daughter Mary who married Francis Mackilwean and sold Feb. 4, 1764 by Francis Mackilwean & wife Mary to Charles Hollinsworth; & (b) 150 ac in the fork between Blossoms Br & Canarys Br; border: begins at a pine on SE side of Canarys Br opposite Crany Gallberry "about" 5 miles from New Topsail Sound, joins Stokeley Bishop, & Blossoms Br; granted Sept. 26, 1766 by King George III to Charles Hollinsworth. (signed) Charles "Hollinsgsworth"; (witness) Thos Tzenn [or Fzerr]; [note at end indicates Chevers & Forbes paid Hollingsworth £750]; dower renounced Nov. 6, 1778 by Mary Hollingsworth, wife of Charles, before James "Buges" & Thos Fzer (signed) Mary Hollingsworth & C Hollingsworth (sic); wit. oath Jun. 2, 1779 by James Burges; Jan. 17, 1789 registered; book I p. 3 [4].

2347. May 14, 1787 John Ashe & Sam Ashe esq (New Hanover Co) to S Erickson, merchant; for £500 sold 500 ac in Bladen Co; border: begins at a sweet gum on W side of Alligator [Cr ?]. (signed) John Ashe & Saml Ashe; (witness) Sampson Mosely & Edward Wood; wit. oath Jul. 1788 by Sampson Mosely; Jan. 27, 1789 recorded; book I p. 6 [7].

2348. Mar. 12, 1788 John Rutherford (NC), by his attorney Archibald Maclaine, to George Mackenzie esq (Brunswick Co, NC); on dated Oct. 17 "last" for £0.5 John Rutherford agreed to deliver to George Mackenzie in Jan. "next" John's share or a third of Negroes in estates of Mrs. Jean Corbin deceased & Mrs. Frances Rutherford deceased, mother of John Rutherford; George agreed to pay John £40 sterling Great Britain money for each slave "to be paid in Kingdom of Great

Britain" in 3 equal payments: (a) a third on Jan. 1, 1789, (b) a third on Jan. 1, 1790, & (c) a third on Jan. 1, 1791 with interest from Jan. 1, 1788; to secure payment, George agreed to mortgage the slaves to John; a division of the slaves was made and John received a third or 24 and they were delivered to George; SO for £960 Great Britain money or £40 for each slave sold Nanny, Gray, James, Cumberland, Qua, Fanny, Joe, Quamina, Minga, Toney, Katy, Virgil, Tamar, Quash, Rachael & her child, Jack, Joe, Sarah, Dinah, Violet, Peter, Peg, Jemmy, & Hylas & increase of female slaves. (signed) John Rutherford, by A Maclaine; (witness) John Maclellan & Jos G Wright; wit. oath Jul. 1789 by J G Wright; book I p. 7 [8].

2349. Oct. 17, 1787 John Rutherford esq (NC) to George Mackenzie (or McKenzie) esq (Brunswick Co, NC); an agreement with bond of £2,000 sterling Great Britain money: for £0.5 John agrees to deliver in Jan. "next" his share or third of Negroes in estate of Mrs. Jane Corbin deceased & Mrs. Frances Rutherford deceased, mother of John; George agrees to pay John £40 sterling Great Britain money for each slave "to be paid in Kingdom of Great Britain" in 3 equal payments: (a) a third on Jan. 1, 1789, (b) a third on Jan. 1, 1790, & (c) a third on Jan. 1, 1791 with interest from Jan. 1, 1788; to secure payment, George agreed to mortgage the slaves to John; if any of the slaves has a child between now & date delivered, then the children are George's property free of any cost; if any accident prevents delivery, then a further credit of 1, 2, & 3 years is to be given from delivery date. (signed) John Rutherford; (witness) L McPherson & R Bradley; wit. oath Jul. 1789 by R Bradley; book I p. 9 [10].

2350. [blank] "7788" [or Jun. 1, 1788] John Wilkinson, gentleman (New Hanover Co), legatee of William Wilkinson esq, to Robert Scott, merchant (Wilmington, NC); fir £100 NC money sold [omitted] ac in Brunswick Co on Eagles Island opposite Wilmington; border: joined on S by a small creek which is boundary of land that was owned by Richard Eagle deceased, on N by a "square" acre formerly owned by John Rutherfurd deceased, on E by the river, & runs W back from the river [no more description]; part of 640 ac sold by John Watson, original grantee, to Michael Higgans [or Higgens] who sold Oct. 20, 1740 to Robert Walker deceased and sold Apr. 20, 1765 by Ann Walker, executrix of Robert Walker's will, to Wm Purviance deceased who sold Dec. 18, 1767 to William Wilkinson. (signed) John Wilkinson; (witness) Geo Hooper & Thos Wright; [note at end indicates Scot paid Wilkinson £100]; wit. oath Jul. 1788 by Tho Wright; book I p. 9 [11].

2351. Jul. 9, 1788 Rebecca Green to Henry Toomer; for £45 NC money sold my claim to Negroes in estate of Woodman Bishop deceased or a sixth of the Negroes. (signed) Rebecca Green; (witness) Wm Nutt [no more description]; wit. oath Jul. 1788 by Wm Nutt; Feb. 1, 1789 recorded; book I p. 11 [13].

2352. Jan. 29, 1788 Hannah Green (New Hanover Co) to my daughter Julia [Green]; for £0.5 & natural loves & affection sold a Negro girl Peggy & her increase. (signed) Hannah Green; (witness) Peter Harris & William Green; wit. oath Jan. 1788 by William Green esq; Feb. 2, 1789 recorded; book I p. 12 [14].

2353. Jul. 7, 1788 Thomas Wright, sheriff (New Hanover Co) to William Green esq (same); for £200 NC money sold 640 ac on E side of Cape Fear R; border: begins at a cypress on "the" river; known as Bevis' Point; sold [blank], 1786 at New Hanover Co court house due to writ of fieri facias from New Hanover Co Pleas & Quarter Sessions Court returnable to court first Monday in Jul. 1786 for £172.8.3 damages & £2.3.9 costs against Doctor Samuel Green deceased, in hands of William Green administrator "with the will annexed", due to suit by Thomas Craike; land sold because no goods or chattels found. (signed) Tho Wright, sheriff; (witness) John Bradley & Thos Brown; [note at end indicates Green paid Wright £200]; Jul. 1788 acknowledged; Feb. 2, 1789 recorded; book 2 p. 12 [15].

2354. Jul. 7, 1788 Mary Hanson, "former" widow of John Campbell deceased (late of Wilmington, NC), and Mary Campbell & Rachael Campbell, 2 of daughters of John Campbell & all devisees of John Campbell, to Henry Toomer, merchant (Wilmington, NC); for £120 sold part of lot (no number) in Wilmington on N side of Market Street & W side of Third Street; border: begins at corner of Market Street & Third Street, 33 feet on Market Street, & 132 feet on Third Street; sold May 1, 1754 by Caleb Grainger & wife Mary to John Campbell who willed it to Mary Hanson, then Mary Campbell, Mary Campbell, & Rachael Campbell. (signed) Mary Hanson, "Rachel" Campbell, & Mary Campbell by A Maclaine her attorney; (witness) Jos G Wright [only one witness]; [note at end indicates Toomer paid the women £120]; wit. oath Jul. 1788 by J G Wright; Feb. 10, 1789 recorded; book I p. 16 [18].

2355. Jun. 26, 1788 Edward Chevers & his brother William Chevers and "with" their nephew George Chevers are heirs of Norman Harrison Chevers deceased (late of New Hanover Co) to John "Ablen" Campbell (same); for £242 NC money sold two-thirds of 390 ac on New Topsail Sound; border: begins at John Simpson's corner stake "in" the sound; part of 500 ac granted May 4, 1728 by Lords Proprietor to Richard Nixon who willed it Mar. 5, 1745/6 to his daughter Mary who married Francis "Meckelwean" and sold Feb. 4, 1764 by Francis & Mary Meckelwean to Charles Hollinsworth who sold Nov. 6, 1778 to Norman Harrison Chevers & David Forbes deceased who said Norman Harrison [Chevers] survived. (signed) William Chevers & Edward Chevers by his attorney Wm Chevers; (witness) Jos G Wright & A Maclaine; [note at end indicates Campbell paid Wm Chevers £242]; wit. oath Jul. 1788 by J G Wright; book I p. 17 [21].

2356. Jun. 26, 1788 John Ablen Campbell (New Hanover Co) first part, William Chevers, gentleman ("present" of Wilmington, NC) second part, & Archibald Maclaine, attorney ("same") third part; Campbell paid Chevers (sic) [amount blank] & £0.5 which Maclaine paid Campbell; SO Campbell sold to Chevers 2 tracts: (a) 150 ac between Blossoms Br & Canarys Br; border: begins at a pine on S side of Canary Br opposite Crany Galberry about 5 miles from New Topsail

Sound, joins Stokely Bishop, & Blossom Br; granted Sept. 26, 1766 to Charles Hollinsworth who sold NOv. 6, 1778 to Norman Harrison Chevers deceased & David Forbes deceased but N H Chevers was surviving joint tenant; & (b) an undivided third of 100 ac on N side of Blossom Cr; border: begins at a bay tree "in" Bay Br, joins Thomas Tyer, Charles Hollinsworth, & Stokley Bishop; sold Jan. 13, 1778 by Aaron Dixon to John Collins who sold Apr. 8, 1783 to Norman Harrison Chevers and a third descended to his nephew George Chevers, one of the 3 heirs of N H Chevers, and sold [date blank by George Chevers to J A Campbell; Maclaine can sell the land for as much as he can get. (signed) John A Campbell, William Chevers, & A Maclaine; (witness) Jos G Wright [only one witness]; [note at end indicates Chevers paid Campbell £15 and Maclaine paid Campbell £0.5]; wit. oath Jul. 1788 by J G Wright; Feb. 13, 1789 recorded; book I p. 19 [24].

2357. Apr. 28, 1788 John Ashe (New Hanover Co) to Samuel Ashe (same); for £175 sterling sold 2 Negroes Cato & Simon. (signed) John Ashe; (witness) Lee "DeKeyser"; wit. oath Jul. 1788 by L DeKeyser; Feb. 13, 1789 recorded; book I p. 22 [28].

2358. Oct. 13, 1787 Abraham Beesly [or Busly], planter (New Hanover Co) to Daniel Bourdeaux (same); for £130 NC money sold 164 ac in 2 adjoining tracts on Long Cr: (a) 160 ac; border: begins at second corner pine of the patent on E side of Long Cr & crosses Long Cr twice; being upper half a grant (no date) to Anthony Bourdeaux; except 11 ac that Beesly sold in 1783 to said Danl Bourdeaux for £11 specie; & (b) 15 ac; border: begins at a stake on Rolling Road opposite Abraham Beesly's house; sold in 1786 for £15 specie by Gibs Lamb to Abraham Beesly. (signed) Abraham Beesly; (witness) John Jones, John Bloodworth, & David Jones; wit. oath Jul. 1789 by John Jones "esquire"; Feb. 14, 1789 recorded; book I p. 22 [29].

2359. Jan. 10, 1788 Thomas Wright, high sheriff (New Hanover Co) to Duncan Stewart (Bladen Co, NC); for £82 sold 100 ac on South R; border: joins Bennet [or Robt] Smith & said Duncan Stewart's land formerly owned by William Stewart deceased; called "Oat" field; includes land sold by Bennet [or Robt] Smith to said Hainey; includes said Hainey's improvement; sold Jan. 10, 1788 due to an execution from Sampson Co court against John Hainey for £62.6.9 due to suit by Daniel Williams; land sold because no goods or chattels found; land sold to James Speller, attorney for said Stewart. (signed) Thos Wright, shff; (witness) John Hill & W H Hill; Jul. 1788 acknowledged; book I p. 24 [32].

2360.)Wilmington, NC) Apr. 8, 1788 Woney Maclamy [or MaClamy], planter (New Hanover Co) to Thomas Simmons, inn keeper (same); for [amount omitted] sold a Negro man Dublin about 35 years old. (signed) "Wonne" Maclamy; (witness) Morris Ward; [no wit. oath mentioned]; book I p. 26 [34].

2361. Apr. 5, 1788 John Morris, planter (New Hanover Co) to William Cutlar, gentleman; for £60 NC money sold [omitted] ac on Island Cr, a branch of NE River; border: begins at head of a small branch of Island Cr, joins Gregg's formerly Croker's land, crosses Island Cr, joins a savanna, point of a pocosin near main branch of Island Cr, a small pond, & Musquitoe Br; granted Apr. 13, 1780 by Gov. Richd Caswell to William Morris and at his death descended to his brother John Morris. (signed) John Morris' mark "X"; (witness) Hiram J Richards & Benjn. Liddon; [note at end indicates Cutlar paid Morris £60]; wit. oath Jul. 1788 by Benjn Liddon; book I p. 27 [35].

2362. "Jun. 1786" William Campbell & company to William Green; for £130 sold a Negro fellow Gabriel. (signed) Wm Campbell & co; [no witness]; Jul. 1788 acknowledged by John Bradley (sic); book I p. 28 [37].

2363. Sept. 6, 1786 James Morris to John Ablin Campbell; for £800 NC money sold 3 tracts: (a) 730 ac; border: begins at a great pine by Bear Cr on Topsail Sound, joins a great pond, W side of Mill "Creek branch", crosses Jumping Run, & Nichols; sold (no date) by James Morris to John Ablin Campbell; 520 ac is the manor "plantation" where James Morris lately lived "when I gave said Campbell possession"; willed to me by my grand father William Morris; (b) 110 ac; border: begins at a pine on New Topsail Cr, joins a branch, Thomas Nixon, mouth of another branch, Saw Pond, & William Morris; willed to me by my grand father William Morris and sold Jul. 8, 1747 by William Nichols to William Morris; & (c) 100 ac; border: joins "the" land on N side of "the" late "Peter McClammy esq", joins SW side of above land sold by William Nichols to William Morris; includes a grist mill; sold Jul. 9, 1785 by Thomas Maclammy to me for £340. (signed) James Morris; (witness) Robert Nixon & Will M Waca; wit. oath Jul. 1788 by Robt Nixon esq; book I p. 29 [38].

2364. Jul. 10, 1788 Thomas Wright, sheriff, to Edward Russell; for £6.2 sold right of John Nichols jr in [omitted] ac on "the" sound known as Tabby House; & (b) said Nichols' undivided right to a Negro fellow Johnny taken in an execution of a suit by the government against said Nichols for arrearages of taxes. (signed) Thos Wright, sheriff; [no witness]; Jul. 1788 acknowledged; book I p. 31 [41].

2365. Nov. 15, 1782 David Jones, widower (New Hanover Co) to Margaret Jones, widow of William Jones deceased (same); a marriage contract has been agreed on between David & Margaret: David agrees for Margaret to have full power to dispose of her estate, which she now owns, after the marriage and she can will it to anyone; if Margaret dies intestate or without disposing of her estate, then her estate descends to her heirs as if the marriage hadn't happened; David "disclaims" any interest in Margaret's estate. (signed) David Jones; (witness) Thos Bloodworth, James Larkins, & John Kennier; wit. oath Jul. 1788 by Jas Larkins; book I p. 31 [42].

2366. Jul. 1, 1788 Arthur Mabson (New Hanover Co) to Daniel Bourdeaux (same); for "valuable consideration" sold 2 young Negro girls Caroline & Doll.

(signed) Arthur Mabson; (witness) Aaron Messick [only one witness]; wit. oath Jul. 1788 by Aaron "Messck"; book I p. 32 [43].

2367. Mar. 9, 1788 James Malpus sr (New Hanover Co) to James "Fleeming", merchant (same); for £30 sold 2 tracts: (a) 100 ac on Cypress Br of Long Cr; border: begins at a black oak below "the old tract path", crosses Cypress [Br], & joins a small savanna; & (b) 200 ac on widow Moores Cr; border: begins at a small pine in a small marsh on E side of the creek, joins open woods, & crosses Bear den Br. (signed) John Malpus; (witness) John Williamson & Fras. Williamson; wit. oath Jul. 1788 by J Williamson; book I p. 33 [44].

2368. Nov. 18, 1773 Elizabeth Miller (Dobbs Co, NC) to my beloved children John Miller, Richard Miller, Anne Miller, Jean Miller, & Sarah Miller, children of my deceased husband John Miller; for natural love & affection gave all my interest in real & personal estate in the attached inventory dated today. (signed) Elizabeth Miller; (witness) Zenas Parker & Philomene Noble; [note at end:] a gray mare delivered in name of the "articles" mentioned in the inventory;
      Nov. [blank], 1773 inventory annexed to deed of gift from Elizabeth Miller: a "plantation" where I live, 2 beds, 2 ruggs, 3 sheets, 2 bolsters, a blanket, 2 bedsteads, 2 cords, 9 silver spoons, a pair of silver clasps, a Negro girl Sarah, 3 axes, an iron kettle, a gray mare, a black walnut table, a pine table, a tea kettle, 10 spoons, 2 iron potts, 4 ash chairs, a hand mill, a pewter bason, a pewter dish, 6 pewter plates, a trunk, a 500 "sta", 3 juggs, a stone crock, a butter pot, a spice morter & pestal, a pair of cotton cards, an iron trammel, a linnen wheel, a wollen wheel, a hand saw, a grindstone, a flat iron, a box iron, a pocket book, a glass pepper box (signed) Elizabeth Miller [same witnesses]; wit. oath Jul. 1788 by Richd Miller who believes "E Miller" is in handwriting of Elizabeth Miller; book I p. 34 [46].

2369. Jul. 10, 1788 William Hill to William Lamb; for £20 specie & £30 "in currency" sold a little Negro girl Rhina. (signed) "W H Hill"; (witness) Saml Buxton; Jul. 1788 acknowledged; book I p. 35 [48].

2370. May 11, 1788 Henry Cummings, constable (New Hanover Co) to (New Hanover Co) to William Miller (same); for £10 sold 100 ac on S side of 640 ac granted Feb. 4, 1773 to James Blythe; border: begins at a corner of 100 ac "lately" granted to Saml Swann sr being a line of "an old survey" by said Swann being southermost corner of said 640 ac and joins eastermost corner of 320 ac granted by said Swann; part of 640 ac sold by James Blythe to William Purviance now deceased and taken by execution in suit by Peter "Hewston" against said Purviance's estate and "warrant tried" before Maurice ward JP and execution issued with stay agreeable to law in such cases but now sold. (signed) Henry Cumming, constable; (witness) Edwd Jones & Anthy B Toomer; wit. oath Jul. 1788 by Edward Jones; Apr. 7, 1789 recorded; book I p. 36 [49].

2371. (Wilmington, NC) Jul. 10, 1788 John Cholwell to Henry Rooks; for £20 sold 2 feather bes, 3 tables, 3 pair of blankets, a tea kettle, a "duch" oven, a spider, 2 skillets, a pot rack, a bedstead, ten plates, 2 juggs, 2 earthen potts, an earthen kettle, 2 dishes, 3 delph pans & dishes, 5 cups & saucers, a sugar dish, a small bowl, a chest & trunk, 3 pails, 2 piggons, a chamber pot, a bedstead, 2 candle molds candlestick, 2 pair of snuffers, 6 knives & forks, 2 axes, 2 hatchets, 2 hammers, 2 hoes, a keg, & a pair of mill stones. (signed) John Cholwell; (witness) Joel Parish [only one witness]; wit. oath Jul. 1788 by Joel Parish; Apr. 22, 1789 recorded; book I p. 37 [51].

2372. Feb. 12, 1788 Thomas Jones (New Hanover Co) to Edward Jones, merchant; for £85 NC money sold a Negro boy Prince about 13 years old. (signed) Thos Jones; (witness) Patk Brennan [only one witness]; wit. oath Jul. 1788 by P Brennan; book I p. 38 [52].

2373. Jan. 27, 1788 John Wilkinson (New Hanover Co) to John Coleman (same); for £300 NC money sold part of lot #11 in Wilmington in Blackmore's Alley; border: 42.5 feet front & runs back 41 feet. (signed) Jno Wilkinson; (witness) J L Moran & Henry Rooks; [note at end indicates Coleman paid Wilkinson £300]; wit. oath Oct. 1788 by H Rooks; book I p. 38 [52].

2374. Nov. 12, 1788 Elizabeth Wimble (Boston, Suffolk Co, Massachusetts) widow of William Wimble mariner deceased (late of Boston), Rebecca Bass wife of Gillam Bass trader (Boston) late Rebecca Wimble & daughter of William, Catherine Marrisquell wife of Lewis Marrisquell (Dracut, Middlesex Co, Massachusetts) late Catherine Wimble daughter of William, & Elizabeth Bass (Boston) grand daughter of William to our trusty friend Gillam Bass, trader (Boston, Suffolk Co, Massachusetts); power of attorney to receive from anyone the money owed for land lately owned by William Wimble in Wilmington or elsewhere in North Carolina. (signed) Elizabeth Wimble, Rebecca Bass, Lewis "de" Marrisquell, Catherine "Maresquell", & Elizabeth Bass; (witness) Samuel Barrett & Patty S Barrett, witnesses to signing of Mrs. Wimble and Mrs. & Miss Bass, and Parker Varnum & Abigal Nanomd; (Boston, Suffolk Co) Nov. 12, 1788 acknowledged by Elizabeth Wimble, Rebecca Bass, & Elizabeth Bass before Samuel Barrett JP; (Middlesex) Nov. 17, 1788 acknowledged by Lewis de & Catherine Marrisquell before Parker Varnum JP; (Mass.) Dec. 2, 1788 Gov. John Hancock certifies Saml Barrett is justice in Boston & Parker Varnum is justice in Dracut (signed) John Hancock & John Avery jr, Secretary; (New Hanover Co) Jan. 1789 presented in court & ordered recorded; May 8, 1789 recorded; book I p. 39 [54].

2375. Feb. 10, 1789 Mary Harnett (New Hanover Co) to Sarah Issabella Purviance, daughter of late William Purviance (same); for £25 sold 100 ac on "the" sound; border: joined on W by George Stemire, on E by land of late William Purviance, on N by George Hooper & A Maclaine, & on S by a creek; Ezekiel Johnston lives on part of the land; formerly sold by William Dry to [omitted]. (signed) Mary Harnett; (witness) Alexander Hostler & James Moore; [note at end indicates Mary received £25 on the same day]; wit. oath Mar. 6, 1789 by James Moore before Judge Ashe; book I p. 42 [58].

2376. Jul. 19, 1788 John Thomson to Mrs. Margaret Hill; for £50 sold a Negro boy Hope. (signed) John Thomson; (witness) W H Hill [only one witness]; wit. oath Oct. 1788 by Wm Hill; book I p. 43 [59].

2377. Jun. 27, 1788 Edward Chevers & William Chevers, surviving brothers of George Chevers their nephew & heirs of Norman Harrison Chevers deceased (late of New Hanover Co) to Archibald Maclaine, attorney (Wilmington, NC); for £0.5 sold in trust their undivided two-thirds of 2 tracts: (a) 150 ac in the fork between Blossom Br & Canarys Br; border: begins at a pine on SE side of Canary Br opposite Crany Galberry about 5 miles from new Topsail Sound, joins Stokely Bishop, & Blossom Br; granted Sept. 26, 1766 to Charles Hollinsworth who sold Nov. 6, 1788 to Norman Harrison Chevers & David Forbes also deceased & N H Chevers is surviving joint tenant; & (b) 100 ac on N side of Blossom Br; border: begins at a bay tree "in" Bay Br, joins Thomas Tyer, Charles Hollinsworth, & Stokely Bishop; sold Jan. 10, 1778 by Aaron Dixon to John Collins who sold Apr. 8, 1783 to Norman Harrison Chevers; both tracts "lately" in public sale by Edward Chevers, William Chevers, & "the grantee" of said George Chevers to William Chevers (sic) for £45 NC money; Maclaine to try to sell the land for £30 or two-thirds of £45 with any excess going to William Chevers. (signed) William Chevers & Edward Chevers, by Wm Chevers his attorney; (witness) Jos G Wright [only one witness]; wit. oath Oct. 1788 by J G Wright; book I p. 43 [60].

2378. May 14, 1788 Edmund Moore, planter (New Hanover Co) to Jesse Rooks (same); for £40 NC money sold a Negro man Friday about 20 years old; sale void if Moore pays Rooks £40 NC money by Dec. 1 next. (signed) Edmd Moore; (witness) John Jones [only one witness]; [note at end indicates Rooks paid Moore £40 May 14, "178"]; [another note:] May 14, 1788 Moore has hired Negro man Friday from Rooks until Dec. 1 next for £0.40 (sic) and Moore is to find him cloth & pay his tax (signed) Edmd Moore (witness) John Jones; Dec. 22, 1788 received of Jesse Rooks £0.40 for hire of Negro Friday (signed) Jesse Rooks (sic); wit. oath Apr. 1789 by John Jones esq; book I p. 46 [64].

2379. Feb. 4, 1786 Thomas Loper, planter (New Hanover Co) to Oswell Sill, taylor (same); for £290 sold, due to court order, 320 ac on head of Bridgen Cr; border: begins at mouth of Yellow Spring Br of said creek, runs up "the" great Spring Br, up a small branch, joins Porters Neck Road, & Rous' back line. (signed) Thomas Loper's mark [script "T"] & Ann Loper (sic); (witness) Michael "Lober", Jno Stone, & "Sweet" Ashford; wit. oath Oct. 1788 by Michael Lober; Jun. 2, 1789 recorded; book I p. 47 [66].

2380. Apr. 22, 1788 Elizabeth Moore, widow ("at present" of Craven Co, NC) first part, John Hill esq (New Hanover Co) second part, & William Henry Hill esq (New Hanover Co) third part; a marriage is intended between W H Hill and

Elizabeth Moore; Elizabeth owns "considerable" personal estate principally slaves; W H Hill wants to secure part of the estate to Elizabeth's sole use; SO for £0.5 paid by John Hill to Elizabeth, Elizabeth with consent of W H Hill sold in trust following Negroes to John Hill: Quacas, Sinah, Bob, Hannah, Daniel, Austin, Polly, Abram, Bacchas, Fed, Betty, Sue, Harding, Catey, Tom, Burke, & Ned with increase of females; Elizabeth to receive profits from labor of the slaves but W H Hill can direct their labor after the marriage; after William & Elizabeth die, slaves go to any issue they have, but if not issue, then slaves go to survivor of William & Elizabeth. (signed) E Moore, John Hill, & W H Hill; (witness) M Nash & Thos Hill; wit. oath Oct. 1788 by Thos Hill; book I p. 49 [69].

2381. (Wilmington, NC) Dec. 5, 1788 Wm Hill to Alfred Moore esq; for £450 sold 4 Negroes: Quaco, Mary, Cupid, & Celia. (signed) W Hill; (witness) T Hill [only one witness]; Jun. 16, 1789 acknowledged; book I p. 51 [71].

2382. Nov. 21, 1788 James "Fleeming", merchant (Wilmington, NC) to George MacKenzie (Brunswick Co, NC); for £0.5 and for love & affection towards my child Annabella Fleeming & children of my dear wife: Henry Yonge, Christiana [Yonge], Elizabeth [Yonge], Claudia [Yonge], & William Campbell Yonge sold in trust following slaves: [men] Will, Scull, August, Quashie, Bob, & Hermes and women: Janie, Clhoe, Janie (sic) & their future increase; slaves sold for benefit of my child Annabella, said children of my wife, & any future children I may have by my wife. (signed) Jas Fleming; (witness) John Howell [only one witness]; wit. oath Jun. 13, 1789 by John Howell before Judge Ashe; Jun. 15, 1789; book I p. 51 [72].

2383. (Wilmington, NC) Jun. 8, 1789 Wm Hill to Alfred Moore esq; for £250 sold 2 Negro fellows: Scipio & Alick. (signed) W Hill; (witness) P Mallett [only one witness]; Jun. 16, 1789 acknowledged before Saml Spencer, JSCLE; book I p. 52 [73].

2384. Sept. 9, 1788 Margaret Hill, executrix of will of my husband William Hill esq deceased, to my son William Henry Hill; for a relinquishment made today by William Henry Hill to me for £2,234 "from my husband's estate" as his share sold (a) a moiety or half of "plantation" called "Forceput" on "the" river near Wilmington; land is divided by line beginning on the river at a small cypress notched opposite land of Joshua Grainger Wright, runs W to a large notched pine at edge of a bay at the foot & S side of a hill knows as John's Hill, runs due W until it is at right angles to back line of said tract, runs "thro" the high land; said dividing line is intended to be northern boundary of that part of the land intended to be sold; W H Hill gets land S of the dividing line; & (b) sold 12 Negroes: Any a wench & her children Balaam, Jack, Grace, Fed, & Bess, Dianna & her children Jupiter, Bella, & Dy, & 2 fellows Jim & Limping Balaam; & (c) sold Stephen Daniel's bond & mortgage, Maurice Moore's note, Jehu Davis' note. (signed) Margt. Hill; (witness) Tho Callender & John Hill; wit. oath Oct. 1788 by T Callender; book I p. 52 [73].

2385. Oct. 10, 1788 George Hooper, merchant (Wilmington, NC) to John Allen, carpenter (same); for £65 NC money sold part of lot #32B in Wilmington on N side of Princess Street; border: joined on W by part of same lot owned by William Campbell, S by Princess Street, E by part of same lot "agreed to be purchased" of George Hooper by William Gordan sadler, & N by lot #33 owned by William Campbell; western boundary is equal distant or 165 feet from Front Street & Second Street and width on Princess Street is 18 feet & running back 66 feet to lot #33. (signed) G Hooper; (witness) Will Hooper jr & Richard Watson; [note at end indicates Allen paid Hooper £65]; wit. oath Oct. 1788 by Richd Watson; book I p. 53 [75].

2386. (Wilmington, NC) May 29, 1788 Margaret Hill to James walker; for £150 sold Negro London. (signed) Margaret Hill; (witness) W H Hill [only one witness]; wit. oath Oct. 1788 by Wm Hill (sic); book I p. 56 [78].

2387. Oct. 29, 1787 Gov. Richard Caswell (Kingston, NC) to John Jones; grant #214; for £0.50 per 100 ac granted 50 ac on W side of Black R & W side of Buckle Swamp; border: begins at northermost line of "your" late survey 14 poles from the corner, joins Rowe, & crosses "Buckel" Br. (signed) Rd Caswell & W Williams, D Secretary; Jul. 7, 1789 recorded; book I p. 56 [79].

2388. Oct. 29, 1787 Gov. Richard Caswell (Kingston, NC) to John Filyaw; grant #210; for £0.50 per 100 ac granted 200 ac on NW side of NE Cape Fear R & both sides of Lewis Cr; border: begins at a hickory near Blackmon's line, crosses a branch, & joins said Filyaw. (signed) Rd Caswell & W Williams, D Secretary; Jul. 7, 1789 recorded; book I p. 57 [80].

2389. (Wilmington, NC) Jan. 8, 1789 Edward Jones, merchant (New Hanover Co) to Pettigrew Moore, planter; for £200 NC money sold a Negro woman Lucy about 25 years old of yellow complexion country born and a Negro girl Sukey, Lucy's daughter, about 5 years old yellow complexion. (signed) Edw. Jones; (witness) John Colvin [only one witness]; Jan. 1789 acknowledged; Jul. 8, 1789 recorded; book I p. 58 [81].

2390. Feb. 9, 1788 John Wilkinson (New Hanover Co) to Richard Rundle (same); for £3,000 NC money sold part of lot No.[blank] in Wilmington fronting on Front Street; border: 50 feet in front and runs back to low water mark of Cape Fear R. (signed) John Wilkinson; (witness) Jona. Robeson & Wm Ewans; [note at end indicates Rundle paid Wilkinson £3,000]; wit. oath Oct. 1789 by Wm Ewans; book I p. 58 [82].

2391. (Wilmington, NC) Jan. 18, 1788 Elenor Routledge to Charles Simpson; for l25 sold a Negro boy Doctor "until" I return him £25 when he will return the Negro boy to me. (signed) Elenor Routledge; (witness) David James [only one witness]; wit. oath Oct. 1788 (sic) by David James; book I p. 59 [83].

2392. Oct. 7, 1788 George McCulloch (New Hanover Co) to Alexander McCulloch; for £42 proclamation money sold 67 ac; border: begins at a cedar post on Barren Inlet Cr & joins the old patent line; part of 2,500 ac granted Jul. 15, 1725 to Saml Swann. (signed) Geo McCulloch; (witness) Dd Williams & Samuel Bunting; wit. oath Oct. 1788 by David Williams; book I p. 60 [84].

2393. (Wilmington, NC) Dec. 22, 1787 Robert Daniel to Mrs. Margaret Hill; for £70 sold a Negro girl Judy. (signed) Rt Daniel; (witness) W H Hill [only one witness]; wit. oath Oct. 1788 by W Hill; book I p. 61 [85].

2394. Jun. 17, 1786 Gibbs Lamb, planter (New Hanover Co) to Abraham Beesly (same); for £15 [14--lined out] specie sold 15 ac on Long Cr; border: begins at a stake on Rolling Road opposite Abraham Beesly's house where he lives. (signed) Gibbs Lamb's mark "X" & Margaret Lamb's mark "X" (sic); (witness) Richd Proby & Sarah Proby; wit. oath Oct. 1788 by Richard Proby; Jul. 11, 1789 recorded; book I p. 62 [86].

2395. [blank], 1786 William Wright (New Hanover Co) to Gibbs Lamb (same); for £100 sold 100 ac on W side of Horse [Cr ?]; border: begins at a pine on James Williams' line, joins a bay pond, upper edge of Kieth Savanna, & said William [Wright's] line; surveyed Sept. 30, 1786 by Wm Wright. (signed) Wm Wright; (witness) Richard Proby & Thomas Lamb; wit. oath Oct. 1788 by Richard Proby; book I p. 63 [88].

2396. May 29, 1788 (Wilmington, NC) May 29, 1788 James Walker to William Henry Hill; for £150 sold a Negro Jim [or Jem]. (signed) James Walker; (witness) Alexander Hostler [only one witness]; Oct. 1788 acknowledged; book I p. 65 [90].

2397. Nov. 23, 1785 Samuel Buxton, planter (NC) to James Smyth (NC); for £50 NC money sold 300 ac on E side of Black R; border: begins at a pine about 0.5 miles below the thorofare on the swamp side; known as Orrs thorofare; granted Mar. 22, 1771 by Gov. Josiah Martin to William Orr and sold by his heir Nathan Orr to Bryant Buxton who gave it to Samuel Buxton. (signed) Saml Buxton; (witness) Jacob Lewis & Abraham Lewis; wit. oath Oct. 1788 by Jacob Lewis; book I p. 65 [91].

2398. Jul. 2, 1787 John Magee, gentleman ("near" Wilmington, New Hanover Co) to William Fairer [or Fairor], planter (Duplin Co, NC); for £100 NC money sold 7 ac near Wilmington; border: begins at a stake in middle of run of Toomers mill Br on N edge of "the" main road. (signed) John Magee; (witness) Justus Miller & John "Farrior"; (Duplin Co, NC) Apr. 1788 acknowledged & wit. oath (New Hanover Co) Oct. 1788 by Justus "Mill"; book I p. 66 [92].

2399. Apr. 28, 1788 John Ashe esq (New Hanover Co) to Samuel Ashe, the younger esq (same); due to a marriage contract, John Ashe secured to his "now" wife Elisabeth about Oct. or Nov. 1783 all his real & personal estate reserving to himself the use & profits thereof for his natural life; about Mar. 20, 1783 Samuel Ashe became bound with John Ashe to Nathaniel Moore for £1,000 sterling Great Britain money conditioned on payment of a "clear" yearly annuity of £50 like money free from all deductions for natural life of Nathaniel Moore; there is now due from John to Samuel, including part of the annuity which has been paid by Samuel, £400 like money exclusive of 3 years of the annuity; SO to secure Samuel for £400 sterling & sums due on bond & annuity and for £0.5 NC money sold all land, Negro slaves, & increase of female slaves for natural life of John; Samuel to pay £0.1 yearly on Jan. 1 of each year to John if demanded with first payment due Jan. 1, 1789; Samuel to pay taxes due. (signed) John Ashe & Saml Ashe; (witness) A Maclaine [only one witness]; wit. oath Oct. 1788 by A Maclaine; Jul. 18, 1789 recorded; book I p. 67 [94].

2400. May 19, 1787 John Hill esq ("near" Wilmington, N) to Peter Mallett esq (Wilmington, NC); for £100 sold 10 ac; border: begins at William Campbell's corner or upper line formerly the dividing line between Cornelius Harnett & said Campbell and joins "the" river; part of "plantation" where said Hill lives; sold May 31, 1786 by Mary Harnett to said Hill; reserving to Hill the present straight road from Hill's house to Wilmington not less than 66 feet wide and Mallett isn't to build or place any building in the "range" or prevent the "prospect" from the house as above of a full view of the river. (signed) John Hill; (witness) W H Hill & J Bernard; [note at end indicates "Mallet" paid Hill £100]; wit. oath Jun. 15, 1789 by J Bernard before Sam Ashe esq; book I p. 69 [97].

2401. Mar. 3, 1788 Robert McLorinan, gentleman (Mansion House, city of London, Great Britain) to Jonathan Tompkins, merchant (Wilmington, NC); power of attorney to sell my part of land on N side of Wilmington or part of lot #27A [in Wilmington]; border: joined on E by a house presently "or lately" occupied by Maj. John Walker, on W by house lately owned by Cornelius Harnett deceased, 25 feet in front, & runs "back" North 132 feet; land to be sold to John Campbell, book seller (of Wilmington, NC); land was part of estate of Henry McLorinan deceased who devised it to me & my brother James McLorinan, confectioner (of Abbey Street, city of Dublin). (signed) Robert McLorinan; (witness) Thomas Younger [only one witness]; wit. oath Oct. 1788 by Thos Younger; Jul. 20, 1789 recorded; book I p. 71 [99].

2402. Oct. 10, 1788 Morris Fennel (New Hanover Co) to James Spiller (Sampson Co, NC); for £120 NC money sold 3 Negroes: John, Hagar, & Cloe. (signed) Morris Fennel; (witness) Tho Maclaine [only one witness]; [note at end indicates Spiller paid Fennel £120 Oct. 10, 1788]; Oct. 1788 acknowledged; Jul. 20, 1789 recorded; book I p. 72 [101].

2403. (Wilmington, NC) Jun. 13, 1788 Robert Howe to James Walker; for £321 in bonds & money sold Negro Sue & her 3 children Sampson, Josh, & Jacob "all boys" being slaves belonging to estate of late Gen. Robert Howe & sold at public auction to discharge debts of Gen. Robt Howe "by" Thomas Wright. (signed) R Howe, admr; (witness) Saml Vance [only one witness]; wit. oath Oct. 1788 by Saml Vance; book I p. 73 [102].

2404. Mar. 18, 1788 John Wilkinson, gentleman (Wilmington, NC) to Aulay Macnaughton, merchant (same); for £450 NC money sold part of lot #16 in Wilmington on Front Street; border: 25 feet in front & runs back 73 feet on Wilkinsons Alley. (signed) John Wilkinson; (witness) Geo Reid & John Macauslan; [note at end indicates "MacNaughton" paid Wilkinson £450]; wit. oath Jun. 18, 1789 by John Macauslan before Judge Williams; book I p. 73 [102].

2405. Mar. 20, 1788 John Wilkinson (Wilmington, NC) Aulay Macnaughton (same); for £700 NC money sold [part of] lot #16 in Wilmington on Front Street; border: 75 feet in front, joins Front Street on E, the river on W, Wilkinson Alley on S, & Hendersons Alley on N; deed void if Wilkinson pays Macnaughton £700 NC money & interest by Mar. 20, 1795; otherwise Macnaughton can occupy the land for 30 years Macnaughton is free to build on all foundations on the premises on lots "on the street" or on the wharf "intended" for warehouse; Macnaughton can enjoy the house so built for 8 years from today free of rent; at end of 8 years the building will be valued by 4 skillful workmen with 2 chosen by each party & their valuation will be binding and amount paid to Wilkinson; any building to be of brick or stone and roof covered with slate or tile; if warehouse is built, Macnaulton to have free use of the wharf to land & ship goods; until default Wilkinson can enjoy the land except buildings erected by Macnaulton. (signed) Jn. Wilkinson; (witness) John Gardner & Joseph Milne; [note at end indicates Macnaughton paid Wilkinson £700]; wit. oath Jun. 18, 1789 by Joseph Milne before Jno Williams, JSCLE; Jul. 26, 1789 recorded; book I p. 75 [104].

2406. Sept. 17, 1787 Richard Miller (New Hanover Co) to John Miller (same); for love & affection & for a silver watch sold [omitted] ac on E side of Long Cr [no more description]; where I live; sold after death if me & my wife Catherine "or her removal" from said land after my death; Richard & wife Catherine to pay yearly tax as General Assembly directs. (signed) Richd Miller; (witness) J Rhodes [only one witness]; wit. oath Dec. 23, 1788 by Jacob Rhodes before Judge Spencer; Jul. 25, 1789 recorded; book I p. 79 [110].

2407. Sept. 1, 1788 Archibald Macalister (Brunswick Co, NC) to Auley Macnaughton (Wilmington, NC); for £400 NC money sold part of lot 8A in Wilmington being a water lot fronting on Front Street; border: begins at lot #9, runs 40 feet S, W to the river, 40 feet up the river, & E to Front Street. (signed) A "McCalester"; (witness) James walker & John Macauslan; [note at end indicates Macnaughton paid McCalester £400]; wit. oath Jun. 18, 1789 by John Macauslan before Judge Williams; Jul. 31, 1789 recorded; book I p. 80 [111].

2408. May 20, 1789 Jonathan Tomkins [or Tompkins] (New Hanover Co) to Henry Toomer, merchant (same); for £600 NC money sold part of lot (no number) in Wilmington on S side of Market Street; border: begins at corner of part of lot owned by George Bell, runs a "direct" line on the street to the low water mark, runs back 33 feet from the street to lot owned by estate of John Quince deceased; part of lot taken by execution by Sheriff Thos Wright to Jonathan Tomkins, due to "sundry" writs of fieri facias against Jonathan Dunbiban deceased due to suits by Thomas Brown, Thos Henderson, Chas Jewkes, Peter Mallet, & others; writs from New Hanover Pleas & Quarter Sessions Court "first Monday" & returnable to succeeding court; includes the wharf which is said to contain [blank] feet. (signed) Jonathan Tomkins; (witness) Wm Nutt & LBerry Stokes; [note at end indicates Toomer paid Tomkins £600]; wit. oath Jun. 13, 1789 by William Nutt before Judge Williams; book I p. 83 [115].

2409. Mar. 31, 1789 George Hooper, merchant (Wilmington, NC) to William Gordan, sadler (same); for £100 NC money sold lot #32B in Wilmington on N side of Princess Street; border: joined on W by part of same lot owned by George Hooper, on N by lot #33 owned by William Campbell esq, E side is 110 feet from Second Street, width of Princess street is 37 feet, & runs back 66 feet to lot #33. (signed) Geo Hooper; (witness) Wm Hooper jr & Thos Anderson; [note at end indicates Gordan paid Hooper £100]; wit. oath Apr. 1789 by William Hooper; book I p. 85 [117].

2410. Jan. 29, 1789 [29th year of reign of George III] William Gordon Rutherfurd, esq (Cornhill, London, Great Britain), second son of John Rutherfurd deceased late Receiver General of his majesty's quit rents in the "late province" but now state of NC, and Alexander Shaw, esq (Plymouth Dock, Devon Co, Great Britain), store keeper of his majesty's ordinance, & wife Frances who is only daughter of John Rutherfurd deceased to John Rutherfurd, esq (town of St. John's, New Brunswick Province, North America), eldest son of John Rutherfurd deceased; W G Rutherford, Frances Shaw, & John Rutherfurd are only children & legal representatives of John Rutherfurd deceased and legatees of Jane Corbyn widow deceased; W G Rutherford, A Shaw, & F Shaw give power of attorney to John Rutherfurd to receive from anyone in North Carolina or elsewhere in United States the money owed to us for work of any slaves owned by us; attorney can sue for nonpayment, occupy the land, houses, or mills, possess the slaves & all real & personal estate of John & Jane C Rutherfurd deceased; attorney can sell the property & do anything we would do. (signed) Wm Gordan Rutherfurd, Alexr Shaw, & Frances Shaw; (witness) Wm Shackley & John Atkinson for W G Rutherfurd and Stephen Haddy & Wm Foot for A & F Shaw; Aug. 20, 1789 "authendicated" before Saml Ashe, JSCL&E; wit. oath Feb. 6, 1789 by William Shackley before William Gill, Lord Mayor of city of London (signed) "Nash" (sic); Feb. 6, 1789 William Shackley (Morship Street, Middlesex Co) swears he saw W G Rutherfurd sign the deed & John Atkinson was also a witness (signed) Wm Shackley & Wm Gill, mayor; Jan. 29, 1789 Peter Tonkin, mayor (of borough of Plymouth, Deven Co, Great Britain) certifies William Foot, gentleman (of Plymouth Dock) swore to above deed (signed) Peter Tonkin; Jan. 29, 1789 William Foot swears he saw A Shaw & Frances Shaw sign the deed (signed)

William Foot & Peter Tonkin; Sept. 6, 1789 recorded; book I p. 86 86 [119].

2411. Jun. 17, 1789 Henry Toomer & wife Magdalen (Wilmington, NC) to George Logan, taylor (same); "about" Nov. 15, 1784 Henry Toomer & wife Magdalen sold at lot in Wilmington to George Logan; but Magdalen didn't renounce dower, so deed was invalid; SO for £250 NC money sold lot #28 in Wilmington on E side of Front Street between Market Street & Princess Street; border: between Cornelius Harnett's lot now Mary Harnett's and Henry Toomer's lot, 15 feet 4 inches in front on "said" street, runs back 50 feet to John Campbell's land. (signed) Henry Toomer & "M M" Toomer; (witness) John Lord; [note at end indicates Logan paid Toomer £250]; Jun. 17, 1789 acknowledged by Henry & Magdalen Toomer and Magdalen renounced dower before Jno Williams, JSCL&E; Sept. 9, 1789 recorded; book I p. 92 [128].

2412. May 20, 1789 Jonathan Tomkins (New Hanover Co) to Henry Toomer (same); for £600 NC money sold part of lot [no number] in Wilmington on S side of Market Street; border: begins at corner of part of lot owned by George Bell, runs a "direct" line along the street to low water mark, & runs 33 feet back from the street to lot owned by estate of John Quince deceased; includes the wharf which is said to be [blank] feet; lot was sold by Sheriff Thomas Wright to Jonathan Tomkins, due to "sundry" writs of fieri facias against Jonathan Dunbiban deceased by suits of Thomas Brown, Thomas Henderson, Charles Jewkes, & "others"; writs from New Hanover Co Please & Quarter Sessions Court on first Monday in [blank] & returnable to succeeding court [maybe same as deed on p. 115]. (signed) Jonathan Tomkins; (witness) Wm Nutt & LBerry Stokes; book I p. 95 [132].

2413. Apr. 17, 1789 Daniel Mallett, merchant (Wilmington, NC) Stephen Austin (city of Philadelphia, PA, but now in Wilmington); for £0.5 leased for a year 241 ac; border: begins at a gum & water oak on the river bank on N side of a high bluff on SW side of NE River & near head of a marsh; being 141 ac of swamp & marsh and 100 ac of high land; Austin to pay yearly rent of a pepper corn if demanded. (signed) D Mallett; (witness) Ed Jones & Elijah Austin; [note at end:] Apr. 18, 1789 my instructions are to pay Stephen Austin half of my mortgage by Jan. 1 next and he leaving sufficient power to receive it (signed) Mallet; wit. oath Jun. 13, 1789 by E Jones before Judge Williams; book I p. 96 [134½, which follows unnumbered page after p. 132].

2414. Apr. 18, 1789 Daniel Mallett, merchant (Wilmington, NC) Stephen Austin, merchant (city of Philadelphia, PA, but now in Wilmington); upon settlement of accounts with Austin, it was found Mallet owed Austin 2,003 Spanish milled dollars & a third of "a dollar" to secure payment of a bond dated today for $4006 (sic) conditioned on Mallett paying Austin 2,003 1/3 Spanish milled dollars & interest by Jan. 1, 1791; to secure payment & for £0.5 sold 241 ac; border: begins at a gum & water oak on the river bank on N side of a high bluff on SW side of NE River & near head of a marsh; being 141 ac of swamp & marsh and 100 ac of high land; sold Apr. 7, 1787 by Peter Mallett & wife Sarah to Daniel Mallett recorded in New Hanover Co Register's office book H p. 59 & 60; sale to Austin void if debt is paid by Jan. 1, 1791; Daniel can occupy the land until default; deed void if Daniel pays debt. (signed) D Mallett & Stephen Austin; (witness) Edwd Jones & Elijah Austin; wit. oath Jun. 13, 1789 by Edwd Jones before Jno Williams, JSCLE; Dec. 8, 1789 recorded; book I p. 98 [134, which follows p. 133 which is after 134½].

2415. Nov. 1, 1789 Thos Haslin, gentleman (Craven Co, NC) to Alfred Moore esq; for £100 sold a Negro woman Nanny. (signed) Thos Haslin; (witness) Thos W Pearson [only one witness]; Dec. 1, 1789 acknowledged before Judge Williams; book I p. 102 [139].

2416. Jun. 13, 1787 Thomas Wright, sheriff (New Hanover Co) to William Hoskins (Massachusetts Bay); for £400 NC money sold part of lot #2B in Wilmington on S side of Market Street; border: joined on E by part of same lot now owned by Margaret Hill, on W by part of same lot owned by Henry Hoskins, 25 feet in front on Market Street, & runs S back 66 feet; owned by Henry Young at his death; sold Jun. 13, 1787 at the court house in Wilmington due to writ of fieri facias from New Hanover Co Pleas & Quarter Sessions court returnable to court first Monday in Jul. 1787 against late Henry Young, in hand of Catherine Young administratrix, for £250 damage & £2.4.1 cost due to suit by Alexander Hostler. (signed) Thos Wright, sheriff; (witness) Mar. Robt Willkings & Anthony Ward; [note at end indicates Hoskins paid Wright £400]; wit. oath Jan. 1789 by M R Willkings; Jan. 11, 1790 recorded; book I p. 102 [139].

2417. (Wilmington, NC) Jun. 8, 1789 Alfred Moore to William Henry Hill; for £130 sold a Negro fellow Jacob. (signed) A Moore; (witness) P Mallett; Dec. 11, 1789 acknowledged before Judge Ashe; Jan. 11, 1790 recorded; book I p. 105 [143].

2418. Jun. 10, 1789 Robert Howe, administrator of estate of "Major" Gen. Howe "with will annexed", to Peter Mallett (Wilmington, NC); for £1,268 sold 12 Negroes: Job a man, Toney a carpenter, Charles & his wife Sindar & their children James, Abigal, Bubo, & Cate, Peter a boy, Himbo a girl, Ansaw a man, & Nanny a cook; sold Dec. 12, 1787 at public vendue to said Mallett due to advertisement by New Hanover Co sheriff. (signed) R Howe, admr; (witness) John Lord & Stepn. Daniel; wit. oath Jun. 17, 1789 by John Lord before Judge Williams; book I p. 105 [144].

2419. Jul. 11, 1789 John Mauger, merchant (Wilmington, New Hanover Co) to Peter Mangeon, merchant (same); for £1,000 NC money sold part of lot #1A in Wilmington on N side of Market Street; border: 31 feet front on the street, runs 66 feet back from the street, joined on E by land "now said to be" owned by Thos Maclaine, on N by lot formerly owned by Alexander Duncan, & W by house & land of James Moran; presently occupied by H P Morfets & Lewis McPherson;

sold Aug. 25, 1783 by Joseph Eagles & wife Sarah to Marshall Robert Willkings who sold Nov. 6, 1784 to Jonathan Tomkins who sold in 2 deeds Dec. 9, 1785 and Apr. 11, 1789 to John Mauger with two-thirds in one deed & remaining third is other deed. (signed) John Mauger; (witness) W Claypoole & Peter Carpenter; [note at end indicates Mangeon paid Mauger £1,000]; wit. oath Jul. 1789 by Peter Carpenter; book I p. 106 [145].

2420. Nov. 20, 1788 Gov. Samuel Johnston (Fayetteville, NC) to James Read; grant #462; for £2,205 specie "secured to be paid" granted [blank] ac in #176 lot in Wilmington; border: begins at SW corner stake of the lot on the river, runs E on N side of Castle Street to Front Street at SE corner of the lot, N 66 feet on Front Street to NE corner of the lot, & W parallel to Castle Street to a stake on the river; includes the wharf & other improvements; sold due to act of General Assembly as confiscated property of estate of John McDonald. (signed) Sam Johnston & J Glasgow, Secretary; Jan. 20, 1790 recorded; book I p. 108 [148].

2421. Feb. 17, 1789 James Reed to Peter Maxwell, merchant (Wilmington, NC); for £840 sold all my interest in "within mentioned" lot [see deed above]. (signed) James Read; (witness) Robt Muter [only one witness]; Apr. 1789 proved; Jan. 20, 1790 recorded; book I p. 109 [149].

2422. Mar. 17, 1789 Peter Maxwell, merchant (Wilmington, NC) to Alexander Riddell [or Riddle], merchant (New York City); for £960 NC money sold lot #176B in Wilmington; known as McDonald's lot & "lately" divided by a New Street established by law; border: joined on S by Castle Street, on E by Front Street; sold Nov. 20, last as confiscated property by the State to James Read esq who sold Feb. 17, 1789 to Peter Maxwell. (signed) Peter Maxwell; (witness) Robert Muter & Robt Conn; [note at end indicates Riddell paid Maxwell £960]; wit. oath Apr. 189 by R Muter; book I p. 109 [150].

2423. Mar. 7, 1789 Peter Maxwell, merchant (Wilmington, NC) to Alexander Riddell & company, merchant (New York City); for £182.14.3 NC money sold an undivided half of [blank] ac with a distillery lately destroyed by fire; border: joins upper part of Wilmington; sold (no date) by William Campbell to Lewis McPherson who sold to Peter Maxwell by 2 deeds Jun. 1, 1784 and Apr. 8, 1786. (signed) Peter Maxwell; (witness) Robert Muter & Robt Conn; [note at end indicates Riddell paid Maxwell £1,082.18.3 (sic)]; wit. oath Apr. 1789 by Robt Muter; Jan. 24, 1790 recorded; book I p. 112 [153].

2424. Nov. 9, 1784 Gov. Alexander Martin (New Bern, NC) to David Jones; grant #195; for £0.50 per 100 ac granted 101 ac on Rockfish [Cr]; border: begins at mouth of Sills [or Sculls] Cr at Rockfish [Cr] & joins "the bite" of a branch. (signed) Alex Martin & J Glasgow, Secretary; Jan. 20, 17090 recorded; book I p. 114 [156].

2425. Oct. 29, 1787 Gov. Richard Caswell (Kingston, NC) to David Jones; grant

#207; for £0.50 per 100 ac granted 158 ac on N side of Rockfish [Cr]; border: begins at a pine in Governor Tryon's line, joins the governor's corner, Fusel [or Fussel], & Matthew Johnson. (signed) Rd Caswell & W Williams, D Secretary; Jan. 30, 1789 recorded; book I p. 115 [157].

2426. Oct. 24, 1786 Gov. Richard Caswell (Kingston, NC) to David Jones; grant #198; for £65 "to be paid" granted 180 ac below the Welsh tract Road; border: begins at a "branch" of small pines by a pine being upper corner of "another" survey of 450 ac of said Tryon's, joins Benjamin Fussel's old line on upper edge of "the" great road, & Ferguson's old patent; sold at public vendue due to act of General Assembly as confiscated property in estate of Wm Tryon esq. (signed) Rd Caswell & J Glasgow, Secretary; Jan. 30, 1790 recorded; book I p. 116 [158].

2427. Oct. 24, 1786 Gov. Richard Caswell (Kingston, NC) to David Jones; grant #199; for £45 specie secured to be paid granted 250 ac; border: begins at "his" corner hickory & pine on S edge of Rockfish Cr [on] upper part of said Tryon's 450 ac survey, joins a pine, "the" main road, Benjamin Fussel, & a bridge over the creek; sold at public vendue due to act of General Assembly as confiscated property as estate of William Tryon esq. (signed) Rd Caswell & J Glasgow, Secretary; Jan. 30, 1790 recorded; book I p. 117 [159].

2428. Oct. 24, 1786 Gov. Richard Caswell (Kingston, NC) to David Jones; grant #200; for £345 specie secured to be paid granted 450 ac on S side of Rockfish Cr; border: begins where Rockfish Cr joins the river on lower side of the creek, joins lower edge of James Padget's field on a high bluff, & a pond; includes a "large" number of old boxed trees & a little improvement of James Padget; sold at public vendue due to act of General Assembly as confiscated property in estate of William Tryon esq. (signed) Rd Caswell & J Glasgow, Secretary; Jan. 30, 1790 recorded; book I p. 118 [160].

2429. Oct. 29, 1787 Gov. Richard Caswell (Kingston, NC) to David Bloodworth; grant #253; for £0.50 per 100 ac granted 100 ac on W side of NE [River]; border: begins at a pine in a meadow & crosses "the" main road. (signed) Rd Caswell & W Williams, D Secretary; Feb. 5, 1790 recorded; book I p. 119 [162].

2430. Dec. 9, 1788 John Hill esq (New Hanover Co) to William Henry Hill esq (same); for £3,800 NC money sold 272 ac near Wilmington; border: begins at the Ferry Landing on Smiths Cr, joins the main road to Wilmington, 2 pines & an oak where line of a grant Nov. 5, 1728 to John Gardner Squires crosses the road, point of a marsh at mouth of the creek; called "Hillton"; one part is 128 ac but called 150 ac and sold May 30, 1753 by William Moore esq deceased to Cornelius Harnett esq deceased and remaining 144 ac was sold Nov. 9, 1756 by executors of William Moore to Cornelius Harnett and sold May 31, 1784 by Mary Harnett to John Hill recorded in New Hanover Co register's office book H p. 465-467 [sic, 427] where the land was called Maynard; part of said grant to J G Squires; "at time of delivery mention made" of 10 ac sold [no date] out of the tract by John

Hill to Peter Mallet. (signed) John Hill; (witness) T Hill & Wm Cutlar; [note at end indicates William paid John £3,800]; Jan. 1789 acknowledged; Feb. 9, 1790 recorded; book I p. 120 [163].

2431. Jan. 22, 1789 Samuel Ashe, gentleman (New Hanover Co) to Samuel Ashe esq ; for £80 NC money sold a Negro girl Molly; lately owned by my late father Maj. Gen. John Ashe and "may be" subject to payment of his debts and was "delivered" to me as part of my proportion of his estate; if Molly is taken to pay debts of John Ashe, I promise to deliver in her place another young female Negro slave of equal value. (signed) Saml Ashe; (witness) William Mabson; Dec. 17, 1789 acknowledged before Judge Spencer; Feb. 13, 1790 acknowledged; book I p. 122 [166].

2432. (Brunswick Co, NC) Dec. 24, 1780 Stephen Daniel to William Henry Hill; today Hill has endorsed a mortgage by me to Margaret Hill, executrix of Wm Hill deceased, for £230; "several" Negroes, including the following, are in the mortgage: Toney & Bess; mortgage is to secure payment of a debt in a bond signed by me with Jacob Leonard & Schenking Moore as securities for a "considerable" sum; SO for £0.5 sold 2 Negroes a fellow Toney & a girl Bess. (signed) Stepn. Daniel; (witness) John Ashe & J Leonard; wit. oath Jan. 1788 by J Ashe "esquire"; Feb. 20, 1790 recorded; book I p. 123 [167].

2433. Nov. 28, 1788 William Larkins, planter (New Hanover Co) to Sweeting Bond (same); for £60 specie sold 150 ac on E side of Long Cr; border: begins at a black gum in James McGufford's line in run of James McGufford's Br, runs up the branch to "the" upper line, & "crosses" James Gufford's line; part of 640 ac granted Apr. 25, 1767 to Wm Larkins. (signed) Willm Larkins; (witness) John Larkins, Robt Larkins, & William Blake; [note at end indicates Bond paid Larkins £60 Nov. 28, 1788]; [no wit. oath mentioned]; book I p. 123 [168].

2434. Nov. 15, 1786 Fredrick Ward (New Hanover Co) to John James (same); for £40 sold 106 ac on Lewis' Cr, a branch of NE River; border: begins at a maple at mouth of Old Field Br, joins Reas Evans, & a small branch. (signed) Fred Ward; (witness) David James, John James (sic), & Anthony Ward; Jan. 1789 acknowledged; Feb. 20, 1790 recorded; book I p. 125 [170].

2435. Aug. 12, 1788 Robert Muter (Wilmington, NC) to William Nichols; for £70 NC money sold a Negro slave James. (signed) Robert Muter; (witness) Morris Ward [only one witness]; Jan. 1789 acknowledged; Feb. 20, 1790; book I p. 126 [171].

2436. Dec. 9, 1788 Charles Jewkes, merchant (Wilmington, New Hanover Co) to John Hill esq (New Hanover Co); for £2,800 NC money sold 1,000 ac on E side of NE Cape Fear R; border: begins at a cypress at mouth of a creek about 1.5 miles above Smiths Cr on NE River, joins mouth of Ness' "or Nesbys" Cr, a savannah, & a bay pond; granted Oct. 22, 1728 by Lords Proprietor to Humphry Johnston who sold Sept. 8 & (, 1729 to Joseph Wragg esq deceased (of SC) who sold Dec. 26, 1759 to Thomas Wright deceased father of sheriff Thomas Wright who sold Jul. 23, 1778 to Charles Jewkes recorded in New Hanover Co register's office book G p. 200 [265—lined out]. (signed) Charles Jewkes & Ann Jewkes (sic); (witness) T Hill & Wm Cutlar; [note at end indicates Hill paid Jewkes £2,800]; dower renounced Jan. 8, 1789 by Ann Jewkes before John Huske JP; Feb. 20, 1790 recorded; book I p. 127 [172].

2437. Jan. 5, 1789 John Guerard to James White; for 300 Spanish milled dollars sold a Negro slave Tom. (signed) John "Geurard"; [no witness]; wit. oath Jan. 1789 by John Fergus (sic); Feb. 20, 1790 recorded; book I p. 130 [178].

2438. Feb. 28, 1788 James Walker to Timothy Bloodworth; for £80 sold 320 ac on W side of NE River; border: joins 50 ac tract, Wm Jones, the river, & "runs out for complement". (signed) James Walker; (witness) Jas Walker (sic) [only one witness]; [note at end:] Mar. 1, 1788 I assign my right to within land to Stephen Filyaw (signed) Timothy Bloodworth (witness) Wm Jones & Jeremiah Hand; Jan. 1789 acknowledged by James Walker; book I p. 131 [179].

2439. Oct. 24, 1788 William H Hill to William Lamb; for £70 sold a Negro boy Valentine. (signed) W H Hill; (witness) T Hill [only one witness]; Jan, 1789 acknowledged; Feb. 20, 1790 recorded; book I p. 132 [180].

2440. Nov. 15, 1788 William H Hill to James Larkins; for £150 sold a Negro wench Nanny & her 2 children Catey & Desseau. (signed) W H Hill; (witness) Thos Moore [only one witness]; Jan. 1789 acknowledged; Feb. 20, 1790 recorded; book I p. 132 [180].

2441. Dec. [blank], 1786 William "McGee", planter ("Wilks" Co, GA) to Samuel Portevint, planter (New Hanover Co); for £500 sold 300 ac; border: begins at a pine, joins Bland, & Sampson's line. (signed) William Magee; (witness) Benjamin Highsmith & William Bland; wit. oath Jan. 1789 by Samuel Portevint (sic); Feb. 21, 1790 recorded; book I p. 133 [181].

2442. Apr. 9, 1788 Jean Overhison (New Hanover Co) to James Smith (same); for £80 specie sold 320 ac on the Welsh tract on W side of NE River; border: begins at a white oak on the river "just above" Watermelon Run; half of 640 ac sold by John Cook (of Duplin Co, NC) to David "David". (signed) Jean Overhison's mark "X" [female]; (witness) John James, Stephen "Fillyaw", & Jas Harper; [note at end indicates Smith paid Jean £80 Apr. 9, 1788]; wit. oath Jan. 1789 by Jno James; book I p. 134 [183].

2443. Sept. 20, 1786 Matthew Johnston (New Hanover Co) to William Jones (same); for £50 sold 210 ac on S side of Rockfish [Cr] & E side of Sills Cr; border: begins at a hickory on bank of Rockfish Cr, joins David Jones, & joins another creek. (signed) Matthew Johnston's mark "X"; (witness) Dd Jones jr & Thos

English; wit. oath Jan. 1789 by Dd Jones; Feb. 21, 1790 recorded; book I p. 136 [185].

2444. Nov. 28, 1788 John Thornber, merchant (Philadelphia [PA}) to my trusty & loving friend John Bradley esq (Wilmington, NC); power of attorney to recover money due to me by executors of estate of Wm Wilkinson deceased (late of Wilmington, NC) and anyone residing in North Carolina. (signed) John Thornber; (witness) Joseph Dugan & Alexr Tod; wit. oath Jan. 1789 by Jo Dugan; Feb. 22, 1790 recorded; book I p. 137 [187].

2445. (Wilmington, NC) Dec. 10, 1788 Wm H Hill to John Hill; for £250 sold 2 Negroes: Jim a fellow & James; "Jem" is now hired to a Cross Creek boat and is at "risque" of John Hill. (signed) W H Hill; (witness) Michl Sampson [only one witness]; Jan. 1789 acknowledged; Feb. 22, 1790 recorded; book I p. 138 [188].

2446. Jan. 13, 1783 Arthur Pitman (New Hanover Co) to Bartholomew Burns; for £28 specie sold 160 ac; border: begins at a gum on W side of widow Moores Cr below mouth of White oak [Cr] & joins mouth of Tuckho [Cr ?]; part of 320 ac granted Sept. 1, 1753 to [omitted]. (signed) Arthur Pitman's mark "X"; (witness) Anthony Burns, John Burns, & Amos Pitman; wit. oath Jan. 1789 by J Burns; Feb. 22, 1790 recorded; book I p. 139 [189].

2447. Apr. 5, 1790 James Fleeming, planter (Bladen Co, NC) to John Kennedy, boat master (Cumberland Co, NC); for £100 NC money sold a Negro fellow Bob about 26 years old a cooper now working in Fayetteville "valued" at £160 & a silver watch valued at £10. (signed) Jas Fleeming; (witness) Ed Jones [only one witness]; wit. oath Apr. 1790 by Ed Jones "esquire"; Apr. 7, 1790 recorded; book I p. 140 [191].

2448. (Wilmington, NC) Apr. 9, 1790 James Moran (Wilmington, NC) John Walker esq (same); for £65 NC money sold a Negro girl Annie about 10 years old. (signed) J Moran; (witness) R Howe & Jo Walker jr; [note at end indicates Walker paid Moran £65]; wit. oath Apr. 1790 by "Js" Walker; Apr. 14, 1790 recorded; book I p. 141 [192].

2449. Mar. 13, 1790 William Blount, esq (Greenville, Pitt Co, NC) to William Henry Hill (New Hanover Co); for £1,200 sold 315 ac on E side of NE Cape Fear R & N side of Smiths Cr "so called"; border: begins at Joshua Grainger Wright's lower corner on E side of NE Cape Fear R nearly opposite the dwelling house now standing on Forceput plantation 160 poles from mouth of Rass' Cr, joins NW corner of Toomers Bridge over Smith Cr, & where Smith Cr "empties"; known as Grainger's "plantation"; includes 140 ac supposed to be tide swamp. (signed) Wm Blount; (witness) James Read & Thos Read; [note at end indicates Hill paid Blount £1,200 Mar. 13, 1790; wit. oath Apr. 1790 by James Read; Apr. 15, 1790 recorded; book I p. 142 [193].

2450. Feb. 28, 1788 James McLorinan, confectioner (Abbey Street, city of Dublin) to Jonathan Tomkins, merchant (Wilmington, NC); power of attorney to sell lot #27A in Wilmington; border: joined on E by house "presently or lately" occupied by John Walker, W by house lately owned by Cornelius Harnett deceased, 25 feet front, & runs N 132 feet back; lot to be sold to John Campbell, book seller (of Wilmington, NC); lot was part of estate of Henry McLorinan deceased who devised it to me & my brother Robert McLorinan, gentleman (of Mansion House, city of London). (signed) James McLorinan; (witness) James Enekin & Corns. McAulay; Feb. 28, 1788 John Talbot Ashenhurst, public notary by royal authority (city of Dublin) certifies power of attorney was executed in my presence by J McLorinan (signed) J T Ashenhurst; Jan. 1789 presented to court & ordered recorded; Apr. 19, 1790 recorded; book I p. 144 [195].

2451. Jan. 5, 1789 Joseph Portevint, planter (New Hanover Co) to my brother Isaac Portevint & my brother-in-law Roger Larkins (same); power of attorney to receive from John Devane (of Bladen Co, NC) money due me from my father's [no name] estate in hands of said Devane. (signed) Joseph Portevint's mark "X"; (witness) Chs. Cogdell & Jas Larkins; wit. oath Jan. 1789 by Jas Larkins; Apr. 19, 1790 recorded; book I p. 145 [197].

2452. Dec. 16, 1788 John Fergus, John Oveler & wife Amelia, Mary Meek, William E Lord, executor of William Lord deceased, to Henry Urquhart; for £200 sold water lot #101 in Wilmington; border: joined on N by Joshua Potts & on S by Hugh Waddle. (signed) John Fergus, John Overler, "Amealia Ovelia", Mary Meek, & Will E Lord; (witness) Robert Scott, Lewis McPherson, & Alexr Urquhart; wit. oath Jan. 1789 by Robert Scott; Apr. 20, 1790 recorded; book I p. 146 [198].

2453. Jan. 10, 1787 Samuel Portevint (New Hanover Co) to Bryant Buxton; for £100 cash sold 88 ac on or near "Brydle" Br & on W side of Long Cr; border: begins at a pine in William Walker's line; granted Mar. 2, 1775 by Gov. Josiah Martin to Samuel Portevint. (signed) Samuel Portevint; (witness) Chs. Cogdell & Benja Robinson; wit. oath Jan. 1789 by Charles Cogdell; Apr. 20, 1790 recorded; book I p. 148 [200].

2454. Nov. 9, 1784 Gov. Alexander Martin (New Bern, NC) to Peter Portevint; grant #188; for £0.50 per 100 ac granted 320 ac on E side of Black R; border: begins at a pine in Timothy Bloodsworth's line, joins Duplin [County] line, crosses Stephens Br, joins open woods, & crosses 2 prongs of Stephens Br. (signed) Alexander Martin & J Glasgow, Secretary; Apr. 21, 1790 recorded; book I p. 149 [202].

2455. Nov. 27, 1789 Gov. Samuel Johnston (Fayetteville, NC) to Robert Nixon; grant #260 [see shuck 2173 in New Hanover Co in Secretary's grant files]; for £10 per 100 ac granted 40 ac between Old Point Cr & Nixsons Cr; border: begins at a stake on the sound channel; includes a place called Little Hamock. (signed)

Sam Johnston & J Glasgow, Secretary; Apr. 21, 1790 recorded; book I p. 150 [203].

2456. Nov. 27, 1789 Gov. Samuel Johnston (Fayetteville, NC) to Robert Nixon; grant #259; for £10 per 100 ac granted 160 ac on S side of Trumpeter Swamp; border: begins at 2 cypress trees on side of "the" run, joins Stokely Bishop, & side of Bay Br. (signed) Sam Johnston & J Glasgow, Secretary; Apr. 21, 1790 recorded; book I p. [205; not in copy of book I].

2457. Mar. 4, 1789 George Davis to William Henry Hill; for £80 sold a Negro boy Scipio. (signed) Geo Davis; (witness) T Hill; wit. oath Apr. 1789 by Thos Hill; Apr. 21, 1790 recorded; book I p. 151 [206].

2458. (Wilmington, NC) Dec. 5, 1788 Alfred Moore to William Henry Hill; for £250 sold 2 Negro slaves: a fellow Christmas & a wench Sally. (signed) A Moore; (witness) T Hill; wit. oath Apr. 1789 by Thos Mill; Apr. 21, 1790 recorded; book I p. 151 [206].

2459. Dec. 30, 1788 Patrick Brenan, publican (Wilmington, NC) John O'Neill, merchant (same); for £50 sold a lame Negro fellow York. (signed) Patk. Brenan; (witness) H Clark; [note at end indicates "Oneile" paid Brenan £50]; wit. oath Apr. 1789 by Henry Clark; Apr. 21, 1790 recorded; book I p. 152 152 [207].

2460. Dec. 13, 1788 Patrick Brenan, publican (Wilmington, NC) John Oneill [or Oneile], merchant (same); for £150 NC money sold following household furniture: 4 beds, bolsters, & pillows, 7 pair of blankets, 15 pair of sheets, 4 quilts, 5 table clothes, 10 towels, 4 large window curtains, 4 dining tables one a large mahogany the others maple & walnut, 6 chairs walnut with hair bottoms, an arm chair "same quality", 6 red turned rush bottom chairs, 6 plain back rush bottom chairs, a card table, a small tea table, 2 pine kitchen tables, a large metal kettle, a copper kettle, a gridiron, a kettle stand, 2 metal pots, a dutch oven, 5 dozen plates, 12 dishes of various sizes, a tureen, 2 coffee pots, 18 cups & saucers, 10 tea spoons & sugar tongs, 3 tea pots, 2 cream jays, 7 china plates, 6 waiters, 2 tea chests, 3 large canisters, 4 large china bowls, a desk, a looking glass, 4 bedsteads, 10 decanters, 18 wine glasses, 24 tumblers, 6 sets of knives & forks, 24 pewter spoons. (signed) Patk. Brenan; (witness) H "Clarke" [only one witness]; [note at end indicates Oneill paid Brenan £150]; wit. oath Apr. 1789 by Henry Clark; Apr. 21, 1790 recorded; book I p. 153 [208].

2461. Oct. 8, 1788 Jacob Stokeley (New Hanover Co) to Peter Smith; for £100 sold a bark bay mare about 13.5 hands high, an iron gray mare about 14 hands high branded ["I" and backward "S"] on rising buttock, a red & white cow & calf marked with a crop in left "year", a black cow & calf with crop [in] left year, a brown cow & calf marked with [blank], a pided(?) heffer marked with a cross in left year, a brown heffer marked with a crop in left year, a red & wife heffer marked with a crop in left "one", 2 sows, 2 pigs, 4 bedsteads, 3 beds & furniture,

2 tables, 6 "chears", 12 earthen plates, 2 pewter dishes, a pair of "fuer" tongs, 2 pot racks, a chest & vase, 3 large pails, a bucket, a "wheal and" linen wheal, 2 iron pots, a tea "cittle", a skillet, a shot gun, a Negro wench Jenney, & 2 plows. (signed) Jacob Stokeley's mark "Ŧ", John Hurst's mark "Ŧ", & Josep. Stokeley (sic); [no witness]; wit. oath Apr. 1789 by John "Heast"; Apr. 21, 1790 recorded; book I p. 154 [210].

2462. Jul. 11, 1788 James Walker, merchant (Wilmington, NC) to William Jones, planter (New Hanover Co); for £400 sold on E side of NE Cape Fear R & near the Welsh tract; border: begins at first station of the patent at mouth of Cypress Cr, joins upper, back, & lower lines of the patent, & the river; being front part of 1,000 ac granted Mar. 5, 1729 by Lords Proprietor to Col. Maurice Moore who sold Dec. 5, 1731 to John Bevan who sold to Evan Jones sr, recorded in New Hanover Co register's office, who sold Jun. 30, 1752 to his son Evan Jones jr who sold Sept. 23, 1756 to Lewis Henry "Deroset" who sold Apr. 21, 1779 to Thomas Fisher and sold [date blank] by Sheriff Thomas Wright, due to execution against Thomas Fisher, to James Walker. (signed) James Walker; (witness) Henry "Watters" & John Bradley; [note at end indicates Walker received £400]; Jan. 1789 acknowledged; Apr. 22, 1790 recorded; book I p. 155 [211].

2463. Aug. 15, 1786 Donald Bain, merchant (Wilmington, NC) to Thomas Maclaine, merchant (same); for £250 sold part of lot #1A in Wilmington on N side of Market Street; border: begins at an oak stake, runs 17 feet "outward" up the street to Farios' [sic Farris] formerly Veale's corner, N 66 feet to Robert Schaw's lot formerly Rutherford's, 17 feet parallel with Market Street to land lately owned by Joseph Eagles, & 66 feet on "the" line to beginning. (signed) Donald Bain; (witness) A Maclaine & Thos Craike; [note at end indicates Maclaine paid Bain £250]; wit. oath Jan. 1789 by Archibald Maclaine; Apr. 22, 1790 recorded; book I p. 157 [214].

2464. May 1, 1788 William James, planter (Duplin Co, NC) to Stephen Filyaw, planer (New Hanover Co); for £100 sold 320 ac on W side of NE Cape Fear R; between William Jones on lower side & Filyaw's "plantation" on upper side; border: joins lower end of said plantation on the river & runs "out"; granted (no date) to Richard James, father of William. (signed) William James; (witness) John Bloodworth & Thomas James jr; wit. oath Apr. 1789 by John Bloodworth; Apr. 26, 1790 recorded; book I p. 159 [216].

2465. Sept. 24, 1788 Thomas Loper, planter (New Hanover Co) to Thomas Sill (same); for £0.5 sold 100 ac near New Topsail Sound; border: begins at said Loper's, John Nichols sr's, & Benjamin Mott's corner lightwood tree "marked 4 ways", joins a big pond, near a small pond, & joins Marshy Br. (signed) Thomas "Lowper"; (witness) Elijah St. George & Oswell Sill; [note at end indicates Sill paid Lowper £0.5 Sept. 24, 1788]; wit. oath Apr. 1789 by Oswell Sill; Apr. 26, 1790 recorded; book I p. 160 [218].

2466. Apr. 8, 1789 Robert Bannerman, planter (New Hanover Co) to Peter Portevint, sadler; for £30 sold 640 ac in Davidson Co [TN} on Cumberland R; border: begins at an ash & box elder on the river bank at mouth of third creek below Cross Cr; granted Nov. 12, 1785 to John Barns now deceased and [now] sold by Robert Bannerman, administrator of said Barns' estate [grant #368 in issued Sept. 15, 1787 (sic), see shuck #396 in Davidson Co, TN in Secretary's grant files, military bounty warrant #650 issued to former Pvt. John Barns for 7 years service in NC Continental Line; John "Barnes" served for 3 years in first Battalion (see Colonial & State Records vol. 15 p. 718) and John Barnes a gunner in Capt. John J Kingsbury's Artillery (see Colonial & State Records vol. 15 p. 735)]. (signed) Rt Bannerman; (witness) Thos Devane jr & Saml Buxton; wit. oath Apr. 1789 by Thos Devane jr; Apr. 26, 1790 recorded; book I p. 162 [220].

2467. Dec. 17, 1788 Thomas Wright, sheriff (New Hanover Co) to Henry Urquhart (same); for £25 sold a fifth of a water lot #101 in Wilmington; border: joined on N by Joshua Potts, on S by Hugh Waddle; taken by execution due to writ of fieri facias from New Hanover Co Pleas & Quarter Sessions Court "in Wilmington District" against Peter Lord (of Bladen Co, NC) due to suit by John Burgwin; writ issued "first Monday in October" & returnable to succeeding court. (signed) Thos Wright, sheriff; (witness) Mar. R Wilkings & Anthy. Ward; [note at end indicates Urquhart paid Wright £25]; Jan. 1789 acknowledged; Apr. 27, 1790 recorded; book I p. 163 [222].

2468. May 14, 1784 John Burgwin esq (Wilmington, NC) to Donald Bain, merchant (same); for £0.5 NC money sold part of lot #1 in Wilmington on N side of Market Street; border: begins at an oak stake, runs E 17 feet up the street to John Farris' formerly Francis Veal's corner, back 66 feet from the street to Messrs. Aneram & Schaw's lot formerly John Rutherford's, 17 feet towards the river to late Richard Eagle's lot, & 66 feet along his lot to beginning; sold Jul. 4, 1764 by Henry Toomer & wife Mary to John Jones (of Wilmington) who with wife [no name] sold May 23, 1770 to John Burgwin. (signed) Jno Burgwin; (witness) John London & Geo Lucas; [note at end indicates Bain paid Burgwin £0.5]; wit. oath Jan. 1789 by John London; Apr. 27, 1790 recorded; book I p. 165 [224].

2469. Jan. 1, 1789 William Lamb & wife Abigal (New Hanover Co) to James Smith (same); for £80 NC money sold 294 ac on W side of NE Cape Fear R; border: begins at a cypress on the river bank where David David's deed calls for a pine, joins Jeremiah Hand's line formerly Dougless', joins an old line called Dougless' or Hand's, a branch, back line of the patent, & said Smith's corner of another deed that was upper part of David David sr's 640 ac; being lower part of 1,280 ac granted (no date) to Evan Jones and John Cook (of Duplin Co, NC) sold 640 ac to David David (of New Hanover Co). (signed) William Lamb & Abigail's mark "+"; (witness) John Larkins sr & Thomas Lamb; wit. oath Apr. 1789 by John Larkins "junior" (sic); Apr. 27, 1790 recorded; book I p. 167 [227].

2470. Feb. 12, 1788 Hardy Parker, planter (New Hanover Co) to Joseph Eakens, school master; for £60 sold 320 ac "chiefly" on E side of widow Moore's Cr; border: begins at a sweet gum & 2 dogwoods beside a swamp; includes his improvement; granted May 6, 1769 to Hardy Parker. (signed) Hardy Parker & Mary Parker's mark "/" (sic); (witness) Archibald Cook & "Henery" Holley; wit. oath Apr. 1789 by Archibald "Cooke"; Apr. 27, 1790 recorded; book I p. 169 [229].

2471. (Wilmington, NC) Jul. 9, 1788 Wm Moseley to John Huske; for £140 sold a Negro fellow Slylas [or Hylas] about 27 years old. (signed) Wm Moseley; (witness) Wm Watson [only one witness]; Apr. 1790 acknowledged; book I p. 1710 [231].

2472. Apr. 1, 1789 John Huske to John Hogg; for £90 sold a Negro fellow Tomside. (signed) John Huske; (witness) Galvin Alves [only one witness]; Apr. 1790 acknowledged; book I p. 171 [231].

2473. Oct. 18, 1788 Daniel Mallett (Wilmington, NC) James Read (same); for £180 NC money sold a Negro man Andrew; (signed) D Mallett; (witness) Thos Read [only one witness]; Apr. 1790 acknowledged; May 1, 1790 recorded; book I p. 171 [232].

2474. Dec. 10, 1788 Robert Howe, admr. of estate of my deceased father Brig. Gen. Robert Howe (Brunswick Co, NC) to Alexander Hostler; for £121 NC money sold a mullato boy Paul "or any other name he may go by" 10 or 12 years old; "some time ago" New Hanover Co sheriff sold at public vendue "sundry" Negro & mullatto slaves belonging to Robt Howe deceased's estate to pay debts due by the estate. (signed) R Howe, admr; recorded; P Carpenter [only one witness]; [note at end indicates Hostler paid Howe £121]; wit. oath Apr. 1790 by Peter Carpenter; May 1, 1790 recorded; book I p. 172 [233].

2475. (Craven Co, NC) Feb. 5, 1784 I certify the bearer, Hannah Lewis commonly called free Hannah, was "admitted to her freedom" in Dec. court 1781 "to best of my remembrance" by Craven Co court "who" are vested with full power & authority to do the same; I "drew" the petition for her freedom & was her attorney on the occasion. (signed) "Jo C (the name so worn that the regr. could not make it out)";

(Craven Co, NC) Feb. 6, 1784 I certify that the bearer, Hannah Lewis, fully proved before Craven Co court she was born free & admitted to her freedom agreeable to above certificate. (signed) Willm Tisdale JLd & Richd Ellis JLd; (New Hanover Co) Apr. 1790 exhibited & court & ordered registered (signed) Thos Maclaine, clerk; May 1, 1790 recorded; book I p. 173 [234].

2476. Aug. 27, 1786 David Bloodworth jr (New Hanover Co) to David Bloodworth sr, planter (same); for "a pees" of land "made over" by David sr to David jr on Watermellion Run gave to David sr 480 ac on W side of NE River;

border: begins at a gum on a "crick" near the "torn" of the river; formerly occupied by his grandfather Evan "Jons". (signed) David Bloodworth jr; (witness) W Jones jr; wit. oath Apr. 1790 by W Jones; May 8, 1790 recorded; [note at end:] memo the original very badly spelled & figures inserted; book I p. 174 [235].

2477. May 8, 1789 John Nutt, cabinet maker (New Hanover Co) to Elizabeth Wimble (Boston, Suffolk Co, Massachusetts), widow of William Wimble marriner (late of Boston, Mass), and Gilliam Bass merchant & wife Rebecca (Boston, Mass), Lewis Marresquille gentleman & wife Kathrine (Dracut, Middlesex Co, Mass), & Elizabeth Bass grand daughter of Elizabeth Wimble (Boston, Mass); for £300 NC money sold lot #201B in Wilmington on New Street; border: joined on S by Mr. Craike, on N by Thomas Clark, & on E by Front Street; sold the day before this by Elizabeth Wimble, "Gillam" Bass & wife Rebecca, Lewis Marresquill & wife Kathrine, & Elizabeth Bass to John Nutt; sale void if Nutt pays grantees £300 by May 8, 1790. (signed) John Nutt; (witness) Joshua Potts & Henry Hoskins; [note at end indicates Nutt paid Gillam Bass, attorney for heirs of William Wimble deceased, £50 (sic) May 8, 1789]; wit. oath Jul. 1789 by Henry Hoskins; May 8, 1790 recorded; book I p. 175 [236].

2478. Jul. 22, 1769 James Bland, planter (New Hanover Co) to John Lyon, merchant (Wilmington, NC); for £12 proclamation money sold 300 ac; border: begins at John Reeves' [or Reoves] corner pine in a savannah & joins Joseph Blake; includes the place called White Oak Swamp & "some" meadows at "the" great road on E side of Black R about 2 miles from the river. (signed) James Bland; (witness) Elizabeth Henekly & Thomas Sewell; wit. oath Feb. 2, 1790 by Thomas Sewell before Saml Ashe, JSC; May 8, 1790 recorded; book I p. 176 [237].

2479. Jan. 28, 1789 Edmond [or Edmund] Moore, tavern keeper (Wilmington, NC) Fredrick Jones esq (New Hanover Co); for £10 NC money sold 75 ac near Topsail Sound; border: begins at a pine in Mrs. Richey's line and joins Mrs. Collier's now Fredrick Jones' line; granted Oct. 29, 1787 to Edmond Moore. (signed) Edmond Moore; (witness) Thos Callender & Jno Cutlar; wit. oath Apr. 1789 by Thos Callender; May 10, 1790 recorded; book I p. 178 [239].

2480. Mar. 20, 1789 Hugh Campbell, merchant (New Hanover Co) to Archibald Ronaldson, house carpenter (same); for £300 NC money sold part of lot [no number] in Wilmington on S side of Marsden Alley "otherwise" called Quinces Alley; border: 42 feet in front on the alley, runs back 20 feet to house owned by John Bradley, joins house owned by Matthew Johnston; sold (no date) by William Ewans to Peter Brown and sold by Sheriff Thos Wright to Marshall Robert Wilkings, due to execution from New Hanover Co Pleas & Quarter Sessions Court due to suit by Henry Young & Jonathan Dunbibbin against Peter Brown, and sold "now" by M R Wilkings to Hugh Campbell. (signed) Hugh Campbell; (witness) John Allan & Wm Ewans; [note at end indicates Campbell received £300 Mar. 20, 1789]; wit. oath Apr. 1790 by John Allan; May 10, 1700 recorded; book I p. 179 [240].

2481. Mar. 16, 1789 Archibald Ronaldson (New Hanover Co) to Hugh Campbell (same); for £550 sold part of lots #53 & 54 in Wilmington on N side of Market Street; border: joined on E by house where Robert McCracken formerly lived, 32 feet front on Market Street, runs 132 feet back North to Doctor Green's lot; sold (no date) by Caleb Grainger deceased (formerly of Wilmington, NC) to David Brown who sold to Thomas Camber who sold to John Mortimer now deceased who willed it to his sister Mary Mortimer who sold to John Burgwin who sold to Archibald Ronaldson. (signed) Archibald Ronaldson; (witness) Wm Ewans & John Allan; [note at end indicates Campbell paid Ronaldson £550 Mar. 16, 1789]; wit. oath Apr. 1790 by John Allan; May 12, 1790 recorded; book I p. 180 [241].

2482. Feb. 16, 1789 John Burgwin, merchant (New Hanover Co) to Archibald Ronaldson (Wilmington, NC); for £300 sold part of lots #53 & 54 in Wilmington on N side of Market Street; border: joined on E by house where Robert McCracken formerly lived, 32 feet front on Market Street, & runs 132 feet back North to Doctor Green's lot; sold (no date) by Caleb Grainger deceased (formerly of Wilmington, NC) to David Brown now deceased who sold to Thomas Camber who sold to John Mortimer deceased who willed it to his sister Mary Mortimer who sold to John Burgwin. (signed) Jno Burgwin; (witness) John Allan & Hugh Campbell; wit. oath Apr. 1790 by John Allan; May 12, 1790 recorded; book I p. 182 [243].

2483. Apr. 6, 1789 Auly [or Auley] MacNaughton, merchant (Wilmington, NC) to George Logan, taylor (same); for £70 NC money sold 100 ac; border: begins at a glade of marsh being a division between plantations late of Joshua Peavy & Daniel Webb, joins mouth of NE drain of Weys Pond, "a dirty" branch, a dividing line agreed on by Joshua Peavy & Daniel Webb "once proprietors thereof"; half of "plantation" formerly owned by John Watson and by "divers" conveyance became property of Henry McLorinan esq who owned it at his death and willed residue of his real & personal [estate] to his brothers James McLorinan & Robert McLorinan & heirs who on Dec. 1, 1786 "caused" the sale Dec. 5, 1786 at Wilmington to George Reid, merchant (of Wilmington, NC) for £66 and sold Jul. 9, 1787 by said Reid to Auly McNaughton who sold at public vendue Jun. 16, 1788 & Logan was highest bidder. (signed) A "Macnaughton"; (witness) Jos G Wright; [note at end indicates MacNaughton received £70]; wit. oath Apr. 1789 by "J" Wright; May 12, 1790; book I p. 184 [245].

2484. May 31, 1790 Silas Cooke, gentleman (New Bern, NC) to Alfred Moore esq (Orange Co, NC; for £85 sold a Negro girl Sukey. (signed) Silas Cooke; (witness) Tho W "Pearsons" [only one witness]; [note at end indicates Moore paid Cooke £85 May 31, 1790; wit. oath Jun. 1, 1790 by Tho H Pearson before Jno Williams, JSCLE; Jun. 10, 1700 recorded; book I p. 186 [247].

2485. Dec. 21, 1789 Alexander Rouse (New Hanover Co) to Elizabeth Rouse (same); for £150 NC money sold "my preset & future" right to Negro fellow Dick.

(signed) Alexr Rouse; (witness) Jno B Moore [only one witness]; wit. oath Jun. 10, 1790 by Jno B Moore esq before Jno Williams, JSCLE; Jun. 11, 1790 recorded; book I p. 188 (sic) [248].

2486. Jun. 17, 1790 James Walker & Thomas Young, merchants under firm of Walker & Young (Wilmington, New Hanover Co) to Samuel Spencer (Anson Co, NC); for £80 sold a Negro fellow Major about 36 years old. (signed) Walker & Young; (witness) Cornls. H Holt [only one witness]; ; [note at end indicates Spencer paid Cornls. H Holt, for Walker & Young £80 Jun. 17, 1790]; wit. oath Jun. 17, 1790 by Cornls. H Holt before Jno Williams, JSCLE; book I p. 187 [249].

2487. "Jun. 1789" Thos Clark to Alfred Moore esq; I exchanged with Moore a Negro boy Ned, Negro girl Clarinda, & Negro boy Johnny children of Mary "A Moore's cook wench" FOR a woman Judy & her child Mary; I confirm the exchange to remove doubts. (signed) T Clark; (witness) Thos Craike [only one witness]; wit. oath Jun. 17, 1790 by Thos Craike before Saml Spencer, JSCLE; Jun. 19, 1790 recorded; book I p. 189 [250].

2488. Jun. 18, 1790 Robert Howe, administrator of late Gen. Robt Howe, to Alfred Moore esq (Orange Co, NC); for £270 sold, by consent of John Burgwin, following Negroes: Isaac and Mary & her child Renchey; I have already received Mr. Moore's note for £120 "being the ballance". (signed) R Howe; (witness) Geo Gibbs; [note at end:] (no date) I assent to above sale due to mortgage I have from General Howe where above Negroes were included (signed) John Burgwin (witness) Geo Gibbs; wit. oath Jun. 18, 1790 by Geo Gibbs before Saml Spencer, JSCLE; book I p. 191 (sic) [251].

2489. Jun. 14, 1790 Thos Neale jr, planter (Brunswick Co, NC) to Alfred Moore esq (Orange Co, NC); for £470 sold following Negroes: a "prime" man Job, his wife a prime woman Sarah, their children Mathew, Daphne, Job, & their last child name unknown about 7 or 8 months old, & a Negro boy Aberdeen about 6 or 7 years old; all the Negroes except Aberdeen are now in Bladen Co, NC, in possession of Capt. James Bradley; I bind myself to deliver the slaves to Moore or his attorney at one of his plantations on Cape Fear [R]. (signed) Thos Neale jr; (witness) James Moore [only one witness]; wit. oath Jun. 15, 1790 by James Moore before Saml Spencer, JSCLE; book I p. 192 (sic) [252].

2490. (Wilmington, NC) Feb. 8, 1790 Mary Sampson to Alfred Moore esq; by hands of Mr. James Walker received £80 for Negro boy Peter (signed) Mary Sampson; (witness) Jno Mackenzie [only one witness]; wit. oath Jun. 12, 1790 by John Mackenzie before Saml Spencer, JSCLE; book I p. 190 (sic) [253].

2491. Jun. 15, 1790 Arthur Howe, gentleman (Bladen Co, NC) to Alfred Moore esq, on behalf of his niece Sarah Nash; for £317 sold & delivered to Sarah Nash following Negroes: Beck & her children Elsey & Amey and Flora & her child Himbo. (signed) Arthur Howe; (witness) James Moore [only one witness]; Jun.

15, 1790 acknowledged before Saml Spencer, JSCLE; book I p. 190 (sic) [253].

2492. Jun. 13, 1790 John Wilkinson, gentleman (Wilmington, NC) to John Bradley (same); for £2,550 NC money sold part of lots #16 & 21 in Wilmington; border: 75 feet in front, joins Front Street on E, the river of W, Wilkinsons Alley on S, & Hendersons Alley on N. (signed) Jno Wilkinson; (witness) John Maclellan [only one witness]; [note at end indicates Wilkinson received £2,550; Jun. 18, 1790 acknowledged before Saml Spencer, JSCLE; Jun. 19, 1790 recorded; book I p. 193 [254].

2493. Jun. 16, 1790 John Bradley to Auly Macnaughton; for £1,3300 NC money sold [part of lots #16 & 21] in Wilmington; border: joins Front Street on E, the river on W, Wilkinsons Alley on S, & Hendersons Alley on N; being land I lately purchased of John Wilkinson; deed void if Bradley pays Macnaughton £1,247 NC money & interest due by bond dated today. (signed) John Bradley; (witness) Joseph Milne [only one witness]; wit. oath Jun. 18, 1790 by Joseph Milne before Saml Spencer, JSCLE; "reced. the tax of 5/" (signed) Saml Spencer; Jun. 19, 1790 recorded; book I p. 194 [255].

2494. (Wilmington, NC) Apr. 1, 1790 James DuBois (Wilmington, NC) to Auley Macnaughton [or McNaughton] (same); for £100 sterling Great Britain money and £80 sterling Great Britain money to be paid on May 1, 1791 and £80 sterling to be paid May 1, 1792 sold part of lot #21 on Front Street in Wilmington; border: 33 feet in front, joins Front Street on E, Cape Fear R on W, Wilkinson's property of N, & Abigal Gregory's property on S; sale void if DuBois repays Macnaughton £260 sterling Great Britain money by May 1, 1794 OR the amount Macnaughton spends in erecting buildings on the premises; buildings to be valued by 2 or more skillful tradesmen mutually chosen; otherwise Macnaughton can sell the lot to pay the debt; DuBois to have property insured for £300 sterling in an insurance office in Britain until property is sold or is destroyed by fire. (signed) James "Dubois" & A McNaughton; (witness) Daniel McNeill & John McAuslan; Jun. 18, 1790 acknowledged & wit. oath by John McAuslan before Saml Spencer, JSCL&E; "recd. the tax of 5/" (signed) Saml Spencer; Jun. 21, 1790 recorded; book I p. 196 [257].

2495. Apr. 6, 1790 Peter Mangeon (Wilmington, NC) to Auley McNaughton (same); on Apr. 6, 1790 Mangeon signed a bond with McNaughton for £428.15.6 NC money; to secure payment & for £0.5 sold lot 1A on N side of Market Street in Wilmington; border: 31 feet front on the street, runs back 66 feet from the street, joined on E by land "said to be" owned by Thomas MacLaine, N by lot formerly owned by Alex Duncan, & W by house & land of James Moran; presently in occupation of Peter Mortin & John Manger with appurtenances; McNaughton can possess the land after Jul. 6, 1790; sale void if Mangeon pays McNaughton £428.15.2 & interest from "Jul. 6" by Aug. 1 next. (signed) P Mangeon; (witness) Joseph D Milne [only one witness]; [note at end indicates McNaughton paid Mangeon £0.5]; wit. oath Jun. 18, 1790 by Joseph Milne before Samuel Spencer,

JSCL&E; "recd. the tax of 5/" (signed) Samuel Spencer; Jun. 21, 1790 recorded; book I p. 197 198 [260].

2496. Jan. 10, 1789 Hugh Waddell, eldest surviving son of late General Wadddell first part, John Burgwin Waddell, son of General Waddell second part, & John Burgwin (Wilmington, NC), guardian of John Burgwin Waddell third part; in his life time, General Waddell owned (a) land on Prince George's Cr; between Leger's upper line & "the" main road; known as Castle Haynes "plantation"; (b) a corner lot in Wilmington between Market Street & Second Street with 2 dwelling houses thereon one presently occupied by Mrs. Sarah Lord & other by Mrs. Hanson; General Waddell made a will Nov. 10, 1772 giving Castle Haynes, the lot, & houses to his eldest son Haynes Waddell; Haynes Waddell died prior to age 21 so property descended to Hugh Waddell & John B Waddell jointly; they intend to divide the property with consent of John Burgwin, guardian; SO Hugh is to have Castle Haynes and John B Waddell to have the houses & lot in Wilmington "with garden & improvements" which are estimated at £600 less than value of the plantation given to Hugh; so Hugh agrees to pay J B Waddell £600 with interest from today. (signed) Hu. Waddell, Jno B Waddell, & Jno Burgwin; (witness) Geo Gibbs & Henry Hunter;

[note at end:] Mar. 3, 1789 it is further agreed between Hugh Waddell & John B Waddell that land below Leger's [or Liger] given to us by our uncle John Brugwin is to be divided in most equitable manner, except that the part E and S of a straight line to be run from a white maple about 100 yards above Minots Bluff on Prince George's Cr in northerly court to a cypress on N side of Spring Br nigh said Hugh Waddell's rice clearing about 100 yards from the high land & a direct line to Leger's Fence and contains about 50 ac which we agree to give to our uncle for his many services in our minority and for £0.5. (signed) Hu. Waddell & Jno B Wadell (witness) Geo Gibbs & Henry Hunter; wit. oath Jun. 17, 1790 by George Gibbs before Jno Williams, JSCLE; Jul. 9, 1790 recorded; book I p. 201 [261].

2497. Jul. 13, 1789 John Wilkinson, gentleman (New Hanover Co) to John Walker esq (same); for £200 NC money sold 320 ac on Smith's Cr; border: begins at a hickory on the creek at mouth of a branch of the creek, joins "the" main road, & the bridge on Mill Cr; part of 640 ac granted in 8th year of reign of George II to John Hodgeson and sold Oct. 21, 1736 by [omitted] to Robert Halton and taken by execution due to sit by John Rutherford, Thomas Jones, & Barbara Clark, administrators of Thomas Clark deceased against estate of Robert Halton deceased and sold Apr. 22, 1763 by Sheriff Caleb Grainger to John Rutherford and sold Aug. 3, 1773 due to decree of Chancery Court by John Rutherford to John Murray who with wife Janet sold Aug. 14, 1773 to William Wilkinson who willed it Sept. 22, 1780 to his nephew John Wilkinson, grantor of this deed. (signed) John Wilkinson; (witness) Henry Hoskins & James Walker jr; [note at end indicates Walker paid Wilkinson £200]; wit. oath Jul. 1789 by James walker; Jul. 12, 1790 recorded; book I p. 205 [264].

2498. Jan. 9, 1779 John Moore esq & wife Martha (New Hanover Co) to John

Walker esq (same); for £500 NC money sold in Brunswick Co on W side of Cape Fear R; border: runs down the river to a small creek on N side of an old field, runs up the creek to the head, N70W "length of the upper line", & down upper line to first station; called Deep water Point; sold May 31, 1739 by Joseph Sherburn, mariner, to Roger Moore esq who willed it to his son George Moore esq and after his death was sold at public vendue by order of John Moore esq, son of George & executor of his will, to John Walker. (signed) Jno B Moore exr & Martha Moore; (witness) Thomas Moore & Simon Mason; [note at end indicates Walker paid Moore £500]; wit. oath Jun. 15, 1790 by Thomas Moore before Saml Ashe, JSCLE; Jul. 12, 1790 recorded; book I p. 208 [267].

2499. Jan. 6, 1790 Hugh Waddell & John Burgwin Waddell, sons & heirs of late General Hugh Waddell deceased (Bladen Co, NC) to John Burgwin (Wilmington, NC); for £354 NC money sold part of lot #27 on N side of Market Street in Wilmington; border: begins at Daniel Dunbibbin's corner on Market Street, 27.5 feet on Market Street to corner of lot formerly owned by Samuel Swann, back at right angle 128 feet, 27.5 feet parallel with Market Street, & along Daniel Dunbibbin's line to beginning; sold (no date) by John Sampson & wife Anne to Edward Forbes who sold to Hugh Waddell since deceased who willed it to his son Hugh, one of grantors of this deed. (signed) Hu. Waddell & Jno B Waddell; (witness) Geo Gibbs [only one witness]; wit. oath Jun. 17, 1790 by George Gibbs before Jno Williams, JSCLE; Jul. 13, 1790 recorded; book I p. 210 [268].

2500. Sept. 20, 1786 Thomas Wright, sheriff (New Hanover Co) to John Walker esq (same); for £16 NC money sold 300 ac on E side of NE River & on branches of Merrick's Cr; between Cat Skin Br & Trumpeter Br; border: begins at a pine; called Juniper Swamp; granted Apr. 22, 7th year of "present" king to John Ashe deceased; sold due to an execution from New Hanover Co Pleas & Quarter Sessions Court in Oct. 1786 returnable to court first Monday in Jan "next" against John Simpson for £311.18.6 damages & £3.12.7 costs due to suit by Archibald Jameson. (signed) Thos Wright, sheriff; (witness) Mar. Robt. Willkings, J Fergus jr, & Ja Walker jr; [note at end indicates Walker paid Wright £16]; Jul. 1790 acknowledged; Jul. 23, 1790 recorded; book I p. 212 [270].

2501. Dec. 31, 1787 Thomas Wright, sheriff (New Hanover Co) to John Walker esq (same); for £28 sold 100 ac on Rocky Point; border: joins Edward Moseley's property now owned by Sampson Moseley, James Moore, & said John Walker; sold Feb. 3, 1729 by Sarah Porter to her son John Porter (late of New Hanover Co) and part of a larger tract granted (no date) to John Porter deceased; sold due writ of fieri facias due to suit by William Dry esq against John Porter; sold Sept. 24, 1751 by Sheriff Caleb Grainger to William Dry who sold Mar. 9, 1764 to General John Ashe who willed it Feb. 23, 1774 to his son John Ashe who sold May 14, 1787 to his brother Major Samuel Ashe; now sold due to writ of fieri facias from New Hanover Co Pleas & Quarter Sessions court Oct. 1787 returnable first Monday in Jan. "next" for £89.6.11 and £3.3 costs against Samuel Ashe, son of John Ashe deceased, "garnishee" of Nathaniel Moore "by" said John Walker.

(signed) Thos Wright; (witness) Richard Watson & Mar. R "Willkings"; [note at end indicates Walker paid Wright £28]; Jul. 1790 acknowledged; Jul. 24, 1790 recorded; book I second p. 213 [272].

2502. Jan. 21, 1790 Michael Keenan, cabinet maker (New Hanover Co) to John Macklehany, pilot (same); for £50 NC money sold a fourth of lot #68 in Wilmington between Orange Street & Ann Street; border: 33 feet on E of Second Street, runs E 165 feet, joined on N by another fourth of the lot owned by Michael Keenan, & on S by lot #73. (signed) Michael Keenan; (witness) John Brown & Shederick [or Michael] Springs; [note at end indicates Macklehany paid Keenan £50]; [another note:] Keenay & Macklehany agree an alley will be left between the "half" lot joining within mentioned half lot owned by Keenan "and within mentioned half lot" 7 feet wide & 35 feet back from the street easterly, under penalty of £100 to be paid by either party who attempts to hinder or stop free passage through the alley, 6 feet of alley to come off the half lot owned by Macklehany (signed) Michael Keenan & John Macklehany; wit. oath Apr. 1790 by John Brown; Jul. 29, 1790 recorded; book I p. 216 [274].

2503. Feb. 23, 1790 John Hall & wife Elizabeth (Brunswick Co, NC) to John Nutt, cabinet maker (Wilmington, New Hanover Co); for £175 NC money sold part of lot #31A in Wilmington on S side of Princess Street; between Front Street & Second Street; border: joined on W by part of John Hall's lot, on S by John Nutt's lot, on E by "ground" formerly occupied by Lehantius Dekeyser, on N by Princess Street, 27.5 feet on Princess street, & 66 feet deep; sold (no date) by Donald Bain to John Hall recorded in book F (sic) p. 474. (signed) John Hall & Elizabeth Hall; (witness) Arthur Howe & John Porter "Grainge"; [note at end indicates Nutt paid Hall £75 (witness) Wm Nutt]; wit. oath Jul. 1790 by Arthur Howe; Jul. 29, 1790; book I p. 218 [276].

2504. Oct. 18, 1788 Hannah Lyon, spinster (Kingston upon Hull town & county) and Mary Brown, widow (same) to Mary Sampson, widow (of Sampson's Hall, Sampson Co, "North America") & Thomas Sewell, merchant (of same county); power of attorney to receive from trustees or executors of John Lyon esq deceased (late of Wilmington, NC) or whoever is concerned £936.6 due to Hannah and £108.6.1 due to Mary from John Lyon deceased & all interest; the money is in default. (signed) Hanh. Lyon & Mary Brown; (witness) (witness) J Porter, mayor [only one witness]; wit. oath Feb. 15, 1790 proved "under attestation" of mayor of Kingston upon Hull (signed) Saml Ashe, JSCLE; Jul. 30, 1790 recorded; book I p. 220 [277].

2505. Nov. 20, 1784 Elizabeth Boone (New Hanover Co) to my children Cathrine Gaillard, Mary Gaillard, & John Gaillard "alias" Cathrine Boone, Mary Boone, & John Boone; for natural love & affection gave (a) following Negroes: Chloe, Abbey, Tom, Ceasar, & Bill with their increase; Negroes & increase to be equally divided among 3 children when children come of age or marry; (b) to Cathrine Gaillard & Mary Gaillard each a good feather bed & furniture; & (c) to John

Gaillard l50 specie when he comes of age or marries. (signed) Elizabeth Boone; (witness) Jno Fergus & John Fergus jr; wit. oath Jun. 18, 1787 by Doctor John Fergus before Saml Spencer, JSCLE; Jul. 30, 1790 recorded; book I p. 221 [278].

2506. Apr. 16, 1787 Sarah Lillington, Henry Watters, & George Moore (New Hanover Co) to George Lillington, gentleman (same); a bond for £8,000 NC money; Sarah is entitled to half of personal estate of her father Alexander Lillington esq deceased exclusive of "some" specific legacies; this part has been valued & delivered today to Sarah by George who is administrator of the will of Alexander Lillington; bond void if Sarah Lillington, Henry Watters, or George Moore pay to George Lillington for Sarah's "ratable" proportion of the debts now due of Alexander Lillington with costs and in future punctually pay proportionable part of debts of the estate if suits are commenced against the estate & judgments issued; George Lillington is authorized to "point out" to the sheriff the property now received by Sarah & [her agreement] to pay proportionable part of debts. (signed) Sarah Lillington, Henry Watters, & Geo Moore; (witness) Sampson Moseley & Saml Watters; wit. oath Jul. 1789 by Sampson Moseley; Jul. 30, 1790 recorded; book I p. 222 [279].

2507. Nov. 27, 1789 Gov. Samuel Johnston (Fayetteville, NC) to James Spiller; grant #262; for £10 per 100 ac granted 110 ac on E side of South R; border: begins at a small bay on bank of the river, joins a marsh, & a "few" yards from corner of "the" county line near the river. (signed) Saml Johnston; (witness) & J Glasgow, Secretary; Jul. 30, 1790 recorded; book I p. 223 [280].

2508. Aug. 6, 1785 John Beck to Charles Jewkes & company; for l100 NC money sold a Negro girl Nancy about 13 years old. (signed) John Beck; (witness) Geo Gibbs [only one witness]; wit. oath Jul. 1790 by Geo Gibbs; book I p. 224 [281].

2509. Oct. 1, 1790 Mildred Swann & F Jones, administrators of estate of Saml Swann esq deceased, to John Jones; for 90 sold a Negro girl Violet. (signed) Mildred Swann & F Jones; (witness) Wm Wright [only one witness]; wit. oath Oct. 1790 by Wm Wright; book I p. 224 [281].

2510. Apr. 24, 1789 James Towning (New Hanover Co) to Joseph Walls (same); for £25 NC money sold 100 ac on S side of Cat Skin Swamp; border: begins at a pine; part of a grant in 1765 by Gov. Wm Tryon to Solomon Towning. (signed) James Towning; (witness) James Jennett & Sarah Jennett; wit. oath Oct. 1789 by James Jennett; Oct. 9, 1790 recorded; book I p. 225 [282].

2511. Jan. 15, 1788 Alexr. McCulloch (Wilmington, New Hanover Co) to John Walker esq (same); for £120 NC money sold a Negro boy Qua. (signed) Alexr. McCulloch; (witness) Geo McCulloch & Ja Walker jr; [note at end indicates McCulloch received £120]; wit. oath Jul. 1789 by "Jas Walker"; Oct. 1790 recorded; book I p. 226 [284].

2512. May 13, 1789 Geo McCulloch & Alexr. McCulloch (New Hanover Co) to John Walker (Wilmington, New Hanover Co); for £120 NC money sold a Negro fellow Dick about 27 years old. (signed) Geo McCulloch & Alexr. McCulloch; (witness) (witness) Ja Walker jr; [note at end indicates Walker paid George & Alexr. £120 May 13, 1789]; wit. oath Jul. 1789 by James Walker (sic); Oct. 1790 recorded; book I p. 227 [285].

2513. Jul. 2, 1790 Richard Price & Michael Molten (New Hanover Co) to Barney Fuller; for 40 cattle sold a Negro boy Matt "or one as likely" by judgment of 3 indifferent people about 16 years old. (signed) Michael Molten & Richd Price; (witness) John Thomson [only one witness]; wit. oath Oct. 1790 by J Thomson; Oct. 1790 recorded; book I p. 228 [286].

2514. Jun. 11, 1790 Thomas Callender, executor of will of Parker Quince deceased, and Richard Quince sr (sic), admor de honis non" of Richard Quince sr deceased, to John Hill, Wm Henry Hill, & Nathl Hill; John Hill, Wm Henry Hill, & Nathl Hill, executors of will of Wm Hill deceased, have discharged a judgment due on execution from Wilmington Dist. Superior Court in favor of Wm Hill's estate against estate of P Quince deceased amounting to £1,500 and agreed to take "certain" Negroes in full payment thereof "at a valuation" AND for £0.5 paid to Callender & Quince sold following 20 Negroes: Ishmael a carpenter, his wife Virtue, their children Sally & Monimia, Robin a cooper, his wife Pindar, their children Johnny, Mary, Bob, Harry, Peggy, Judy, & Becky, Jamey, his wife Jenny, & their children Matty, Tommy, James, & Tetta, & a fellow Huckey and future increase of female slaves. (signed) Richd Quince & Thos Callender; (witness) Henry Kingsburry & Philip Spaulding; wit. oath Jul. 1790 by H Kingsburry; book I p. 228 [287].

2515. Apr. 21, 1790 Mary Harnett (New York City, NY) to John Hester esq (Wilmington, New Hanover Co); power of attorney to sell to George Logan (of Wilmington, NC) a "piece of ground" in Wilmington on E side of Front Street between a lot with 2 tenements owned by me being 2 feet 6 inches wide & runs back East between said lots to E end of my lot. (signed) Mary Harnett; (witness) Alexr. Riddell & Amherst Bartlett; wit. oath Jun. 16, 1790 by Alexander Riddell before Jno Williams, JSCLE; Oct. 14, 1790 recorded; book I p. 230 [288].

2516. Aug. 24, 1788 Thomas Howe, gentleman (New Hanover Co) to James Moore, gentleman (same); for £75 proclamation money sold 320 ac on branches of Smiths Cr; border: begins at a pine by main branch of the creek & joins Jacob Neel. (signed) Thos Howe; (witness) John Moore & John "Olivers"; wit. oath Oct. 1790 by John Oliver; (witness) Oct. 14, 1700 recorded; book I p. 231 [289].

2517. Feb. 4, 1790 Thomas Nixon, planter (New Hanover Co) to Nicholas Nixon, planter (same); for £20 NC money sold 100 ac near New Topsail Sound; border: begins above Bishop Dudley's land where said Dudley formerly lived, begins at a pine near said Dudley's line, & near John Ashe. (signed) Thomas Nixon; (witness) Alexander Jernigan & Robert Nixon; wit. oath Apr. 1790 by Robert

Nixon; Oct. 14, 1790 recorded; book I p. 232 [290].

2518. Jul. 7, 1790 Ceasar Ausustus Beloat & wife Margaret (New Hanover Co) to Charles Simpson (same); for £51 NC money sold 100 ac on NW Cape Fear R in Bladen Co; border: begins at John Singletary's lower corner on E side of the river opposite mouth of Hammonds Cr & joins Singletary's Cr. (signed) C A Beloat & Margaret Beloat; (witness) Alex Carmichaell [only one witness]; dower renounced (no date) by Margaret Beloat before J B Moore; wit. oath Jul. 1790 by Alexr Carmichaell; Oct. 15, 1790 recorded; book I p. 234 [292].

2519. Apr. 29, 1789 Arthur Mabson (New Hanover Co) to Nicholas Nixon (same); for £160 sold 100 ac on New Topsail Sound; border: begins at a line of John Ablin Campbell's survey "since" sold to John Spicer deceased on the sound side & joins "the" patent line; sold (no date) by John Ashe to Ezekiel Alexander who sold to John Ablin Campbell who sold to Arthur Mabson. (signed) Arthur Mabson; (witness) Robert Nixon & Walter Nichols; [note at end indicates Mabson received £160 Apr. 29, 1789]; wit. oath Jan. 1789 by Robert Nixon; Oct. 15, 1790 recorded; book I p. 235 [293].

2520. May 15, 1790 Jonathan Robeson (New Hanover Co) to John Nichols sr (same); for £100 NC money sold two-thirds [omitted] ac of near "the" sound on head of Lees or Licks Cr; border: begins at a pine called in one [of] the conveyances Cannon's now Cuningham's corner on S prong of Lees or Licks Cr, joins corner between this two-thirds & a third conveyed to Messrs. Hane & Burk of Charleston merchants, runs parallel with the sound, joins an old line, main branch of Lees or Licks Cr, above "the" main road, & southermost fork of a branch; known as Erwins place; includes the old "plantation" & buildings or improvements; left by Francis Irwin to his son John [Irwin] who sold Oct. 14, 1785 to Henry Emanuel Lutterloh who "seems" to have sold to Henry Lewis Lutterloh who sold to Henry Tucker merchant (of Wilmington, NC) "et appears to have admitted to be subject to a suit" against Henry Emanuel Lutterloh and Jonathan Robeson & James Moran as securities and judgment against said Lutterloh and land sold by sheriff to Jonathan Robeson. (signed) Jona. Robeson; (witness) Robert Scott & Mar. R Willkings; [note at end indicates Robeson received £100]; wit. oath Jul. 1790 by Robert Scott; Oct. 16, 1790 recorded; book I p. 236 [294].

2521. Sept. 3, 1787 Joseph Alexander, planter, & wife Esther (Onslow Co, NC) to Thomas Nixon, planter (same); for £40 NC money sold 100 ac near New Topsail Sound; border: begins above Bishop Dudley's land where said Dudley formerly lived, begins at a pine near said Dudley's line, & near John Ashe. (signed) Joseph Alexander & Esther's mark "X"; (witness) Mary James & Thos Bishop; wit. oath Oct. 1790 by Thos Bishop; Oct. 16, 1790 recorded; book I p. 238 [296].

2522. Sept. 3, 1787 Joseph Alexander & wife Esther (NC) to Thomas Nixon, planter (same); for £40 NC money sold 240 ac on E side of Sandy Run & both sides of "the" main road; border: begins at a water oak on Sandy Run below the road near Geo Musick's line, crosses the main road, near Galberry Pocosin, crosses Woolf Ridge, near David Alexander, & on N side of "the wood bitch". (signed) Joseph Alexander & Esther's mark "X"; (witness) Mary James & Thos Bishop; wit. oath Oct. 1790 by Thos Bishop; Oct. 18, 1790 recorded; book I p. 239 [297].

2523. May 17, 1788 Alexander Jernagin, planter (New Hanover Co) to Peter Batson (same); for £100 NC money sold 75 ac on head of Middle Cr on New Topsail [Sound]; border: begins at a pine. (signed) Alexander Jernagin; (witness) Thos Nixon & John Morris; [note at end indicates Batson paid Jernagin £100 May 17, 1788]; wit. oath Oct. 1790 by Thos Nixon; Oct. 18, 1790 recorded; book I p. 240 [298].

2524. Apr. 8, 1790 Archibald Maclaine esq, surviving executor of will of John Lyon esq deceased, to Charles Simpson, planter (New Hanover Co); John Lyon wrote a will May 21, 1775 and directed funeral expenses & just debts to be paid and gave to his executors all his real & personal estate except his Negro slaves & household furniture; real & personal estate were to be sold "for the uses of his will"; until the sale, executors were accountable for profits from estate which was to be "laid out & employed" to best advantage of his legatees; executors were Mildred Lyon & Saml Swann both deceased, Archibald Maclaine, & George Seaman Inman; for £210 for tracts a & b and £8 for tract c: (a) 640 ac on E side of Black R & both sides of Calvins Cr; border: begins at John Marshall's beginning corner bay of another survey on W side of the creek & joins Charles Simpson; 320 ac of this tract is now sold; 640 ac was granted Dec. 24, 1771 to John "Marshal" & John Lyon; (b) 100 ac; border: joins tract a; where John Marshall formerly lived & mortgaged by John Marshall to John Lyon and mortgage elapsed; part of 640 ac granted Feb. 20, 1735 to Charles Harrison; (c) 100 ac on E side of South R & both sides of Marsh Br at its head; border: begins at a pine; granted Dec. 20, 1763 to Soloman Huffham jr; all 3 tracts advertised Feb. 10, 1786 and during following month of March to be sold Apr. 3 next and sale to continue until land was sold; sale was adjourned from day to day until Apr. 7 when sale was held at the court house in Wilmington for 12 months credit. (signed) A Maclaine; [no witness]; Apr. 1790 acknowledged; Oct. 19, 1790 recorded; book I p. 241 [299].

2525. May 19, 1789 George McCulloch (living in Wilmington, NC) to Thomas Lucas (Brunswick Co, NC); for £100 sold following household furniture: 2 square "mohogany" tables, a tea table, a dining table, 7 Windsor chairs, a maple desk, a large looking glass, 3 beds & bed cloths in full, a "mattras", 4 bedsteads, a large quantity of crocery ware, 12 pictures, 3 iron pots, & all my kitchen furniture to tedious to mention; & (b) a mulatto boy Yance about 10 years old. (signed) George McCulloch; (witness) Lawrence A Dorsey & R Bannerman; wit. oath Jul. 1790 by L A Dorsey; Oct. 26, 1790 recorded; book I p. 245 [302].

2526. Dec. 22, 1788 Baker Bouden (New Hanover Co) to Thomas Beesley (Duplin Co, NC); for £60 specie sold 80 ac on E side of Long Cr; between Anthony Bourdeaux & James Portevint; border: begins at a pine by the swamp of the creek & joins James Portevint; granted Feb. 30, 1754 by Gov. Matthew Rowan to Peter Lamb who sold to John Williams who sold to Daniel "Burdox" who sold to Baker Bouden. (signed) Baker Bouden's mark "B"; (witness) Joel Parish & Solomon Beesley; wit. oath Jul. 1790 by Solomon Beesley; Oct. 27, 1790 recorded; book I p. 245 [302].

2527. Jul. 11, 1783 James "Richard", tavern keeper (Wilmington, NC) to John Walker, merchant (same); for 532 silver Spanish milled dollars sold 2 Negroes: a woman Phillis & a young fellow Jim. (signed) John "Bichard"; (witness) William Moseley [only one witness]; [following lined out: deed void if Richard pays Walker 532 silver Spanish milled dollars by Jan. 11, 1784 (signed) Jno Walker]; wit. oath Jun. 15, 1790 by William Moseley before Saml Ashe, JSCLE; Oct. 29, 1790 recorded; book I p. 247 [304].

2528. Dec. 21, 1780 Samuel Campbell, copartner of late copartnership of Hogg & Campbell (Wilmington, New Hanover Co) to James Hogg, heir principal legatee & executor of will of his deceased brother Robert Hogg (Orange Co, NC); for £0.5 British sterling sold & for "diverse other things" mentioned in an agreement between S Campbell & J Hogg dated Dec. [blank], 1780 SOLD (a) a moiety of house & lot in town of Bogue in Onslow Co, NC, on W side of White oak R; border: begins at Mr. Lee's corner, runs 60 feet along the water & Front Street to Second Street, along said street to Stephen Lee's upper corner, down to "the" country road or main street, 200 feet up said street, & "his" line to beginning; being an "exact" parallelogram or oblong square; known as the "Whay"; part of "plantation" where Theophilus & Grace Wicks lived; sold May 11, 1771 by Thoephilus & Grace Wicks to Edward Starkey & purchased Sept. 22, 1775 from him; (b) and sold all land between front line of said lot & the water. (signed) Saml Campbell; (witness) Will Hooper, John Gordon, & Ja Burges; [note at end indicates Campbell received £0.5]; (Cumberland Co, NC) wit. oath Dec. 23, 1782 by James Burges before Saml Spencer, JSCLE; Nov. 7, 1790 recorded; book I p. 248 [305].

2529. Jul. 30, 1790 William Jones (Massachusetts) to Jonathan Huntington (Wilmington, NC); for £109.17 NC money sold a Negro boy I called Virgil. (signed) Wm Jones; (witness) John "Allan" & Wm Gordon; wit. oath Oct. 1790 by John Allen; Nov. 22, 1790 recorded; book I p. 249 [306].

2530. Jun. 11, 1790 James Fleeming, merchant (New Hanover Co) to Joseph Eakens, gentleman (same); for £15 2 tracts: (a) 100 ac on Cypress Br of Long Cr; border: begins at a black oak below "the" old tract path & joins edge of a small savanna; & (b) 200 ac on widow Moores Cr; border: begins at a small pine in a small marsh near & on E side of the creek & crosses Bearden Br. (signed) Jas

Fleeming; (witness) J Jennings & Pettigrew Moore; wit. oath Oct. 1790 by Jona. Jennings; Dec. 8, 1790 recorded; book I p. 250 [307].

2531. Apr. 29, 1790 John B Moore (NC) to Jane Howe (NC); for £100 sold a Negro boy Toby. (signed) Jno B Moore; (witness) Thos C Howe [or Nowe] [only one witness]; Jul. 1790 acknowledged; Dec. 9, 1790 recorded; book I p. 251 [308].

2532. [blank], 1789 Thomas Gidins [or Giddons] & Benjamin Gidins (New Hanover Co) to Archibald Cook (same); for £32 sold 200 ac on E side of widow Moore's Cr; border: begins at a white oak in Moores Creek Swamp, joins Pettigrew Moore, Gray, John Burns, & crosses "the laurel". (signed) Thomas Giddins' (sic) mark ["X" with half circle above it] & Benjamin Giddins' mark "X"; (witness) Bartholomew Byrns & Joseph Eakens; wit. oath Oct. 1790 by Joseph Eakens; Dec. 11, 1790 acknowledged; book I p. 252 [309].

2533. Feb. 17, 1783 Thomas Davis esq (New Hanover Co) to John Walker esq (same); by attachment, Walker obtained "again" the goods, chattels, land, & tenements of John Downie trader (late of New Hanover Co) returnable to New Hanover Co court Apr. 1782; "then" the sheriff made a return that he levied the same on "plantation" called Cowpen on NE Cape Fear R as John Downie's property; an execution issued from New Hanover Co court returnable to Jan. 1783 court based on judgment on the attachment in favor of Walker for £183.7 specie & costs; land was sold Feb. 16, "instant" for £90 by Sheriff Thomas Wright to Walker; but Walker believes some doubt may arise respecting Downie's title since there doesn't appear to be a deed to Downie from Thomas Davis former proprietor of the land & grantor of present deed; SO Davis says he sold the land to Downie before the attachment; for £0.5 Davis quit claims land to Walker. (signed) Tho Davis; (witness) Thos McLorinan & Thos Callender; [note at end indicates Davis received £0.5 Feb. 17, 1783]; wit. oath Jun. 16, 1790 by Thos Callender before Jno Williams, JSCLE; Dec. 17. 1790 recorded; book I p. 252 [310].

2534. Feb. 16, 1783 Thomas Wright, sheriff (New Hanover Co) to John Walker esq; for £90 sold 200 ac on NE Cape Fear R; called Cowpen [no more description]; formerly owned by George Moore esq who sold to Thomas Davis esq who is "said to have" sold to John Downie; sold Dec. 14, 1782 at Wilmington due to a writ of fieri facias for £183.7 & costs from New Hanover Co court returnable to court Apr. 1783 against John Downie trader (late of New Hanover Co) due to suit by John Walker. (signed) Thos Wright, sheriff; (witness) Henry Young & Henry Toomer; [note at end indicates Wright received £90 "Feb. 16"]; wit. oath Jun. 16, 1790 by Henry Toomer before Jno Williams, JSCLE; Dec. 18, 1790 recorded; book I second p. 254 [311].

2535. Nov. 18, 1790 William Jones, taylor (New Hanover Co), administrator of goods & chattels of Phillip Jones "house wright" (late of Wilmington, NC), to Samuel Lowder, merchant (New Hanover Co); for £320 sold lot [no number] in Wilmington; border: begins on S corner of Forster's line on Second Street, runs

50 feet on Forster's line, S 27 feet, E 50 feet to Second Street, & up Second Street to first station. (signed) William Jones; (witness) Thos Wright & Mar. R Willkings; [note at end indicates Lowder paid Jones £320]; wit. oath Dec. 17, 1790 by Thomas Wright esq before Jno Williams, JSCLE; Dec. 21, 1790 recorded; book I second p. 254 (no p. 255 in copy of book I) [312].

2536. Dec. 27, 1790 Peter Mangeon, merchant (Wilmington, New Hanover Co) to John Burgwin, merchant (same); for £550 NC money sold part of lot #1A on N side of Market Street in Wilmington; border: 31 feet front on said street & runs back 66 feet, joined on E by lot now owned by George Hooper, N by lot formerly owned by Alexander Duncan, & on W by house & land of James Moran; occupied by John Mauger as tenant; sold (no date) by Joseph Eagles & wife Sarah to Marshal Robert Willkings who sold to Jonathan Tomkins who sold to John Mauger who sold to Peter Mangeon who mortgaged it Apr. 6, 1790 to Auly MacNaughton merchant (of Wilmington, NC) as collateral for payment of £428.15.2 NC money with interest; Mangeon defends title to lot except for the mortgage of £428.15.2; on Aug. 6 last Mangeon gave power of attorney to Auly MacNaughton to sell the lot if Mangeon defaulted on the mortgage, but now Mangeon voids that power of attorney. (signed) P Mangeon; (witness) John Mauger & Edwd James; [note at end indicates Burgwin paid Mangeon £550 (witness) John Gibson]; wit. oath Jan. 1791 by John Mauger; Jan. 6, 1791 recorded; book I p. 257 [314].

2537. Apr. 30, 1780 Gov. Richard Caswell (Kingston, NC) to James Moore; grant #104; for £0.50 per 100 ac granted 100 ac on N side of Burgaw [Cr] & W side of NE River; border: begins at a dead pine, joins a pocoson, a savanna, & a bay swamp. (signed) Rd Caswell & Wm Sheppard, D Sec; Jan. 1791 presented to court & ordered recorded (signed) Thos Maclaine, clerk; Jan. 22, 1791 recorded; book I p. 260 [317].

2538. Dec. 4, 1789 Robert Bell (Franklin Co, NC), one of heirs of property of late George Bell, and John Medearis (Wake Co, NC), on behalf of his 2 sons: Washington David Medearis & Ben Whitehead Hix Medearis, heirs of George Bell, to Joshua A Potts (Wilmington, NC); for £350 NC money sold 627 square "or superficial" feet or part of lot in Wilmington on S side of Market Street near the river; border: 19 feet in front on said street, runs at right angle 33 feet South, joined on property of John Brown & Joshua Potts on E, property of heirs of John Quince deceased on S, "present" property of Henry Toomer on W next to the river, & S line of Market Street on N; being a subdivison of lot formerly owned by Jonathan Dunbibbin & part that was sold (no date) by Sheriff Thomas Wright to Jonathan Thompkins who sold to George Bell; being the half of tenement where an old warehouse stands & is lower or W part of the tenement. (signed) Robt Bell & John Medearis; (witness) Wm Nutt & Ge. Logan; wit. oath Jan. 1790 by William Nutt; Feb. 3, 1791 recorded; book I p. 261 [318].

2539. Dec. 4, 1789 John Medearis (Wake Co, NC) to Joshua A Potts, merchant

(Wilmington, NC); a bond for £5,000 NC money; today Joshua A Potts sold two-thirds of a lot or tenement in Wilmington on S side of Market Street near the water; border: 19 feet front on the street & 33 feet deep; sold (no date) by Jonathan D Tomkins to late George Bell an two-thirds descended to Washington D Medearis & Ben L Medearis, infant sons of John Medearis; Robert bell owns other part of the lot according to acts of Assembly regulating descent of real estate; bond void if Medearis keeps Potts harmless from claims by the infants on the title to the lot. (signed) John Medearis; (witness) Wm Nutt [only one witness]; wit. oath Jan. 1790 by Willm Nutt; Feb. 4, 1791 recorded; book I p. 262 [319].

2540. May 9, 1789 Gillam Bass, attorney for widow & heirs of William Wimble deceased who was son & heir of James Wimble deceased [as in records of New Hanover Co court], to Joshua Potts (Wilmington, NC); for £50 NC money sold 0.5 ac in lot [102 on S side of Market Street] in Wilmington; border: begins on E side of Front Street, runs E 330 feet to second street, S 66 feet on second Street, W 330 feet to Front Street, & N 66 feet on Front Street to beginning, joins Front Street on W, William Campbell's or Samuel Campbell's lot #97 on N, Second Street on E, & lot #107 on S. (signed) Gillam Bass, attorney for heirs of Willm Wimble deceased; (witness) Henry Hoskins & John Nutt; wit. oath Jan. 1790 by Henry Hoskins; Feb. 4, 1791 recorded; book I p. 263 [320].

2541. Jan. 1, 1790 Thomas Cunningham sr (New Hanover Co) to Joshua Potts; for £5 and for a dwelling, store house, kitchen, & other necessary buildings erected on part of a lot in Wilmington leased for 10 years 924 [square feet] or part of a lot on W side of Front Street; border: 28 feet on Front Street, runs W 33 feet at right angle, joins Front Street on E, the alley on S, Thomas Cunningham's land on W, "property of a minor" on N which joins Front Street & Dock Street; being front part of lot where Mrs. Kirkwood lives; 5 feet excepted for "common" alley on E side of the part of the lot; within 10 years, Potts is to build on part of a lot a framed house 24 feet long 16.5 feet wide with "proportionable" pitch or height with second story formed with a hipped or Dutch roof so as to have dwelling & lodging rooms above & lower story to be fixed for a store & counting room with a brick chimney & a fire place on each story, house to be set on a foundation of stone or brick at least a foot high from the ground, & house to be finished in a plain workman like manner having necessary doors, windows etc as customary; also to build a kitchen for cooking of common construction joining or separate from the dwelling house; if there is fire or other unavoidable accident, Potts loses his labour & expense of building without Potts having second expense of building; if there is no accident Potts to deliver lot & improvements to Cunningham on Jan. 1 1800. (signed) Thomas Cunningham's mark "X C" & Joshua Potts; (witness) Sedgick Springs & Thos Cunningham jr; wit. oath Jan. 1796 by S Springs; Feb. 5, 1791 recorded; book I p. 264 [321].

2542. Apr. 14, 1779 Lewis Henry DeRosset esq (New Hanover Co) to Charles Jewkes, merchant (Wilmington, New Hanover Co); for £60 sterling Great Britain money sold 0.5 ac in lot #7 on old plan in Wilmington on Front Street; border:

opposite water lot formerly owned by Thomas Sawier, 66 feet in front, back 320 feet, joined on S by lot formerly owned by William Ford, on N by lot "called" Mitchell's, between "middle" Market Street & Ann Street; sold Dec. 16, 1742 by Thomas Sawier to Jno Porter deceased and taken by execution due to suit by Daniel Laroche (of SC) against estate of John Porter an sold Aug. 18, 1749, with other lots & pieces of land taken at same time by execution, by New Hanover Co Sheriff Lewis DeRosset to Daniel Laroche and sold Oct. 29 & 30, 1753 by Daniel Laroche to Lewis Henry DeRosset. (signed) Lewis DeRosset (sic); (witness) Thos Cobham & John DuBois; [note at end indicates Jewkes paid DeRosset £60 Apr. 14, 1779]; wit. oath Dec. 18, 1789 by William Campbell esq, before Saml Spencer JSCLE, & Campbell recognized hand writing of "late" Lewis Henry DeRosset esq "on left hand side of seal" of this deed and recognized hand writing of John Dubois "late" of Wilmington now resident of New York & accepted by Spencer due to act of General Assembly for granting further time for proving old deeds; Feb. 10, 1719; book I p. 266 [323].

2543. (Brunswick Co, NC) Oct. 28, 1790 Benjamin Smith esq (Belvidere, Brunswick Co, NC) to Archibald Maclaine, Thos Maclaine, William Campbell, James Read, James A Campbell, Thomas Withers, Robert Scott, Joshua Potts, Benjamin Smith, Henry Toomer, George Hooper, Aulay mcNaughton, & Robert M Wilkings esqs, commissioner for regulating pilotage & navigation of Cape Fear R "for use of the state"; Smith is willing to promote & encourage trade & navigation in North Carolina, SO for "good causes" gave 10 ac in Cape Fear Island for sole purpose of erecting a light house thereon; border: includes the spot already fixed by the commissioners for a lighthouse [no more description]; part of a grant (no date) to Landgrave Thos Smith; sold under limitations in act of General Assembly passed Dec. 22, 1789 at Fayetteville and provided lighthouse is completed within 10 years from today to be kept up & well maintained for benefit of navigation on Cape Fear [R]. (signed) Benja Smith; (witness) Ed Jones & J G Scull; (Fayetteville, NC) Dec. 9, 1790 acknowledged before John Williams JSCLE; Feb. 11, 1790; book I p. 262 [325].

2544. May 7, 1789 Elizabeth Wimble (Boston, Suffolk Co, Massachusetts), widow of William Wimble mariner deceased, Gillam Bass, merchant, & wife Rebecca (same), Lewis Maresquelle, gentleman, & wife Katherine (Dracut, Middlesex Co, Mass), & Elisabeth Bass (Boston, Mass), grand daughter of Elizabeth Wimble, to John Nutt, cabinet maker (Wilmington, New Hanover Co); for £300 sold lot #202B in Wilmington; border: 66 feet wide, runs from the river water to Front Street, divided by New Street, joined on S by Mr. Craike, on N by Thomas Clark, & on E by Front Street; formerly owned by William Wimble deceased, son & heir of James Wimble mariner deceased. (signed) Elizabeth Wimble, Gillam Bass, Rebecca Bass, Lewis Manesquelle, Katherine Manesquelle, & Elizabeth Bass; (witness) Joshua Potts & Henry Hoskins; wit. oath Oct. 1790 by Henry Hoskins; Feb. 11, 1790 recorded; book I p. 269 [326].

2545. Oct. 9, 1790 Archibald Maclaine, one of executors of will of Francis

Clayton esq deceased, to Brunetta; Clayton signed his will Oct. 2, instant &, for fidelity of Negro woman Brunetta, manumitted the Brunetta; Clayton directed his executors to apply to New Hanover Co court for emancipation, or if that couldn't be obtained, then Brunetta to be sent to most convenient of United States to be liberated; executors were Archibald Maclaine, Henry Urquhart, Henry Toomer, & Thomas Clayton; Maclaine, Urquhart, & Toomer proved the will in court & became executors; Maclaine, empowered by the court present Oct. term, emancipates Brunetta. (signed) A Maclaine; (witness) Thos Maclaine clerk [only one witness]; Oct. 1790 "signed in court" & ordered recorded; Feb. 25, 1791; book I p. 271 [328].

2546. May 16, 1789 Schenking Moore, planter (Brunswick Co, NC) to Henry Watters, executor of Roger Davis; for £510 sold 5 Negroes: 3 fellows Johnny, Hickey, & Quaco and 2 wenches Venus & Minda; Watters holds "several" bonds executed by Moore to Watters as executor of Roger Davis for £510; sale void if Moore pays bonds. (signed) Schk Moore; (witness) T Hill [only one witness]; [note at end indicates Watters paid Moore £510]; wit. oath Jul. 1789 by Thos Hill; Feb. 26, 1791; book I p. 272 [329].

2547. May 1, 1788 Hiram J Richards to William Green; for £360 sold a Negro fellow Cesar, his wife Satira, & 4 children Tom, Sarah, Deny, & Joe; Negroes were in estate of David Forbes deceased and sold today at public vendue by Richards as administrator. (signed) Hiram J Richards; (witness) John Bradley [only one witness]; Jul. 1789 acknowledged; Mar. 1, 1791 recorded; book I p. 273 [330].

2548. May 2, 1788 Hiram J Richards to William Green; for £169 sold a Negro wench Conney & a fellow Vulcan, formerly owned by Norman Harrison Chevers deceased and sold by me as his administrator. (signed) Hiram J Richards; (witness) Richard Bradley [only one witness]; Jul. 1789 acknowledged; Mar. 1, 1791 recorded; book I p. 273 [330].

2549. Mar. 6, 1789 Edmond Moore (New Hanover Co) to Thomas Picket; for £142.10 NC money sold a Negro man Friday. (signed) Edmd Moore; [no witness]; Jul. 1789 acknowledged; Mar. 1, 1791 recorded; book I p. 274 [331].

2550. Jul. 8, 1789 James White to John Fergus; for £150 sold a Negro fellow Tom, gardner [or goudner]. (signed) James White; [no witness; Jul. 1789 acknowledged; Mar. 1, 1791 recorded; book I p. 274 [331].

2551. Jun. 7, 1788 John Holland, merchant (Wilmington, NC) to Messrs Lane, Son & Fraser, merchants (London); Holland owes Lane Son & Fraser a "very considerable sum" and is "strongly solicited" for payment by John Lane, on of the partners of said "house" now in Wilmington; Holland is presently unable to pay the debt; William "Capbell" & Co and Lewis McPherson & Co merchants (of Wilmington) and "sundry" other people in North Carolina owe Holland; notes &

open accounts to a "considerable" sum are owed to me by annexed schedule; to secure payment & for £0.5 sold to John Lane, on behalf of Lane, Son & Fraser, all debts due to me; Holland also gives power of attorney to John Lane & John Burgwin, for benefit of Lane Son & Fraser, to receive money owed to Holland; attorneys can sue for nonpayment. (signed) John Holland; (witness) Hu Waddell & Geo Lucas;

Jun. 7, 1788 schedule of notes & accounts due to John Holland & assigned to Lane Son & Fraser of London: William Campbell & Co note in 1785 besides interest £150; Lewis McPherson & Co ditto £135; Lewis McPherson acct. unsettled about £200; James Fleeming's bonds, notes & accounts unsettled; Patrick Travers acct signed; Saml Gates note; Wm Campbell & Lewis McPherson acct to Lewis McPherson & by him assigned account to about £560 (signed) John Holland (witness) Hugh Waddell; Jun. 15, 1789 acknowledged before Saml Ashe, JSCLE; Mar. 7, 1791 recorded; book I p. 275 [332].

2552. Jul. 7, 1789 Daniel Mallet (New Hanover Co) to William Walker, planter (same); for £100 NC money sold a Negro girl Bridget about 14 years old & her increase. (signed) D Mallett; (witness) Arthur Stuckey & Presley Simpson; wit. oath Jul. 1789 by Arthur Stuckey; Mar. 9, 1791 recorded; book I p. 277 [334].

2553. Aug. 9, 1788 William Wilkinson (or Wilkeson) (Duplin Co, NC) to George Jacobs (Wilmington, NC); for £150 sold part of lot #4 in Wilmington on Market Street; border: joins the church lot, 41 feet wide fronting on Market Street, runs 66 feet back to lot owned by Benjamin Heron esq, 41 feet along said lot, & 66 feet to Market Street. (signed) Wm Wilkinson; (witness) Henry Hoskins, Robt Wells, & Jacob "Friout"; [note at end indicates Jacobs paid Wilkinson £150 Aug. 11, 1788]; wit. oath Jul. 1789 by Henry Hoskins; Mar. 10, 1791 recorded; book I p. 274 [334].

2554. Jan. 23, 1789 James Howard (New Hanover Co) to mark McClamey (same); for £104 sold on Topsail Sound & E side of Stockley Bishop's mill Cr; border: begins at the crossing place of School house Br, joins fork of the branch at said Mill Cr, & a branch that divides said Howard from Atkinson; sold (no date) by Thomas Merrick and Mark & Luke "McClamy" to James Howard "both" deeds included in this deed. (signed) Jams. Howard; (witness) Thos Bishop & John Batt; wit. oath Jul. 1789 by John Batt; Mar. 11, 1791 recorded; book I p. 279 [336].

2555. Mar. 3, 1789 Mark McClamay [or McClammy] (New Hanover Co) to Philip Clayton, planter (same); for £25.19 NC money sold 820 ac in 4 tracts: (a) 300 ac on both sides of "the" main road E of "the Punch Bowl"; border: begins at a pine on E side of a pond on N side of the road, crosses the road, joins John Coston, & a gallberry [swamp ?]; granted in 1767 by Gov. William Tryon to [omitted]; (b) 250 ac on N side of "the" main road, back of the Punch Bowl Ridge & Pond; border: begins at a pine near middle of Punch Bowl Ridge near a pond & joins edge of a gallberry; granted (no date) by Gov. Wm Tryon to [omitted]; (c) 200 ac on NW side of "the" main road, on head of Whitehouses Cr, & on a ridge joining Reedy Neck; border: begins at a lightwood stake near head of Whitehouses Cr "or rather" George Merrick esq's corner, joins "the" cowpens, & edge of a gallberry; & (d) 70 ac on N side of "the" main road "the island" called Whitehouses Cowpens; border: begins at a crooked pine in the bottom of said cowpens & joins Thomas Barlow; except the timber of whatever kind growing on the land reserved for McClamay. (signed) Mark McClamay; (witness) M F [or T} Blake [only one witness]; Jul. 1789 acknowledged; Mar. 11, 1791 recorded; book I p. 280 [337].

2556. Jul. 11, 1788 Gov. Samuel Johnston (Fairfield, NC) to Benjamin Smith; grant #178; for £0.50 per 100 ac granted 153 ac in Brunswick Co, NC; border: begins at Thomas Craik's corner on Black R, joins "the thoroughfar", & Bendeau. (signed) Sam Johnston & W Williams, D Secretary; Mar. 15, 1791 recorded; book I p. 282 [339].

2557. Jul. 11, 1788 Gov. Samuel Johnston (Fairfield, NC) to Benjamin Smith; grant #209; for £10 per 100 ac granted 230 ac in Brunswick Co, NC; border: begins at a stake on a line of land laid out to Jos Waters, joins Lyon Cr, & Benjamin Smith. (signed) Sam Johnston & W Williams, D Secretary; Mar. 15, 1791 recorded; book I p. 283 [340].

2558. Mar. 4, 1789 John Erwin, planter (New Hanover Co) to Thomas & William James, sons of David James factor (same); for £200 NC money sold 2 tracts: (a) 200 ac; border: begins at David Morgan's corner white oak on Morgans Cr "a little" below an old mill dam, joins a dividing line of "the" old tract, & Rurks; & (b) 200 ac; border: begins at a red oak on said creek swamp "a little" above Sawyer's Landing & joins a marsh; sold (no date) by Ezekiel Morgan to John Erwin. (signed) John Erwin; (witness) Benjn. Gardner & David James (sic); [note at end indicates Thomas & William James, "by hands" of their father David James, paid Erwin £200 Mar. 4, 1789]; Jul. 1789 acknowledged; Mar. 17, 1791 recorded; book I p. 284 [341].

2559. Jan. 19, 1778 Lewis Henry DeRosset esq & wife Margaret (New Hanover Co) to Peter Mallet, merchant (Wilmington, NC); on Nov. 29, 1770 DeRosset sold to Mallet a water lot in Wilmington; border: 66 feet wide, joined on S by lot now "or lately" owned by William Purviance esq, on N by lot lately owned by James Henderson deceased now occupied by Ancrum & Brice, & between Orange Street & Ann Street; known is town plan as 71B but "in Wimble's plan" #11; formerly owned by Robt Walker esq deceased; DeRosset agreed to take as consideration for the lot 3 Negro slaves "such as mentioned" in the deed and £20 proclamation money; in Sept. 1772 Mallet delivered 3 Negroes to DeRosset & paid £20; Mallet has made a wharf, built houses, & at "very considerable expense" erected several valuable improvements thereon; SO for said Negroes & £20 and for £0.5 sold the above lot 71B between Orange Street & Ann Street. (signed) Lewis DeRosset & Margaret DeRosset; (witness) Wm Campbell & Jas Porterfield; [note at end indicates Mallet paid DeRosset 3 Negro men & £20 in Sept. 1772 & £0.5 today];

wit. oath Dec. 18, 1789 by William Campbell esq, due to act of General Assembly in such cases, before Saml Spencer, JSCLE; Mar. 17, 1791 recorded; book I p. 286 [343].

2560. Dec. 11, 1790 John Ashe esq (New Hanover Co) to Samuel Ashe esq (same); for £200 sold his moiety of [omitted] ac on New Topsail Sound [no more description]; devised by General John Ashe by will to his sons William "Algernoon" Ashe & Acourt Ashe or survivor of them and if survivor died without heirs land to be divided between his 2 other sons said John & Samuel Ashe and which "he" now owns by death of William Algernoon Ashe & Acourt Ashe without heirs. (signed) John Ashe; (witness) Jonn Huntington & Robt Harley; [note at end indicates John received £200]; wit. oath Mar. 12, 1791 by Jonathan Huntington before Sam Ashe, JSC; Mar. 18, 1791 recorded; book I p. 288 [345].

2561. Oct. 10, 1788 Richard Quince "now the elder", gentleman (New Hanover Co), only son & heir of Richard Quince jr deceased (late of Brunswick Co, NC) to Lewis McPherson, merchant (Wilmington, NC); for £135 NC money sold his undivided half of water lot #22A in Wilmington; formerly owned by trading house of Campbell, Hooper, & company and at "general" sale of said company's property was bought by Richard Quince jr deceased & Parker Quince now also deceased. (signed) Richd Quince; (witness) John Bradley [only one witness]; [note at end indicates McPherson paid Quince £130]; wit. oath Jul. 1789 by J Bradley; Mar. 19, 1791 recorded; book I p. 289 [346].

2562. Dec. 23, 1790 John Grange, gentleman (Bladen Co, NC) to Alfred Moore esq; for £160 sold a Negro man Joe a black smith & his wife Pegg. (signed) Jno Grange sr; (witness) Arthur Howe & James Grange; [note at end indicates Moore paid Grange £160]; wit. oath Mar. 15, 1791 by Arthur Howe before Jno Williams, JSCLE; Mar. 24, 1791 recorded; book I p. 290 [348].

2563. Dec. 23, 1790 John Hall esq (Brunswick Co, NC), administrator of Thomas Neal (late of Brunswick Co, NC) to Alfred Moore, on behalf of Sarah Nash a minor; for £100 sold a Negro woman Betty & her child Josey; sold due to order of Brunswick Co court for selling slaves belonging to said estate to pay debts. (signed) John Hall; (witness) Arthur Howe [only one witness]; wit. oath Mar. 15, 1791 by Arthur Howe before Jno Williams, JSCLE; Mar. 31, 1791 recorded; book I p. 291 [348].

2564. Dec. 24, 1790 Mary Hanson, widow "formerly" widow & devisee of John Campbell deceased (late of Wilmington, NC) and Rachel Campbell, daughter & devise of John Campbell, to John Walker esq (Wilmington, NC); for £22 sold two-thirds of an undivided lot (no number) on N side of Market Street; border: begins 145 feet from Third Street, runs 50 feet up Market Street, 165 feet N at right angle, W 50 feet parallel with Market Street, & S 165 feet parallel to Third Street to beginning; remaining third of land owned by Mary Campbell (of New

York), daughter of John Campbell; sold [blank], 1744 by Joshua Grainger & wife Katherine to John Campbell who willed it to be equally divided among Mary Hanson then Mary Campbell, Mary Campbell, & Rachel Campbell by will recorded in New Hanover Co. (signed) Mary Hanson & Rachel Campbell; (witness) Amaciah Jocelin, Wm Routledge, & Samuel R Jocelin; [note at end indicates Mary & Rachel received £22]; Mar. 11, 1791 acknowledged by Mary Hanson & Rachel Campbell before Sam Ashe, JSCLE; Apr. 1, 1791 recorded; book I p. 291 [349].

2565. Mar. 29, 1791 Jacob Lewis (New Hanover Co) to Phenly Murphy [or Finely Murphey] (same); for £100 sold part of [omitted] ac on W side of Pinsleys Br; part of a survey that begins at a pine on said branch by a pond, runs S40W 45 chains to a pine, S50E 45 chains to a small pine, N40E 45 chains to a stake, & N 50W 45 chains to first station. (signed) Joseph Lewis; (witness) Charles Murphy & Wm Hennesy; wit. oath Apr. 1791 by C Murphy; Apr. 5, 1791 recorded; book I p. 293 [351].

2566. Mar. 12, 1790 James Flowers (Brunswick, Co, NC), Joshua Potts (Wilmington, NC), & John Hall (Brunswick Co, NC) to James Walker; "sometime ago" Flowers sold to Walker 4 female Negroes: Pheley, Tabb, Polly, & Sally; payment was made to James Hogg by "indorsement of" David Flowers deceased's bond for £350 NC money; SO Flowers, Potts, & Hall agree to warrant title to the Negroes & their increase to Walker against any claims by bond for £1,000 NC money. (signed) Jas Flowers, Joshua Potts, & Jno Hall; (witness) John Brown [only one witness]; wit. oath Apr. 1791 by John Brown; Apr. 9, 1791 recorded; book I p. 294 [352].

2567. Jan. 1, 1791 John Colvin (New Hanover Co) to Mary & Eleanor Scull, daughters of my sister Mary Scull wife of John Gambier Scull (same); for "valuable consideration" sold a young Negro girl Clarinda about 7 year old & her increase. (signed) John Colvin; [no witness]; Apr. 1791 acknowledged; Apr. 9, 191 recorded; book I p. 294 [352].

2568. Apr. 9, 1784 A Maclaine to Caleb Grainger esq; letter of guarantee: you have given or promised my brother Thomas Maclaine a credit in Charleston & another in England; I hereby engage to indemnify you for such money as you may be, on account of these credits, obliged to pay & I intend this engagement is to operate against me & my representatives in favor of you & your estate. (signed) A Maclaine; [no witness]; Apr. 1791 "proved to be hand writing of A Maclaine" (signed) Tho Maclaine, clerk; Apr. 9, 1791 recorded; book I p. 295 [353].

2569. Nov. 26, 1789 Gov. Samuel Johnston (Fayetteville, NC) to Petegrew Moore; grant #276; for £0.50 per 100 ac granted 100 ac on E side of Black R & both sides of "the" main road; border: begins at Solomon Hewes' [or Hewer] corner pine. (signed) Sam Johnston & J Glasgow, Secretary; Apr. 13, 1791 recorded; book I p. 296 [354].

2570. Nov. 26, 1789 Gov. Samuel Johnston (Fayetteville, NC) to Petegrew "Moor"; grant #291; for £0.50 per 100 ac granted 50 ac on E side of Black R, both sides of main road, & both sides of Bear Br; border: begins at a pine on John Lyon's & George Parmer's line. (signed) Sam Johnston & J Glasgow, Secretary; Apr. 13, 1791 recorded; book I p. 297 [355].

2571. Dec. 3, 1790 Gov. Alexander Martin (Fayetteville, NC) to Petegrew Moore; grant #293; for £10 per 100 ac granted 50 ac on E side of Black R; border: begins at a hickory, joins Dennis Moore's thoroughfair, & James Smith; includes James Smith's improvements. (signed) Alexr Martin & J Glasgow, Secretary; Apr. 13, 1791 recorded; book I p. 2987 [355].

2572. Jul. 10, 1790 Thomas Maclaine (Wilmington, New Hanover Co) to George Hooper (same); for £600 NC money sold 2 tracts: (a) part of water lot #1A in Wilmington on N side of Market Street; border: begins at & includes an old cellar wall, joins house of late Arthur Mabson deceased, runs W 16 feet on Market Street towards the river, N 66 feet same width to lot #2 formerly occupied by John Rutherford deceased & lately owned by John Ancrum & Robert Schaw; formerly owned by Francis Veale deceased who devised it to his daughter Ann Veale who sold Aug. 26, 1756 to Isaac Faries deceased (recorded in book D p. 328) and sold by his surviving child & heir Sarah Faries to Thomas Maclaine; & (b) "other part" of same water lot #1; border: begins at western corner of lot on Market Street, runs W 17 feet on said street, N 66 feet same width to lot lately owned by Ancrum & Schaw; formerly in estate of Ann Wright due to deed from Caleb Grainger and Ann sold to John Rutherfurd who sold to Ann Wright (sic) who sold to Thomas Wallace who wold to Henry Toomer who sold to John Jones who sold to John Burgwin who sold to Donald Bain who sold to Thomas Maclaine. (signed) Tho Maclaine; (witness) Thomas Anderson [only one witness]; [note at end indicates Hooper paid Maclaine £600]; Jul. 1790 acknowledged; Apr. 14, 1791 recorded; book I p. 298 [356].

2573. [blank], 1790 Neil Henry (NC) to Charles Henry (New Hanover Co); for £30 sold on Turkey Br; border: begins at Neil Henry's corner black oak & joins Colvin's line on N side of a road. (signed) Neil Henry's mark "X"; (witness) Alexr Campbell & John Henry; wit. oath Apr. 1791 by Jno Henry; Apr. 14, 1791 recorded; book I p. 300 [358].

2574. Sept. 10, 1790 Charles Jewkes, merchant, & wife Ann (New Hanover Co) to Peter Carpenter, trader (same); for £290 NC money sold 0.5 ac in lot #7 in Wilmington on Front Street; border: opposite a water lot formerly owned by Thomas Sawier, 66 feet in front, 330 feet in length, joined on S by lot formerly owned by William Ford, on N by a lot "called" Mitchel's, between middle Market Street & Ann Street; sold Dec. 16, 1742 "among other things" by Thomas Sawier to John Porter deceased recorded in New Hanover Co register's office and sold due to execution, on suit by Daniel Laroche (of SC) against John Porter deceased's estate, Aug. 18, 1749 by New Hanover Co Sheriff Lewis DeRosset to Daniel Laroche together with other lots & land and sold Oct. 29 & 30, 1753 by Daniel Laroche to Lewis DeRosset and sold Apr. 14, 1779 by "said Henry Lewis" DeRosset to Charles Jewkes. (signed) Charles Jewkes & Ann Jewkes; (witness) George Blyth & Michael Keenan; [note at end indicates Carpenter paid Jewkes £290]; wit. oath Apr. 1791 by M Keenan; Apr. 15, 1791 recorded; book I p. 301 [359].

2575. Mar. 31, 1790 Jeremiah McClamey [or McLammy] (New Hanover Co) to John Bradley (same); for £21.19 sold my claim to land my father owned at his death; sole void if McClamey pays Bradley £21.19 & interest by Apr. 1, 1790 (sic). (signed) Jeremiah McClamey's mark "X"; (witness) Morris Ward [only one witness]; wit. oath Apr. 1791 deep presented in court & "the evidence" is dead but hand writing of "Maurice" Ward was "known by the court"; Apr. 16, 1791 recorded; book I p. 303 [361].

2576. Jun. 13, 1790 John Wilkinson to John Bradley; for £2,550 NC money sold water lot #21 in Wilmington; border: joined on E by Front Street, on W by the river, on N by Wilkinsons Alley, & on S by Dubois' Alley; where Richard Rundle lives; lot "may become" liable to pay debts by estate of my uncle William Wilkinson for legacies he left in his will; but if there is no levy on the lot for my uncle's debts & Bradley is "secured in quiet possession" of the lot, then this deed is void (sic). (signed) John Wilkinson; (witness) John Maclellan [only one witness]; wit. oath Apr. 1791 by John Maclellan; Apr. 16, 1791; book I p. 304 [362].

2577. Dec. 8, 1790 Thomas Thompson, planter to David Thompson, planter; for £100 specie sold 2 tracts in Onslow Co, NC: (a) 50 ac; border: begins at George Jenkins' corner pine in fork of Reedy Br & Mill Run and joins a bottom; sold Mar. 5, 1787 by John Armstrong to [me ?]; & (b) on W side of New R; border: begins at a white oak at mouth of a branch that divides Darby Laray's land, joins a "pastine" fence, & a path to John Rhodes' land; lately owned by William Pollock but now owned by Thomas Thompson due to deed Aug. 26, 1780. (signed) Thos Thompson; (witness) William Green & F Lockman [or Lachman]; wit. oath Apr. 1791 by Will Green; Apr. 20, 1791 recorded; book I p. 306 [364].

2578. Dec. 8, 1790 Thomas Thompson, planter to David Thompson, planter; for £300 specie sold 2 tracts in Onslow Co, NC: (a) 100 ac on W side of New R; border: begins at a creek or gut that makes into Stones Creek Bay called Alligator Cr, joins James "Padjet", a dividing line between "Horatia" Woodhouse & James Padjet, Nathaniel Averet, & the bay; where James Padjet lives; (b) 330 ac on W side of New R; border: begins at Isaac Brinson's corner bay tree at head of Alligator "Gut" & joins Nathaniel Averet; granted Apr. 13, 1749 by Gov. Gabriel Johnston to Horatia Woodhouse. (signed) Thos Thompson; (witness) William Green & F Lockman [or Lachman]; wit. oath Apr. 1791 by Will Green; Apr. 21, 1791 recorded; book I p. 307 [365].

2579. Jan. 19, 1791 Thomas Bishop to John Nichols jr; for £47.10 sold a Negro girl "Cassandrai" 4 years old. (signed) Th Bishop; (witness) Nicolas Nixon [only one witness]; [note at end indicates Bishop received £21.11 Jan. 19, 1791]; wit. oath Apr. 1791 by Nicolas Nixon; Apr. 27, 1791 recorded; book I p. 309 [367].

2580. Oct. 5, 1787 Anthony Burns to James Schaw (New Hanover Co); for £100 "in money & cattle" sold 150 ac on E side of "widdow" Moores Cr; border: begins at a pine on side of a swamp being corner formerly made for Daniel Holland "by" Onesymus Futch's lower line; except half of gold & silver mines and any fees or taxes. (signed) Anthony Burns; (witness) Fredk Simpson & Jno Wright; wit. oath Oct. 1790 by Fredk Simpson; Apr. 30, 1791 recorded; book I p. 309 [367].

2581. Nov. 9, 1784 Gov. Alexander Martin (New Bern, NC) to Timothy Bloodworth; grant #160; for £0.50 per 100 ac granted 212 ac on E side of Black R; border: begins at a pine on Fennel's [or Fennell] line on E side of Little Clear Run. (signed) Alex Martin & J Glasgow, Secretary; May 3, 1791 recorded; book I p. 311 [369].

2582. Feb. 28, 1791 Alexander Rouse ("present residing in" New Hanover Co) to Robert Nichols (same); for £120 NC money sold a Negro man Franck. (signed) Alexdr Rouse; (witness) John Nichols & James Towning; Apr. 1791 acknowledged; May 4, 1791 recorded; book I p. 312 [370].

2583. Apr. 13, 1780 Gov. Richard Caswell (Kingston, NC) to Maurice Fennel; grant #76; for £0.50 per 100 ac granted 100 ac on W side of Black R & head of Devans Marsh; border: begins at a pine near Griffins Br & between Devan & Lyons. (signed) Rd Caswell & Wm Sheppard, D Secretary; May 5, 1791 recorded; book I p. 312 [370].

2584. Dec. 15, 1788 Mary Meek, exx, & Henry Urquhart, exr. of will of George Meek deceased, to John Anders, planter (Bladen Co, NC); for £120 NC money sold a Negro boy Abraham 14 years old. (signed) Mary Meek & Henry Urquhart; (witness) David James & Robert Scott; wit. oath Oct. 1789 by David James; May 16, 1791 recorded; book I p. 313 [371].

2585. (Barbados) Mar. 30, 1791 Samuel Went, merchant (St. Michael Parish [Barbados]), surviving partner of Alexander Stevenson esq, to Samuel Vance esq "intending shortly to depart this state for North Carolina" and Edward Jones esq (Wilmington, NC); power of attorney to receive from holders of property & estate of John Rowan deceased the money due me & my partner due to a "writing obligation" Sept. 9, 1777 by John Rowan for £51.9.9 & interest from Sept. 2, 1777 until paid. (signed) Samuel Went; (witness) Nathaniel Lewis & Is Crichlow Wolman; wit. oath May 16, 1791 by Nathaniel Lewis before Sam Ashe, JSCLE; May 18, 1791 recorded; book I p. 314 [372].

2586. (Barbados) Mar. 30, 1790 Samuel Went & James King Went, merchants (Island of Barbados) to Samuel Vance esq "shortly intending to depart this island for North Carolina" & Edward Jones esq (Wilmington, NC); power of attorney to receive from holders of estate & property of John Rowan deceased the money due us due to a bond Nov. 19, 1776 by John Rowan for £200.7.8 Barbados money due to an assignment Jan. 9, 1777 for £16.9.10 Barbados money by George Walroud jr "on a writing obligatory under" hand of John Rowan Feb. 22, 1776 (sic). (signed) Samuel Went & James King Went; (witness) Nathaniel Lewis & Is Crichlow Wolman [or Walman]; wit. oath May 16, 1791 by Nathaniel Lewis before Saml Ashe, JSCLE; May 18, 1791 recorded; book I p. 315 [373].

2587. (Barbadon) Mar. 30, 1790 James King Went, merchant (St. Michael Parish [Barbados]), surviving partner of Mr. Francis Walroud, to Samuel Vance esq "shortly intending to depart this island for North Carolina" & Edward Jones esq (Wilmington, NC); power of attorney to receive from holders of estate & property of John Rowan deceased the money due to me & my partner from John Rowan by 2 notes or writings obligatory dated Nov. 3, 1770 & Jun. 21, 1776. (signed) James King Went; (witness) Nathaniel Lewis & Is Crichlow Wolman [or Nolman]; wit. oath (no date) by Nathaniel Lewis before Saml Ashe, JSCLE; May 19, 1791 recorded; book I p. 316 [374].

2588. Nov. 26, 1789 Gov. Samuel Johnston (Fayetteville, NC) to James White; grant #280; for £0.50 per 100 ac granted 102 ac being Dennis Moore's Thoroughfare Island in Black R; border: begins at a "hehucleberry", maple, & ash at upper point of the thoroughfare & joins mouth of the thoroughfare. (signed) Sam Johnston & J Glasgow, Secretary; may 27, 1791 recorded; book I p. 317 [375].

2589. Mar. 9, 1790 Thomas Wright, sheriff (New Hanover Co) to John Martin (same); for £200 sold corner lot [no number] in Wilmington; border: 22 feet on first or Front Street, joins lot & house owned by John Blakely, & 75 feet on front of Princess Street; sold Oct. 6, 1789 due to writ of fieri facias from New Hanover Co Pleas & Quarter Sessions court returnable to Oct. term 1789 for £1,082.16 & £5.14.11 costs against John Foster, in hands of his attorney Thomas Craike, due to suit by Samuel Donaldson, surviving partner of Willm Gibson & company. (signed) Thos Wright, sheriff; (witness) Mar. R Wilkings [only one witness]; ; [note at end indicates Wright received £200]; Jul. 1790 acknowledged; May 31, 1791 recorded; book I p. 318 [376].

2590. Feb. 1, 1789 Robert McLorinan & James McLorinan, brothers & heirs of Henry McLorinan deceased (late of Wilmington, New Hanover Co) first part, William Campbell esq (Wilmington, NC) brother & heir of James Campbell deceased second part, & John Campbell bookseller (same) third part; William Campbell owned part of lots #27 & 28 in Wilmington on N side of Market Street; border: begins on Market Street at E corner of building & ground formerly owned by Thomas Hedges now part of estate of Cornelius Harnet esq deceased, runs E

25 feet on Market Street to house & lot presently occupied by John Walker, N at right angle with Market Street 132 feet to lot formerly owned by Robt Walker esq deceased now owned by Henry Toomer, W 25 feet on Toomer's line, & S 132 feet to Market Street; on Aug. 11, 1774 William Campbell agreed with Clarissa Catharine McLorinan, wife of Henry McLorinan, to sell the lot for her part of "purchase money"; "soon after" she died; Henry also "lately" died & his executors have satisfied Campbell for residue to the purchase money; Robert & James McLorinan sold their interest in the lot to John Campbell for £800 NC money; SO for £800 paid by John Campbell to Jonathan Tomkins, attorney for Robert & James McLorinan and for £0.5 paid by John Campbell to William Campbell sold above land to John Campbell; sold Jul. 25, 1751 by Caleb Grainger esq deceased to Thomas Campbell who sold Jun. 29, 1756 to James Campbell recorded in New Hanover Co registry book C p. 647 (sic) & book D p. 298 (sic). (signed) Jonathan Tomkins, attorney for Robt & James McLorinan, & Wm Campbell; (witness) Jos G Wright [only one witness]; [note at end indicates John Campbell paid Tomkins £800]; wit. oath Apr. 1789 by J G Wright; Jun. 1, 1791 recorded; book I p. 320 [378].

2591. Nov. 9, 1784 Gov. Alexander Martin (New Bern, NC) to Thomas Lee; grant #170; for £0.50 per 100 ac granted 51 ac on Rockfish [Cr]; border: begins at a maple "afore and aft" tree of Jacob Powell's line, joins Blank, Daniel Highsmith, & Joshua Lee. (signed) Alex Martin & J Glasgow, Secretary; Jun. 11, 1791 recorded; book I p. 323 [381].

2592. Oct. 16, 1790 Nathaniel Pouncey (New Hanover Co) to Martha Jones "alias" Pouncey; for faithful & laborious services for last 18 years emancipated Martha; if New Hanover Co court has any objection to ratifying according to law, I declaim for past 18 years I have been married to her according to law and during that period treated her as my lawful wife. (signed) Nathl Pouncey; (witness) Ed Jones & John "Blakeley"; wit. oath Apr. 1791 by Ed Jones esq; Jun. 11, 1791 recorded; book I p. 323 [381].

2593. Oct. 16, 1790 Nathaniel Pouncey (New Hanover Co) to John Jackson, son of Martha Jones "alias" Pouncey a Negro woman; I declare John to be my son born in lawful "wedwock"; if this is insufficient to secure him rights & privileges of a freeman, I declare him free from all my claims and renounce all my claim to his services which laws of this country might award me; I trust in consequence of this declaration & further assurance, that John has always supported an honest industrious character so the court will not object to my emancipating my own son. (signed) Nathl Pouncey; (witness) Ed Jones & John Blakeley; wit. oath Apr. 1791 by Edward Jones esq; Jun. 11, 1791 recorded; book I p. 324 [382].

2594. Jun. 15, 1789 John Hill, planter (New Hanover Co) to William Cutlar esq (same); for £130 sold a Negro wench Susy. (signed) John Hill; (witness) W Hill; Jul. 1789 acknowledged; Jun. 25, 1791 recorded; book I p. 324 [382].

2595. Mar. 28, 1789 Jno B Moore to Henry Williams (New Hanover Co); for £80 sold a Negro girl Hagar. (signed) Jno B Moore; [no witness]; Oct. 1789 acknowledged; Jun. 27, 1791 recorded; book I p. 325 [383].

2596. Jun. 15, 1789 Francis Brice (New Hanover Co) to William Cutlar; for £72 NC money sold a Negro man Punch. (signed) F Brice; (witness) Benjn. Liddon; [note at end indicates Cutlar received the Negro Jun. 15, 1789]; wit. oath Jul. 1789 by Benjn Liddon; Jun. 27, 1791 recorded; book I p. 325 [383].

2597. Aug. 11, 1789 John M Davis to Marshal Robert Wilkings; for £90 NC money sold a Negro girl Bess about 13 years old. (signed) John M Davis; (witness) Jos Winslow [only one witness]; Oct. 1789 acknowledged; Jun. 27, 1791 recorded; book I p. 326 [384].

2598. Oct. 1, 1785 George McCulloch (New Hanover Co) to Alexander McCulloch (same); for £150 NC money sold 2 Negro "girls" Fanny about 30 years old & Clarissa about 6 years old. (signed) Geo McCulloch; (witness) Jacob Williams & Dd. Williams; wit. oath Oct. 1789 by D Williams; Jun. 28, 1791 recorded; book I p. 326 [384].

2599. Jul. 1, 1789 Henry Toomer to Jacob Fryout (Wilmington, NC); for £30 sold an alley 12 feet wide taken from a lot owned by me; it is understood [alley] is for convenience of Jacob Fryout having a "back out set" from his own lot to Front Street. (signed) Henry Toomer; (witness) Wm Nutt [only one witness]; wit. oath Jul. 1789 by William Nutt; Jun. 28, 1791 recorded; book I p. 327 [385].

2600. Sept. 4, 1789 Joel Parrish (or Parish) (New Hanover Co) to my son James Parrish (same); for love & affection gave a Negro boy Ephraim 14 years old Apr. 15 "last"; if James dies before he is 21, then Ephraim remains my property. (signed) Joel Parrish; (witness) Arthur Crews & Richd Parrish; Oct. 1789 acknowledged; Jun. 28, 1791 recorded; book I p. 327 [385].

2601. Sept. 19 [at top of deed and 20 at bottom of deed], 1788 Edmund [or Edmond] Moore, planter (New Hanover Co) to John Haynes, planter (same); for £80 NC money sold 150 ac [no more description]; where Edmund Moore formerly lived; granted May 4, 1769 to Samuel Collier. (signed) Edmund Moore; (witness) White Barwick [only one witness]; [note at end indicates Moore received £80]; Oct. 1789 acknowledged; Jun. 28, 1791 recorded; book I p. 328 [386].

2602. Mar. 16, 1787 John Harrod, planter (Sampson Co, NC) to Jesse Haynie, planter & son of John Haynie (New Hanover Co); for £100 NC money sold 100 ac on N side of South R above Benit Smith's; border: begins at a red oak in the fork of a branch, joins a marsh, & South R. (signed) John Harrod's mark "F"; (witness) John Haynie & Saml Boozman; wit. oath Oct. 1789 by John "Hanie"; Jun. 29, 1791 recorded; book I p. 329 [387].

2603. May 15, 1789 Henry Waters, planter (New Hanover Co), executor of will of Roger Davis esq deceased (of Brunswick Co, NC) to Schencking Moore, planter (Brunswick Co, NC); for £510 NC money sold 300 ac in Brunswick Co on Town Cr; border: joined on S by William Herd's "plantation", on N by Samuel Rourk's plantation, & on W by Town Cr; known as [name blank]; owned by Roger Davis at his death. (signed) Henry "Watters"; (witness) Michl Sampson & Fredk Jones; wit. oath Oct. 1789 by Michl Sampson; Jun. 30, 1791 recorded; book I p. 330 [388].

2604. May 13, 1789 Hiram Jeremiah Richards (New Hanover Co), administrator of David Forbs [or Forbes] merchant deceased (late of Wilmington, NC), to Lewis McPherson [or Macpherson] (Wilmington, NC); on May 1 "instant", due to public notice, personal estate of David Forbes was sold by New Hanover Co sheriff in Wilmington on 6 months credit; for £332 NC money secured to be paid sold a Negro woman Betty & her 3 children Casar, Phillis, & Bob and increase of female slaves. (signed) Hiram J Richards; (witness) Mar. R "Wilkings" [only one witness]; wit. oath Jul. 1789 by M Robert Willkings; Jul. 1, 1791 recorded; book I p. 331 [389].

2605. Aug. 10, 1788 George Jacobs (Wilmington, NC) Jacob Fryout (same); for £100 sold part of lot #4 in Wilmington on Market Street; border: 41 feet wide fronting Market Street, joins the church lot, runs back 66 feet to lot owned by Benjamin Heron esq, 44 feet on said lot, & 66 feet to Market Street. (signed) Georg. Jacobs; (witness) Hugh Campbell & Henry Hoskins; wit. oath Jul. 1789 by Hu. Campbell; Jul. 1, 1791 recorded; book I p. 332 [390].

2606. Mar. 28, 1789 John Hynes (or Hines), planter (New Hanover Co) to Frederick Jones, planter (same); for £50 sold 150 ac on NW side of New Topsail Sound back of Fredk Jones' formerly Samuel Swann's land; border: begins at a white oak by a red oak stump Michael "Loaper's", Mark McClammy, & Fredk Jones' formerly Samuel Swann's corner, joins Fredk Jones' back line, Stafford, & Collier's old corner; granted May 4, 1769 to Samuel Collier. (signed) John Hynes' mark "Ⅎ"; (witness) Michl Sampson & Jane Sampson; wit. oath Oct. 1789 by Michl Sampson; Jul. 4, 1791 recorded; book I p. 333 [391].
2607. Apr. 7, 1790 James Stephens before Jno B Moore JP swears in New Hanover Co court: Alexander Hostler (late of Wilmington, New Hanover Co) "some days" before his death told Stephens a Negro boy Hector, then bound to & at work with said Stephens at the ship carpenter's trade, was property of Mercer Gabie son-in-lawof Hostler and given to said Gabie by said Hostler. (signed) Jno B Moore JP [Stephens doesn't sign]; [no witness]; Jul. 1790 exhibited in court & ordered recorded (signed) Tho Maclaine, clerk; Jul. 4, 1791 recorded; book I p. 335 [393].

2608. Oct. 29, 1787 Gov. Richard Caswell (Kinston, NC) to John Gambeer Scull; grant #242; for £0.50 per 100 ac granted 320 ac on W side of Black R; border: begins at a large cyprus on the river bank at mouth of a cove & below Cunney

Bluff. (signed) Richd Caswell & W Williams, D Secretary; Jul. 13, 1791 recorded; book I p. 335 [393].

2609. May 5, 1791 James Flowers, administrator of David Flowers, to James Hogg (Orange Co, NC); for £104.10 sold a Negro boy Toney. (signed) Jas Flowers, admr of David Flowers; (witness) Mar. R Willkings [only one witness]; wit. oath Jul. 1791 by Marshall Robt "Wilkins"; Jul. 13, 1791 recorded; book I p. 336 [394].

2610. Nov. 29, 1788 Joseph Richard Gautier, planter (Bladen Co, NC) to Nixon Chester (New Hanover Co); for £110 NC money sold a Negro boy Anser [Answer--lined out] about 16 years old. (signed) J R Gautier; (witness) P N Gautier [only one witness]; Jul. 1791 acknowledged; Jul. 13, 1791 acknowledged; book I p. 336 [394].

2611. Jun. 14, 1785 Robert Bloodworth & wife Rebecca (New Hanover Co) to Eleanor Kenan, widow (same); for £10 NC money sold lot #23 in town of Washington on NE Cape Fear R at a place called the Welsh tract [no more description]. (signed) Robert Bloodworth & Rebecca Bloodworth; (witness) Jno James & William Ware; wit. oath Jul. 1791 by John James esq; Jul. 14, 1791 recorded; book I p. 337 [395].

2612. Jun. 14, 1785 Robert Bloodworth & wife Rebecca (New Hanover Co) to Eleanor Kenan, widow (same); for £10 sold lot #53 in town of Washington on NE Cape Fear R at place called the Welsh tract [no more description]. (signed) Robert Bloodworth & Rebecca Bloodworth; (witness) Jno James & William Ware; wit. oath Jul. 1791 by John James esq; Jul. 14, 1791 recorded; book I p. 338 [396].

2613. May 27 [22 in copy], 1789 Joseph R Gautier (Bladen Co, NC) to Nixon Chester (New Hanover Co); for £110 NC money sold a negro girl Juba. (signed) J R Gautier; (witness) Henry Tucker [only one witness]; Jul. 1791 acknowledged; Jul. 15, 1791 recorded; book I p. 339 [397].

2614. Jan. 1, 1790 R Rowan to Alexander Hostler; for £100, paid by "hands of" Mr. Thomas Davis, sold a Negro girl Nancy. (signed) R Rowan; (witness) Jos G Wright [only one witness]; wit. oath Jul. 1791 by Jos G Wright; Jul. 13, 1791 recorded "book F"; book I p. 340 [398].

2615. Jan. [blank], 1791 Ann Sophia Hasell, widow of honorable President Hasell deceased, to William Green esq (New Hanover Co); for £1,000 sold 10 Negroes: 3 fellows Shonty, Cain, & Hannibal, a wench Rachel & her child Kitty, 4 boys Paulo, Pierre, Cavanno, & Jamy, & a girl Pamelia. (signed) Ann Sophia Hasell; (witness) Jos J Wright [only one witness]; [note at end:] (no date) A S Hasell delivered Cavanno a Negro boy in name of all the slave sold (signed) Jos G Wright; wit. oath Jul. 1791 by Jos G Wright; Jul. 16, 1791 recorded; book I p. 340 [398].

2616. May 15, 1791 Nathaniel Moore, gentleman (Granville Co, NC) to Samuel Ashe esq (New Hanover Co); for quit claim to Ashe, one of the obligors named in 2 bonds, conditioned on payment of 2 "ennuities to" me for £50 sterling Great Britain money each dated "about" Mar. 20, 1783 and the "condition & penalty" of said bonds in all actions or suits against Ashe that my executors or heirs may demand from "beginning of the world until today". (signed) Nathl Moore; (witness) J R Gautier & Henry Watters; wit. oath Jul. 1791 by J R Gautier; Jul. 16, 1791 recorded; book I p. 341 [399].

2617. Oct. 1, 1790 James Jennett ([New] Hanover Co) to Jesse Jennett (Brunswick Co, NC); for £80 sold 2 adjoining tracts: (a) 200 ac; border: begins at a pine tree on the ridge near "the" main road, joins Black Swamp, & a bay swamp; & (b) 125 ac on both sides of "the" main road near his own ditch; border: begins at a red oak on N side of the road by Samuel Collier's beginning corner of a grant to Thos McClamy, crosses the road, near Frederick Jones' line at a pond, & joins John Simson; taken up (no date) by Samuel Lane. (signed) James Jennett & Sarah Jennett (sic); (witness) Thomas Russ & James Russ; Oct. 1790 acknowledged by James & S Jennett; Jul. 21, 1791 recorded; book I p. 342 [400].

2618. Feb. 11, 1791 John Reardan, merchant (Cumberland Co, NC) to John George Mayer (Charleston, SC); for £160 sold [omitted] ac in Fayetteville, Cumberland Co, NC; border: begins at a stake on W side of "the" fifty feet street that runs from corner of Adam's piazza to corner of England's house, runs South "30 minutes" West 30 feet with said street to a stake at intersection of the street & Hay Street, N70W 24 feet on Hay Street to a stake, N20E 29 feet, & S70E to beginning; & a 2 story house or tenement 20 feet by 16 feet with balcony & piazza 8 feet by 20 [feet] built on the lot; deed void if Reardan pays Mayer £160 by Sept. 1 next with interest. (signed) John Reardan; (witness) John Blakeley & Richard Rigby; [note at end indicates Reardan received £160]; wit. oath Jul. 1791 by John Blakeley; Aug. 2, 1791 recorded; book I p. 343 [401].

2619. (Bladen Co, NC) Mar. 27, 1790 John Wilkings to Marshall Robert Wilkings; for £200 NC money sold 2 Negroes a girl Cloey about 14 years old & a boy Jupiter about 12. (signed) John Wilkings; (witness) J Byrne jr; Apr. 1790 acknowledged; Aug. 10, 1791; book I p. 346 [404].

2620. Feb. 14, 1791 John Reardan, merchant (Cumberland Co, NC) to John Wray (Charleston, SC); for £80 sold [omitted] ac in Fayetteville, Cumberland Co, NC; border: begins at a stake on W side of "the" fifty feet street that runs from corner of Adam's piazza to corner of England's house, runs South "30 minutes" West 30 feet with said street to a stake at intersection of the street & Hay Street, N70W 24 feet on Hay Street to a stake, N20E 29 feet, & S70E to beginning; & 2 story house or tenement 20 feet by 16 feet with balcony & piazza 8 feet by 20 feet on the lot; deed void if Reardan pays Wray £80 by Dec. 1 next with interest. (signed) John Reardan; (witness) John Blakeley & Richard Rigby; [note at end indicates Rardan received £80]; wit. oath Jul. 1791 by John Blakeley; Aug. 30, 1791 recorded; book I p. 346 [404].

2621. Apr. 13, 1780 Gov. Richard Caswell (Kingston, NC) to Benjamin Shadwick; grant #80; for £0.50 per 100 ac granted 50 ac on a branch of Merricks Cr; border: begins at Merrick's, Morris', & McAlexander's corner white oak, joins a savanna near McQuillan's line, crosses a swamp, joins a savanna on W side of Player's Swamp, & a pocoson. (signed) Rd Caswell & Wm Sheppard, D Secretary; Aug. 31, 1791 recorded; book I p. 348 [406].

2622. Nov. 17, 1788 Rebecca Green to Mark McClamey; for £150 sold a Negro woman Sue & her child Allin. (signed) Rebecca Green; (witness) Robert Nixon [only one witness]; wit. oath Jan. 1790 by Robt Nixon; Aug. 31, 1791 recorded; book I p. 349 [407].

2623. Aug. 31, 1790 Alexander Rouse (New Hanover Co) to Mark McClammy [or McClamey] sr; for £150 NC money sold a Negro wench Jean, formerly owned by Wonny McClammy deceased, & her male chile "Jam"; slaves became Rouse's property by his wife's part of estate of her father. (signed) Alexr Rouse; (witness) Tho Bishop & John Batt; wit. oath Jan. 1791 by John Batt; Sept. 5, 1791 recorded; book I p. 350 [408].

2624. Aug. 25, 1791 Frederick Ward, gentleman (Brunswick Co, NC) to John Burgwin (New Hanover Co); for £450 NC money sold lot (no number) in Wilmington on N side of Market Street; border: between Mrs. McGregory's & lot formerly owned by John Sampson esq now owned by said Burgwin and runs back 126 feet; sold Jan. 19, 1750 by William White deceased (formerly of Wilmington) to Daniel Dunbibbin who willed it Jul. 28, 1757 to Jean Ward, mother of Anthony & Frederick Ward and wife of Anthony Ward their father, and willed to her son Anthony Ward who sold Dec. 5, 1790 to his brother Frederick Ward for £500. (signed) Frederick Ward; (witness) Geo Gibbs [only one witness]; [notes at end indicate Burgwin paid Ward £450 and on Aug. 29, 1791 Ward delivered to Burgwin quiet possession of lot & premises (signed) Geo Gibbs & James Lovell]; wit. oath Sept. 6, 1791 by George Gibbs before Saml Spencer, JSCLE; received the tax of 5/ (signed) Saml Spencer; Sept. 8, 1791 recorded; book I p. 351 [409].

2625. Jun. 30, 1791 Archibald Ronaldson, house joiner & inn keeper (Brunswick Co, NC) to Dennis Reardan & George Duncan, merchants; for 1200 NC money sold house & lot with improvements "in" Maiden Lane; being third lot on S side of the lane from Front Street in Wilmington [no more description]; sale void if Ronaldson pays Reardan & Duncan £200 by Jul. 1, 1792 with interest. (signed) Archd Ronaldson; (witness) John Brown & William Ferguson; Sept. 7, 1791 acknowledged before Saml Ashe, JSCLE; Sept. 9, 1791 recorded; book I p. 353 [411].
[on p. 414 of original book I: "pages 414 thru 438 not filmed-faded & illegible"]

2626. Nov. 9, 1790 Archibald McAllister (or McCallister) & wife Mary, formerly Mary Grainger (Brunswick Co, NC) to Benjamin Mott (New Hanover Co); for "300 currency" being Spanish mill dollars at £0.12.6 each sold 500 ac on the sound between Mott's land & land owned by Mrs. Alice Heron [no more description]; sold Feb. 28, 1787 by Wm Grainger deceased to Mary McCallister formerly Mary Grainger; except 6 ac reserved to heirs of William Grainger "as by said deed". (signed) A McAllister & Mary McAllister; (witness) Mary Jane Dry & Mar. Robt Willkings; [note at end indicates Mott paid McAllister £300 "currency" at £0.12.6 Spanish milled dollars]; wit. oath Apr. 1791 by M R Willkings; Sept. 20, 1791 recorded; Jan. 6, 1791 Wm Mason & Thos Hall are appointed to obtain dower renouncement of Mary McAllister (signed) Thos Maclaine, clerk; (South Carolina, sic) dower renounced Feb. 2, 1791 by Mary McAllister, formerly Mary Grainger, (of Brunswick Co, NC) before William Mason [almost entire deed repeated in dower renouncement] (signed) Mary McAllister & Wm Mason; Apr. 1791 deed" exhibited in court & ordered recorded (signed) Thos Maclaine, clerk; Sept. 22, 1791 recorded; book I p. 354.

2627. Apr. 23, 1791 Auley McNaughton (Wilmington, NC) to Daniel Ferguson, black smith (same); for £200 sold part of lot in Wilmington on S side of Princess Street; border: joined on W by "ground" owned by Daniel Bain, on E by ground owned by late Col. Thomas Loyd's estate & now owned by Miss Peggy "Lloyd", 55 feet front on said street, & 66 feet back. (signed) A McNaughton; (witness) John McAuslan; [note at end indicates Ferguson paid McNaughton £200]; wit. oath Jul. 1791 by John McAuslan; Sept. 30, 1791 recorded; book I p. 358.

2628. Apr. 17, 1770 Anthony Ward (Wilmington, NC) to William Marshall, mariner (New Hanover Co); for £40 proclamation money sold 106 ac on Lewises Cr, a branch of NE Cape Fear R; border: begins at a maple tree on N of Old Field Br, joins Reas Evans, & a small branch. (signed) A Ward & Jane Ward (sic); (witness) "Jana" Dunbibbin; wit. oath Oct. 1791 by J G Scull who recognized hand writing of Dunbibbin; Oct. 8, 1791 recorded; book I p. 359.

2629. Jan. [blank], 1787 Samuel Swann esq & wife Mildred (New Hanover Co) to John Burgwin, merchant (Wilmington, NC); for 2,000 Spanish milled dollars sold (a) 333 1/3 ac on Price Georges Cr & NE Cape Fear R; border: joins a line of marked trees that divides the land form land where late General Waddell formerly dwelt called Castle Haynes, on N by the main river, on S by Prince George Cr, & on W by a line that divides the land from land formerly sold by Roger Moore esq to Roger Haynes; known as Legar's "plantation"; & for 700 Spanish milled dollars sold (b) 110 ac where a dwelling house & kitchen are erected where late Mrs. Jane Swann resided; on the south within about 2 miles of the plantation & "the" main road called Collier's; where Samuel Swann's mother lately resided; described in deed (no date) from John Simpson & wife Susanna to [Swann ?]; both tracts owned by Samuel Swann. [not signed]; [no witness]; [note at end indicates Burgwin paid 2,000 Spanish milled dollars to (not signed)];

Jan. 5, 1791 Samuel Swann, in his life time sold above land to John

Burgwin and consideration money "appears" to have been received; SO Mildred Swann widow administratrix & Frederick Jones surviving administrator of Samuel Swann, due to act of Assembly in Dec. 1787 called an act to impower administrators to make conveyances for real estate, confirm the land to John Burgwin. (signed) Mildred Swann & Fredk Jones; (witness) Wm Cutlar [only one witness]; wit. oath Jul. 1791 by William Cutlar; Oct. 11, 1791 recorded; book I p. 360.

2630. Mar. 18, 1791 Mathew Johnston (Wilmington, NC) to Robert Wells, James McKoy Stephens, & George Logan (same); grantees and grantor (sic) are securities for Mathew Johnston in bond dated Mar. [blank], 1791 for £2,350 payable to Gabriel Kingsbury deceased; bond was conditioned on payment of £1,175 by Mathew Johnston to Gabriel Kingsbury by Mar. 1, 1792; to secure the grantees & for £0.5 sold (a) house & part of lot #6 in Wilmington; border: joins an alley on N, tenement of estate of John Quince on E, lots of John Bradley & estate of Thomas Henderson on S, & tenement owned by Archibald Ronaldson on W, & 25 feet front on the alley; (b) lot #231 on W side of Front Street; border: 66 feet in front, runs W along South Street to Stony Street, from W side of said Sunony(?) Street down to low water mark on the river; includes a wharf & tenement; being water lot purchased from New Hanover Co sheriff to Mathew Johnston due to execution; (c) lot #1 on S side of Market Street; border: "twenty sixteen inches" in front & runs back 71 feet from the street; improved by a brick tenement thereon; "lately" purchased by Mathew Johnston from executor of John Kingsbury deceased; & (d) Negro slaves: George, Lady, Paul, & Jiny and their increase; sale void if Johnston pays Gabriel Kingsbuy £1,175 by Mar. 10, 1792 due by bond; if there is a default, grantees can sell or rent the property. (signed) Mathew Johnston, Robert Wells, James McKoy Stephens, George Logan; (witness) Mar. Rob Willkings; wit. oath Jul. 1791 by Marshall Robt Willkings; Jul. 1791 recorded; book I p. 362.

2631. May 30, 1791 Mary Harnett (New York City), by her attorney John Huske, to George Logan, tailor (Wilmington, NC); Mary owns "a small piece of ground" on E side of Front Street in Wilmington between "lately" erected tenement of her own & a brick tenement where George Logan lives; border: land is 2.5 feet wide, runs back the depth of Logan's lot to Mary's Harnett's ground, & fronts of N side of Market Street; Logan agreed to buy from Mary the privilege of passage through said ground to back part of his tenement and to be kept open for their joint benefit; SO for £60 NC money Mary sold full & free use & joint privilege of passage through said ground between tenements of Mary & Logan for Logan's convenience from Front Street to back part of his tenement which is about 50 feet from the street. (signed) Mary Harnett by John Haske atty & George Logan; (witness) Wm Nutt [only one witness]; [note at end indicates Huske received £60];

(no date) in within deed it is mentioned that ground sold to Logan is 2.5 feet wide; but Mary Harnett's tenement approaches nearer in some places; SO, to better explain intentions of the parties, it is understood that space sold for an alley is the space between tenements of Logan's house & [Mary's house]; deed in no way affects Mrs. Harnett's tenement; if Mrs. Harnett's tenement is taken down & another building built, then the 2.5 foot passage is to remain. (signed) Mary Harnett by Jno Huske attorney & George Logan; (witness) Wm Nutt; wit. oath Jul. 1791 by Wm Nutt; Oct. 15, 1791 recorded; book I p. 366.

2632. Dec. 8, 1789 Thomas Craike (New Hanover Co) to Peter Carpenter (Wilmington, NC); for £40 NC money sold 0.5 ac in lot #222 in Wilmington on E side of Front Street; being third lot on S side of Queen (or "Cunn")[Street]; border: 66 feet fronting on Front Street, same width to Second Street. (signed) Thos Craike; (witness) James White & Sedgewick Springs; [note at end indicates Craike received L40 Dec. 19, 1789 (sic)]; Jan. 1790 acknowledged; Oct. 16, 1791; book I p. 367.

2633. Apr. 6, 1785 Thomas Lowber & wife Ann (New Hanover Co) to Michael Lowber (same); for £97.5.9 sold 200 ac on New Topsail Sound; border: begins at a hickory, joins second corner of the patent, Samuel Swann, & head line of the patent; part of land granted Mar. 7, 1736 to Henry Bishop Bearingdall. (signed) Thomas Lowber (Ann doesn't sign); (witness) Michael Kenan & M R Willkings; [note at end indicates Thomas "Lober" received "full consideration"]; wit. oath Apr. 1790 by M "Keenan"; Oct. 17, 1791 recorded; book I p. 368.

2634. Apr. 6, 1789 Edmund Hawes, planter (New Hanover Co) to Michael Lowber (same); for £350 sold 188 ac on W side of Black R; border: begins at a white oak "said to be" Rigby's corner below said Hawes' house, joins head of a branch, & the river; part of 300 ac granted May 17, 1754 to John Howard sr deceased and sold Feb. 20, 1778 to Edmund Hawes sr deceased and upper part was since sold to "one" Roberts; except one-eighth of an acre being place where the family burying ground is and my heirs may have unmolested access to the grave yard. (signed) Edmund Hawes [or Howes]; (witness) Aley Hawes & James Corbett; wit. oath Oct. 1790 by James Corbett; Oct. 20, 1791 recorded; book I p. 370.

2635. Apr. 22, 1786 Arthur Stuckey (New Hanover Co) to James Malpass (same); for £100 sold 200 ac on W side of Moores Cr; border: begins at a pine on upper side of Swanns Br on a hill side, runs up Swanns Br, & near Samuel Ashe; granted Dec. 22, 1768 by Gov. Wm Tryon to Rowan [or Roan] Row who sold to David Masson who sold to Samuel Herring who sold to Arthur Stuckey. (signed) Arthur Stuckey; (witness) John Jones & J Dubose; wit. oath Oct. 191 by John Jones; Oct. 22, 1791 recorded; book I p. 371.

2636. Sept. 10, 1789 John A Campbell (New Hanover Co) to Christopher Howard, planter (same); for £25 sold 300 ac in 2 tracts on N side of New Topsail Sound both granted (no dates) Gov. Wm Tryon to Bishop Dudley: (a) 200 ac; between said Dudley, George Merrick, & John Ashe, begins at a laurel in a branch of "Whitmarshes" Cr "just" above a corner of grant to Abigail Veal, & joins George Merrick's line on Causeway Br; & (b) 100 ac; between said Dudley &

John Ashe's head line, begins at a black jack in "his own" line on a branch of Whitehurst Cr, & joins grant to "Abigal" Veal. (signed) John A Campbell; [no witness]; Oct. 1791 acknowledged; Oct. 24, 1791 recorded; book I p. 373.

2637. Jul. 6, 1790 James Towning, constable, to John Nichols; for £53.10 sold a Negro fellow Jack; sold due to writ of fieri facias due to suit by Luke McLammy against Alexander Rouse, guardian of Woney McLammy; writ issued by Robert Nixon esq. (signed) James Towning; (witness) A Rouse [only one witness]; wit. oath Oct. 1791 by A Rouse; Oct. 20, 1791 recorded; book I p. 374.

2638. Dec. 9, 1790 Amos Love (Onslow Co, NC) to James Howard sr (New Hanover Co); for £160 NC money sold 112 ac on New Topsail Sound & on N side of Whitehurst Cr; border: begins at Andrew Forbs' [or Forbes] corner live oak at mouth of a little branch, joins Rush Watts, & the sound. (signed) Amos Love; (witness) Jno "T" Blake & James Howard jr; wit. oath Oct. 1791 by James Howard; Oct. 26, 1791 recorded; book I p. 375.

2639. Jun. 24, 1791 John Marshall sr (New Hanover Co) to Archibald McFaulton (same); for "15" NC money sold 100 ac on S side of Black R; border: begins at a large cypress at end of Bunn [or Bever] Br, crosses Lyon Swamp & near Gum Swamp; granted Apr. 30, 1780 to said Marshall. (signed) John Marshall; (witness) John G Scull & Edwd Declain; wit. oath Oct. 1791 by John G Scull; Oct. 29, 1791 recorded; book I p. 376.

2640. (Bridgetown, Island of Barbados) Sept. 14, 1791 Wm Boston & Wm Simmons, merchants (St. Michael Parish, Island of Barbados) to Mr. Saml Vance, merchant (Wilmington, NC); power of attorney to receive money owed to us by anyone in Wilmington or any other part of North Carolina including Elizabeth Howell, widow of John Howell merchant deceased (of NC) or heirs or executors of John Howell. (signed) Wm Boston & Wm Simmons; (witness) Wm "Sincalin" & Wm Bycraft; wit. oath Oct. 1791 by Wm Sinclair; Oct. 30, 1791; book I p. 377.

2641. Jul. 30, 1791 David Perkins, planter (New Hanover Co) to my loving son David Perkins (same); for love, good will, & affection gave a bay mare, a sorrel mare, yearling colt, 3 cows, 2 calves, a dark "herifer" yearling, a red stear yearling, a cow called Cherry, another called Spot, a "red furniture cow" called Pink, 10 hogs, a feather bed, a saddle & bridle, a large chest with 5 pint case bottles, a gini, a small pewter dish, 5 small pewter plates, 3 pewter basins, 12 spoons, an iron pot & pot hooks, an axe, a weeding hoe, pair of iron wedges, small iron kettle, a plow, & a table; I have delivered an inventory of the items to Mr. John Nichols sr. (signed) David Perkins; [no witness]; wit. oath Oct. 1791 by John Nichols (sic); Nov. 2, 1791 recorded; book I p. 378.

2642. Jul. 30, 1791 David Perkins, planter (New Hanover Co) to my loving son John Perkins (same); for love, good will, & affection gave a gray mare, a horse yearling, a brinded 2 year old heifer, a cow called Nance, another called Crump, a saddle & bridle, 10 hogs, a bedstead & feather bed & furniture, a linnen wheel, a wolling ditto, a case with 12 bottles, a weaving loom & harness, a large iron kettle, a pewter dish, 6 pewter plates, 12 spoons, 3 pewter basins, 6 knives & forks, a gun, pair of flesh forks, an iron ladle, a reap hook, a grindstone, a pair of hand mill stones, an axe, a weeding hoe, pair of iron wedges, pair of cast wheel boxes, an axle & body bed pins & harmasses, an iron bolt, a box iron & 2 iron heaters, & a table; I delivered an inventory of the items to John Nichols sr. [not signed]; (witness) Thos Blake & John Nichols; wit. oath Oct. 1791 by J Nichols; book I p. 379.

2643. Jul. 30, 1791 David Perkins, planter (New Hanover Co) to my loving son Newton Perkins (same); for love, good will, & affection gave a large bay horse called Snipe, an iron gray horse called Robin, a young bay mare called Feling, a bridle & saddle, 5 cows, 4 calves, 2 heifers & "frosty" and "other" a red white pied cow, one called Pidde & one called Blossom & one called Stately (sic), 60 hogs, a gem, a pot, a skillet, a frying pay, a tea kettle, a feather bed & furniture, a chest & 4 stone jars, 2 narrow axes, a broad axe, 2 grubbing hoes, 2 weeding hoes, a plow & harrow, 12 "clunk" bottles "pattry fowls meet", corn, potatoes, & very other thing to value of 6 pence; I have delivered an inventory of the items to Mr. John Nichols. (signed) David Perkins; (witness) Jno F Blake & John Nichols; wit. oath Oct. 1791 by John Nichols; Nov. 6, 1791 recorded; Aug. 13, 1851 transcribed; book I p. 380.

book K
2644. Sept. 6, 1791 Henry Toomer (Wilmington, NC) to Marshall Robert Willkings (same); for £39 sold land in Wilmington; border: 26 feet on Toomer's Alley, being at corner of lot owned by estate of Abigail Gregory & runs 26 feet on the alley to James "Geekies" lot. (signed) Henry Toomer; (witness) Wm Nutt; [note at end indicates Willkings paid Toomer £39]; wit. oath Oct. 1791 by William Nutt; Dec. 1, 1791 recorded; book K p. 1.

2645. Apr. 6, 1789 Michael "Lobar" to Edmund Hawes sr; for £150 sold a Negro Bailem. (signed) Michael Lobar; (witness) John Herring & John Hawes; wit. oath Apr. 1790 by John Hawes; Dec. 2, 1791 recorded; book K p. 2.

2646. Apr. 6, 1789 Michael Lobar to Edmund Hawes sr; for £85 old a Negro girl Sue. (signed) Michael Lobar; (witness) John Herring & John Hawes; wit. oath Apr. 1790 by John Hawes "sr"; Dec. 2, 1791 recorded; book K p. 2.

2647. Nov. 26, 1789 Gov. Samuel Johnston (Fayetteville, NC) to David James; grant #270; for £10 per 100 ac granted 170 ac; border: begins at a water oak & ash on Darbysagins [or Darbys] Br where "the" main road crosses the branch, joins Frederick Jones, his own land, James Ewin, & Samuel Buntin. (signed) Sam Johnston & J Glasgow, Secretary; Dec. 3, 1791 recorded; book K p. 3.

2648. Nov. 26, 1789 Gov. Samuel Johnston (Fayetteville, NC) to David James;

grant #286; for £0.50 per 100 ac granted 230 ac between his marsh land & Turkey Cr; includes an island called "Derbyagens" Island; border: begins at a gum at mouth of a small creek on Turkey Cr being one of his marsh land corners & joins Derby Br. (signed) Sam Johnston & J Glasgow, Secretary; Dec. 4, 1791 recorded; book K p. 3.

2649. Nov. 26, 1789 Gov. Samuel Johnston (Fayetteville, NC) to Daniel Morgan; grant #289; for £10 per 100 ac granted 100 ac in fork of Long Cr & Morgan Cr; border: begins on Blenning's line & said Morgan's line. (signed) Sam Johnston & J Glasgow, Secretary; Dec. 5, 1791 acknowledged; book K p. 4.

2650. Jul. 28, 1791 Thomas Wright, sheriff (New Hanover Co) to William Green esq (same); for £60 sold 0.25 ac or half of lot #55 in Wilmington on Second Street & N side of Market Street "with letter A"; being third lot West from Market Street; border: joins other half lot & house now owned by William Green, begins 132 feet from corner of Market Street & Second Street, runs N 33 feet with Second Street, E 330 feet parallel to Market Street, S 33 feet on Third Street, & W 330 feet on Market Street to beginning; [reference made to plat of Wilmington authorized by act of Assembly in Mar. 1745]; sold Jun. 29, 1791 at "the most public place" in Wilmington due to writ of fieri facias for £104.2 & interest and £6.1 costs from New Hanover Co Pleas & Quarter Sessions Court returnable to court first Monday in Jul. 1791 against Doctor Samuel Green deceased, in hands of William Green administrator "with will annexed of goods & chattels of said Samuel green unadministered by his late executors" due to suit by John Burgwin. (signed) Thos Wright, sheriff; (witness) Robert Mutee [or Muter] & I Bernard; [note at end indicates Green paid Wright £60]; wit. oath Oct. 1791 by Isaac Bernard; Dec. 6, 1791; book K p. 5.

2651. Oct. 3, 1791 Samuel Ashe & wife [name blank] (New Hanover Co) to James Walker (Wilmington, NC); for £1,000 NC money sold 640 ac in Brunswick Co on N side of Old Town Cr & W side of Cape Fear R about 5 miles above Old Town [Cr ?]; border: begins at a red oak in a branch; known as Spring Garden "Groveley"; granted Jun. 20, 1725 to Maurice Moore (of Bath Co, NC) with annual quit rent of £0.1 per 100 ac and sold Dec. 5, 1727 by Maurice Moore to John Baptista Ashe recorded in Carteret Precinct book C p. 74 & 75 and inherited by Samuel Ashe from J B Ashe. (signed) Saml Ashe; (witness) Jno Hall & Henry "D'hube"; [note at end indicates Walker paid Ashe £1,000 Oct. 5, 1791]; Oct. 1791 acknowledged; Dec. 7, 1791 recorded; book K p. 8.

2652. Oct. 3, 1791 Charles Jewkes & wife [name blank] (Wilmington, New Hanover Co) to James Walker jr (Wilmington, NC); for £1,050 NC money sold 122.5 ac in Brunswick Co; border: begins at a white oak on W side of Cape Fear R on "the great" island called Eagles' Island opposite Wilmington, runs W 173 poles to a red bay on E side of a small creek, S20W 6 poles down the creek to the main creek, S43E 18 poles down main creek, S65E 46 poles, S7W 26 poles, S38E 30 poles, S26W 22 poles, N75E 32 poles, S25W 20 poles, S8W 35 poles, N83E

26 poles, N12E up the river to first station, continued up the river N20E 55 poles to a large cypress on the river, W to main creek, & down the main creek; part of 640 ac granted (no date) by King George II to John Watson with yearly quit rent of £0.3 per 100 ac and sold by Watson to Richard Eagles deceased recorded in New Hanover Co and sold May 17, 1765 by Eagles to Anthony Ward recorded in New Hanover Co book F p. 125 and sold Sept. 28, 1778 by Ward to Alexander Hostler who sold Oct. 6, 1778 to Charles Jewkes recorded in New Hanover Co book G p. 286. (signed) Charles Jewkes; (witness) Jos G Wright & Thomas Younger; [note at end indicates Walker paid Jewkes £1,050 Oct. 3, 1791];

(Wilmington, NC) Oct. 3, 1791 "be it known" Charles Jewkes had reserved for Francis Moon 20 ac of within land; border: "beings & runs all the way through" from the river to the main creek "an equal breadth" to make 20 ac from upper part of within land "the West course" from the large cypress being the last course mentioned in within deed to be upper line of said 20 ac & to begin on the river, to run said breadth "quite" through the ground from East to West to make up 20 ac; but said land never to be claimed by Charles Jewkes or any other person until Francis Moon claims it by good claims, but "to devolve to holder of within mentioned land if otherwise". (signed) Charles Jewkes; (witness) Jos G Wright & Thomas Younger; wit. oath Oct. 1791 by "J" Wright; Dec. 8, 1791 recorded; book K p. 11.

2653. Apr. 13, 1780 Gov. Richard Caswell (Kingston, NC) to Thomas Lamb; grant #47; for £0.50 per 100 ac granted 154 ac on N side of Burgaw [Swamp]; border: begins at an oak in E line of Lamb's "late" survey, joins E edge of Burgaw Swamp, James Moore, Thos Williams. (signed) Rd Caswell & Wm Sheppard, D Secretary; Dec. 8, 1791 recorded; book K p. 14.

2654. Apr. 13, 1780 Gov. Richard Caswell (Kingston, NC) to Thomas Lamb; grant #67; for £0.50 per 100 ac granted 200 ac on S side of Cypress Cr, a branch of Long Cr; border: begins at a large pine on W side of Cypress Cr, near an old tar kiln, & joins Thomas Lamb. (signed) Rd Caswell & Wm Sheppard, D Secretary; Dec. 9, 1791 recorded; book K p. 15.

2655. Apr. 13, 1780 Gov. Richard Caswell (Kinsgton, NC) to Thomas Lamb; grant #68; for £0.50 per 100 ac granted 200 ac on Burgaw "Creek", a branch of NE [River]; border: begins at a stake on S side of Burgaw [Cr], joins a large pocoson, & a savanna between 2 pocosons. (signed) Rd Caswell & Wm Sheppard, D Secretary; Dec. 10, 1794 recorded; book K p. 15.

2656. (Bahama Islands) Oct. 24, 1791 Alexander Lorimer, planter (formerly of Charleston [SC] merchant & now of Island of New Providence, Bahama Islands) to Joseph Shoemaker, planter (of Bahama Islands but shortly to proceed to America); power of attorney to receive from anyone in South or North Carolina or any other state in North America all money due to me. (signed) Alexander Lorimer; (witness) Thos Ritchie & Daniel MacKay; wit. oath Dec. 1, 1791 by Thomas Ritchie before Sam Ashe, JSCLE; Dec. 11, 1791 recorded; book K p. 16.

2657. Feb. 2, 1791 James Moran, gentleman, & wife Margaret (Wilmington, NC) to Gabriel Kingsbury, house wright (same); for £40 sold part of lot #5B in Wilmington on S side of Market Street; border: 40 feet on Market Street, runs back 66 feet the same width, joined on W by part of same lot owned by Samuel Marshall, on E by part of same lot owned by heirs of Richard Player "or howsoever otherwise"; sold (no date) by Richard Player to James Turner. (signed) James "S" Morgan & Margaret Moran; (witness) Robt Harley [or Hailey], John Telfair, & Jno Livingston; [note at end indicates Kingsbury paid Moran £40]; wit. oath Oct. 1791 by John Livingston; Dec. 12, 1791 recorded; book K p. 18.

2658. Apr. 13, 1780 Gov. Richard Caswell (Kingston, NC) to William Lamb; grant #30; for £0.50 per 100 ac granted 100 ac on Cypress Cr, a branch of Long Cr, & below mouth of Bee Br; border: begins at a pine on N side of Cypress Cr. (signed) Rd Caswell & Wm Sheppard, D Secretary; Dec. 14, 1791 recorded; book K p. 19.

2659. Mar. 23, 1789 Robert "Multer" [or Multee] (Wilmington, New Hanover Co) to Peter Carpenter; for £110 NC money sold a Negro man Quashie. (signed) Robert Muter; (witness) J S Moran [only one witness]; [note at end:] Sept. 29, 1790 I assign my right to Mr. Nixon Chester for "value recd." (signed) Peter Carpenter [no witness]; Oct. 1791 acknowledged by said Carpenter; Dec. 15, 1791 recorded; book K p. 20.

2660. Apr. 1, 1790 Peter Carpenter (New Hanover Co) to Nixon Chester (same); for £110 sold a Negro man Crawford. (signed) P Carpenter; (witness) Henry Tucker & J S Moran; "Oct. term" acknowledged; Dec. 17, 1791; book K p. 21.

2661. Apr. 13, 1780 Gov. Richard Caswell (Kingston, NC) to James Kinnear; grant #2; for £0.50 per 100 ac granted 210 ac on "Cypres" Cr, a branch of Long Cr; border: begins at a black jack on W side of Cypres [Cr], joins William Jones, Skybow, Stuckey, Lamb, & Thos Kinnear. (signed) Rd Caswell & Wm Sheppard, D Secretary; Dec. 20, 1791 recorded; book K p. 21.

2662. Apr. 13, 1780 Gov. Richard Caswell (Kingston, NC) to John Stokeley; grant #63; for £0.50 per 100 ac granted 100 ac on Rezoes Swamp; border: begins at Stokeley's SW corner of a "late" survey, joins Francis, & crosses a branch. (signed) Rd Caswell & Wm Sheppard, D Secretary; Dec. 21, 1791 recorded; book K p. 22.

2663. Nov. 9, 1784 Gov. Alexander Martin (New Bern, NC) to John Stokeley; grant #201; for £0.50 per 100 ac granted 152 ac; border: begins at SW corner of "your" late survey & crosses a branch. (signed) Alex Martin & J Glasgow, Secretary; Dec. 22, 1791 recorded; book K p. 23.

2664. Apr. 13, 1780 Gov. Richard Caswell (Kingston, NC) to Hezekiah Bonam;

grant #74; for £0.50 per 100 ac granted 357 ac between Long Cr & Moore's Cr; border: begins at Francis Harvey's corner large pine near Burns Road, joins Malpass' corner at a spring branch, Lewis, & SE side of Beardon Savanna. (signed) Rd Caswell & Wm Sheppard, D Secretary; Dec. 24, 1791 recorded; book K p. 24.

2665. Nov. 9, 1784 Gov. Alexander Martin (New Bern, NC) to William Taylor; grant #191; for £0.50 per 100 ac granted 52 ac; border: begins at a pine in Clark's line, joins Rouse, edge of a glade, & a branch in "the" swamp. (signed) Alex Martin & J Glasgow, Secretary; Dec. 26, 1791 recorded; book K p. 25.

2666. Oct. 29, 1787 Gov. Richard Caswell (Kingston, NC) to William Wright; grant #239; for £0.50 per 100 ac granted 100 ac on W side of Horse Br; border: begins at a pine in Jas Williams' line, joins a bay pond, & upper edge of Kieth's Savannah. (signed) Rd Caswell & W Williams, D Secretary; Dec. 27, 1791 recorded; book K p. 26.

2667. Oct. 29, 1787 Gov. Richard Caswell (Kingston, NC) to John Kenear; grant #246; for £0.50 per 100 ac granted 111 ac on W side of Long Cr; border: begins at a pine on Wm Braxton's line & joins Robert Lamb. (signed) Rd Caswell & W Williams, D Secretary; Dec. 28, 1791 recorded; book K p. 27.

2668. Oct. 29, 1787 Gov. Richard Caswell (Kingston, NC) to David Jones; grant #250; for £0.50 per 100 ac granted 50 ac on W side of NE [River] & S side of Rockfish Cr; border: begins at his own corner hickory in fork of Porters Br & joins Martin Willis. (signed) Rd Caswell & W Williams, D Secretary; Dec. 29, 1791 recorded; book K p. 28.

2669. Nov. 26, 1789 Gov. Samuel Johnston (Fayetteville, NC) to Gibs Lamb; grant #283; for £10 per 100 ac granted 10 ac; border: begins in Marden's line on side of Long Cr & near Geo Moore. (signed) Sam Johnston & J Glasgow, Secretary; Dec. 30, 1791 recorded; book K p. 29.

2670. Dec. 15, 1791 Gov. Alexander Martin (New Bern, NC) to James Jones; grant #295 [sic, #296 see shuck #2212 in New Hanover o in Secretary's grant files]; for £10 per 100 ac granted 220 ac on N side of Pearsells Savanna; border: begins at Owens Kennan's SW corner stake & joins Martin Willis. (signed) Alex Martin & J Glasgow, Secretary; Jan. 1, 1792 recorded; book K p. 30.

2671. Dec. 15, 1791 Gov. Alexander Martin (New Bern, NC) John James; grant [blank, #295 see shuck 2211 in New Hanover Co in Secretary's grant files]; for £10 per 100 ac granted 300 ac on SW side of Lewis Cr and between said creek & Horse Br; border: begins at a spruce pine lower end of "the" Bay Pond & joins edge of North branch. (signed) Alex Martin & J Glasgow, Secretary; Jan. 2, 1792 recorded; book K p. 31.

2672. Dec. 15, 1791 Gov. Alexander Martin (New Bern, NC) to John James; grant #297; for £10 per 100 ac granted 230 ac on E side of Horse Br; border: begins at Hardy Malpus' NW corner "Hardy Parker being patentee" of said land, joins a branch, & land where Col. "Blooworth" lives. (signed) Alex Martin & J Glasgow, Secretary; Jan. 3, 1792; book K p. 32.

2673. Jul. 16, 1791 Charles Cogdell (New Hanover Co) to Richard Roberds (Duplin Co, NC); for £50 sold 100 ac on W side of Black R; border: begins at a white oak on the river bank & runs through lower ford at "the" second branch to back line to Edmund Hawes' "plantation" survey; part of survey where said "Haws" formerly lived. (signed) Richard Roberds' mark [upside down isosceles triangle with wiggly sides]; (witness) Isaac Hynes & Thomas Hunter; wit. oath "Oct. term" by Thomas Hunter; Jan. 4, 1792 recorded; book K p. 33.

2674. Jan. 7, 1786 Thomas Bloodworth (New Hanover Co) to James Bloodworth (same); for 400 ac sold to him by James Bloodworth sold 1,280 ac on W side of Long Cr near "the" bridge [no more description]. (signed) Thos Bloodworth; (witness) Hugh Campbell & John Kinnear; wit. oath Jul. 1790 by Hugh Campbell; Jan. 5, 1792 recorded; book K p. 34.

2675. Aug. 1, 1769 John Kelly (Wilmington, NC) to Anthony Ward (New Hanover Co); for £40 proclamation money sold 106 ac on Lewis Cr, a branch of NE Cape Fear R; border: begins at a "mapell" at mouth of Old Field Br & joins Reas Evans. (signed) John Kelly; (witness) Jno Dubois & John Pensell; [note at end indicates Ward paid Kelly £40 Aug. 1, 1769]; Jan. 1792 "admitted" in court by [omitted]; Jan. 6, 1792 recorded; book K p. 35.

2676. Jun. 31, 1774 Thomas Henderson, mariner (Wilmington, NC) to James White esq (Bladen Co, NC); for £400 proclamation money sold an undivided half of a tenement, saw mill, & 1,410 ac on South R & Lake Cr in Bladen Co [no more description]; sold (no date) by George Palmer & wife Mary Ann to John walker who sold Jan. 30, 1772 to Thomas Henderson recorded in Bladen Co register's office; other half of property sold (no date) by George Palmer & wife to Bunbury Day deceased now owned by James White & wife Bridget. (signed) Thos Henderson; (witness) Peter Mallett [only one witness]; [note at end indicates White paid Henderson £400]; wit. oath Jan. 1792 by Peter Mallett; jan. 8, 1792 recorded; book K p. 36.

2677. Jun. 14, 1790 James Flowers (Brunswick Co, NC), administrator of goods & chattels of David Flowers deceased (late of Brunswick Co, NC), to James Hogg (Orange Co, NC); for £120 NC money, "allowed" by Hogg towards discharge of debt due to executors of Robert Hogg by late David Flowers, sold a Negro Daniel, from estate of David Flowers, 45 years old. (signed) Jas Flowers, admr; (witness) Joshua Potts [only one witness]; wit. oath Jan. 1792 by Joshua Potts; Jan. 10, 1792 recorded; book K p. 38.

2678. Jan. 16, 1790 Rebecca Guerard, widow (New Hanover Co) to John Fergus & James Walker "esquires" (Wilmington, NC); for £0.5 NC money leased for a year 1,600 ac on or near head of "the" sound; where John Guerard deceased (late of New Hanover Co) "usually" resided & presently occupied by said Rebecca Guerard; and sold land "adjoining or adjacent thereto" or all she is entitled to under will of her late husband John Guerard [no more description]; lease begins Jan. 1, 1790; quit rent is 1 pepper corn. (signed) Rebecca Guerard, Jno Fergus, & James Walker; (witness) John Lord & John Fergus jr; wit. oath Apr. 1790 by John Fergus jr; Jan. 12, 1792 recorded; book K p. 38.

2679. Jan. 17, 1790 Rebecca Guerard, widow (New Hanover Co) first part, John Fergus esq & James Walker, merchant (both of Wilmington, NC) second part, & Peter Maxwell, merchant (Wilmington, NC) third part; a marriage is shortly intended between Rebecca Guerard & Peter Maxwell; Rebecca owns, in her own right under will of her late husband John Guerard deceased, divers land, Negroes, stock, household & kitchen furniture, & plantation tools; Rebecca wants to "assure" the same to herself & Peter or longer lived one of them & not be liable for payment of Peter's debts or be at his disposal; SO to secure the estate to Rebecca & for £0.20 NC money paid by Fergus & Walker to Rebecca, Rebecca with consent of Peter sold in trust (a) 1,600 ac where John Guerard deceased (late of New Hanover Co) usually resided & presently occupied by Rebecca and all land adjoining or adjacent thereto which she is entitled to under will of her late husband John Guerard; [above lease of land mentioned]; & (b) all Negroes, horses, neat cattle, hogs, sheep, household & kitchen furniture, plantation tools & implements of husbandry, & other goods & chattels in schedule prefixed to this deed; Fergus & Walker to permit Rebecca, until the marriage, to receive rents & profits from the land for her sole use and after marriage permit Peter & Rebecca to have sole management & direction and take rents & profits of the property for their support, but for no other use or for privae debts of Peter; Fergus & Walker to receive rents & profits from the property for support & education of issue, if any, from the marriage in proportions as Peter & Rebecca direct; if not issue or issue dies under 21 years old or unmarried, then Fergus & Walker to sell the premises to Peter & Rebecca or survivor of them;
schedule of property: male slaves Buck, parker, York, Ben, Will, Sam, George, jack, & Romes; female slaves Pamela, Nancy, Hessy, Abby, Rina, Nancy 2nd, Julia, & Myrtilla; 20 cattle being cows & calves, 25 sheep, 3 horses, a desk, 2 dining tables, 2 tea tables, a marble slab, 24 sitting chairs, 4 bed steads, 5 beds, 3 set curtains, a musquito net, 4 looking glasses, a candle stand, 34 pictures, 5 pair fire dogs, 2 pair shovel & tongs, some china, glass & earthen ware, 12 silver table spoons, 12 tea spoons, a soop spoon, a punch ladle, a milk pot, pair salt sellars. (signed) Rebecca Guerard, Peter Maxwell, Jno Fergus, & James Walker; (witness) John Lord & John Fergus jr; [not at end indicates full possession to items in the schedule was given by Rebecca to Fergus & Walker by delivery of a girl Nancy]; wit. oath Apr. 1790 by Jno Fergus jr; Jan. 30, 1792 recorded; book K p. 40.

2680. Feb. 27, 1788 John Wilkinson (New Hanover Co) to Richard Rundle (same); for £3,000 NC money sold part of lot (no number) in Wilmington fronting on Front Street; border: 50 feet in front, runs back "quiet" to low water mark of Cape Fear R [no more description]. (signed) John Wilkinson; (witness) Wm Ewans & Jona. Robeson; [note at end indicates Rundle paid Wilkinson £3,000]; wit. oath Oct. 1788 by Wm "Ewand"; Jul. 8, 1789 recorded in book "I" p. 82 (sic); [note at end:] May 29, 1790 it is my intention that above "houses & lots be reconvaid" to Mr. John Wilkinson after debts now due "or may become due" to me or wherein I stand security for any sum not due or that may become due "against me to be made out of said estate" (signed) Richard Rundle; book K p. 44.

2681. Oct. 13, 1795 Lucretia Rundle widow of Richard Rundle & administratrix of his goods & "natural" guardian of her minor son Richard, George Rundle eldest son of Richard Rundle & administrator of his goods, & Mary Rundle, only daughter of Richard Rundle, to John Wilkinson, merchant (Wilmington, NC); Wilkinson & Richard Rundle, merchant deceased (of Wilmington) had "sundry" dealings & "pecuninary" transactions with each other and Wilkinson became indebted to Rundle; at Randle's "intercession" Wilkinson sold property to Rundle as collateral for payment of debt owed when accounts were made as by note May 29, 1790 which Rundle added to above deed; SO grantors are "conversant" with above deed and "the parties" have settled all accounts; it appears by Rundle's books a balance of £182.17.6½ is due by Wilkinson; at signing of this "acquittal & discharge" Wilkinson paid Lucretia & George the balance; so grantors quit claim to Wilkinson "any part" of the premises mentioned in deed by Wilkinson to Rundle. (signed) Lucretia Rundle, George Rundle, & Mary Rundle; (witness) Ed Jones & F Lachman; wit. oath Jan. 1792 by F Lachman; Jan. 31, 1792 recorded;
    Dr [by] John Wilkinson in account current with Richd Rundle's estate: (a) to sundry debits on the books as per account rendered him from Jan. to Jun. 6, 1791 £1,107.7.10½; (b) to amount your obligation to Mr. Willm. Wilkinson where late Richd Rundle was security £472.10; [total of a & b] £1,579.17.10½; (c) by amount sundry credits exhibited in the "a/c" rendered you from '87 to Jun. '91 £813; (d) by amount discounted on settlement with Mr. Wilkinson for short credits in rents etc £11.10.4; (e) by amount bond to W Wilkinson cancelled £472.10; (f) by balance due the estate £182.17.6½; [total of c-f] £1,579.17.10½; (signed) Geo Rundle, administr.; book K p. 45.

2682. May 1, 1790 Gillam Bass (Boston, Massachusetts) to William Claypool (Wilmington, New Hanover Co); Rebecca Bass, Elizabeth Bass, Catharine DeMausquell, coheireses of William Wimble deceased are entitled to take possession of lots in Wilmington; so they and Elizabeth Wimble widow of William Wimble & Lewis DeMausquell husband of Catharine authorized Gillam Bass to take possession of the lots and sell them due to power of attorney recorded in New Hanover Co registry book I p. 55 [or 54 in original copy of book]; SO for £85 sold (a) lot #147 in Wilmington; border: begins on N side of Church Street & E side of Front Street, runs E 330 feet on Church Street to Second Street, N 66 feet on Second Street, & W to Front Street; & (b) lot #142; border: begins at NW corner of above [lot], runs E 330 feet along the same to Second Street, N 66 feet,

W to Front Street, & S 66 feet on Front Street to first station; formerly owned by James Wimble deceased, father of William Wimble deceased. (signed) Gillam Bass; (witness) John Huske & Galvin Alves; [note at end indicates Bass received £85]; wit. oath Jan. 1791 by John Huske; Jan. 31, 1792 recorded; book K p. 48.

2683. Jan. 7, 1791 John Abel Campbell esq (New Hanover Co) to James Bloodworth esq (same); for £100 NC money sold a moiety of following 760 ac, on or near Long Cr, formerly in copartnership between Thomas Cobham & Thomas Bloodworth and surviving partner, Bloodworth, sold (no date) to J A Campbell: (a) [omitted, maybe 100] ac on E side of Long Cr; border: begins at a cypress on the creek side & joins Thomas Hutchins; granted Sept. 26, 1766 to Thomas Ready; (b) 320 ac on E side of Long Cr; border: begins at a gum in "the" swamp & joins N side of Hutchins; granted Mar. 15, 1756 to Peter Lovillard [or Dovillard]; (c) 50 ac on both sides of Long Cr; border: begins at Michael Blancher's corner cypress on W side of the creek, joins Charles Bazen, a cypress on the creek 80 yards above Standley's Ford, joins James Standley, Richard Millar; granted Jul. 22, 1774 to Richard Millar; (d) 160 ac on W side of Long Cr; border: begins at a pine beside a small branch on N side of a savannah, crosses the savannah, joins S side of a pond, & Michael Blancher; sold Nov. 10, 1772 by Charles Bazen to Thomas Bloodworth; (e) 100 ac on W side of Long Cr; border: begins at a water oak on the creek side; granted (no date) to Michael Blancher and sold by Arthur Stuckey to Thomas Bloodworth who sold to John A Campbell; (f) 30 ac on E side of Long Cr; border: begins at a cypress, joins Jenkins, & the creek; sold (no date) by James Standley to Thomas Bloodworth who sold Aug. 10, 1780 to John A Campbell. (signed) John A Campbell; (witness) Henry Hoskins & D Jones jr; [note at end indicates Bloodworth paid Campbell £100]; Apr. 1791 acknowledged; Feb. 18, 1792 recorded; book K p. 51.

2684. May 10, 1791 Nathan Crocker, mariner (Wilmington, NC) to George Hooper, merchant (same); for £493.14.8 sold part of lot #12 "in the old plan or #72 in new plan" in Wilmington on E side of Front Street between Orange Street & Ann Street; border: begins at lot formerly owned by Robt Walker (of said town), runs N 33 feet on Front Street, E 165 feet, S 33 feet, & W 165 feet to first station; known as Wimble's lot; sold Feb. 20, 1790 by Peter Mallett & wife Sarah to Nathan Crocker; sale void if Crocker pays Hooper £493.14.8 by Jun. 1, 1793 & "lawful" interest of £6 per year per £100; Crocker can remain on the lot until default. (signed) Nathan Crocker; (witness) Thomas Anderson & John Allan; wit. oath Jan. 1792 by Thos Anderson; Feb. 24, 1792 recorded; book K p. 54.

2685. Feb. 21, 1789 Bridget Snow, widow (Wilmington, NC) to my daughter Elizabeth Snow; for [amount omitted] gave all my furniture "to say" beds, "badsteads", tables "&&", and a Negro girl Phebe. (signed) Bridget Snow; (witness) E [or ED} Levy; wit. oath Feb. 22, 1792 by L A Dorsey & John Stewart who recognize hand writing of Bridget Snow and Lau. A Dorsey also recognizes hand writing of Eleazer "Levey" (signed) Anthy. B Toomer, clerk; Feb. 26, 1792 recorded; book K p. 57.

2686. ("Hilton") Jan. 20, 1792 Thomas Hill to Wm Henry Hill; for £120 sold a Negro boy Joeboy. (signed) Thos Hill; (witness) Nat Hill [only one witness]; wit. oath Feb. 1792 by Nat Hill; book K p. 58.

2687. Feb. 21, 1792 Nathl. Hill to Wm Henry Hill; for £89 sold a boy slave John, son of my carpenter John. (signed) Nathl Hill; [no witness] Feb. 1792 acknowledged; Feb. 27, 1792; book K p. 58.

2688. (Hilton) Nov. 17, 1792 Roger Davis to Wm Henry Hill; for £125 sold a Negro boy Sampson about 18 years old, without ails or disorder. (signed) Roger davis; (witness) John Oliver & Nathl M Hill; wit. oath Feb. 1792 by Nat Hill; book K p. 59.

2689. May 5, 1791 James Flowers to William Henry Hill; for 1160 sold 3 Negroes: a man Pompey, a woman Darinda, & their boy child Oliver. (signed) Jas Flowers, atmr; (witness) John Huske & Mar R Willkings; wit. oath Feb. 1792 by M R Willkings; Feb. 27, 1792 recorded; book K p. 59.

2690. Jul. 30, 1791 John Hall esq & his wife Elizabeth (Brunswick Co, NC) to John Bleakley, merchant (Wilmington, NC); for £150 sold part of lot (no number) in Wilmington; border: joined on S by Princess Street, on W by "lots" owned by John Martin, said John Bleakley, & Mrs. Slingsby or John McAlester, on S & E [by lot owned by ?] John Nutt, 66 feet deep, & 27 feet fronting on Princess Street. (signed) John Hall & Elizabeth Hall; (witness) Thos Fitzgerald, Donald Bain, & William Hall; [note at end indicates "Bleakly" paid Hall £150]; Jan. 1792 acknowledged; Mar. 3, 1792 recorded; book K p. 60.

2691. Nov. 7, 1789 William Wright, planter (New Hanover Co) to Edward Evans (same); for £25 specie sold 100 ac on Horse Br & on W side of Walker's Br; border: begins at Walker's SW corner & joins a savannah. (signed) Wm Wright; (witness) Archd Wright & Thomas Liddon; Jan. 1792 acknowledged; Mar. 6, 1792 recorded; book K p. 62.

2692. Jun. 30, 1791 John Hill (New Hanover Co) to Arthur Mabson (same); for "value received" sold a Negro girl Beck. (signed) John Hill; (witness) Joshua Bradey [only one witness]; wit. oath Oct. 1791 by Joshua Bradey; Mar. 8, 1792 recorded; book K p. 63.

2693. Mar. 12, 1789 Alexr Riddell (presently in Wilmington, NC), for myself & partners, to my trusty & loving friend Mr. Robert Muter, merchant (Wilmington, NC); power of attorney to receive money due to me & to sell half of land & improvements in late distillery near Wilmington due to deed Mar. 7, "instant" from Mr. Peter Maxwell to me & partners and to sell the water lot & wharf in Wilmington sold Mar. 7 instant by Mr. Peter Maxwell to me & partners and to receive from "sundry" persons payment of notes left with said attorney. (signed)

Alexr Riddell, for self & partners; (witness) W Claypoole & John Telfair; wit. oath Jan. 1792 by John Telfair; Mar. 10, 1792 recorded; book K p. 63.

2694. Mar. 13, 1789 Alexr Riddell (presently in Wilmington, NC), on behalf of Riddell, Colquhoun, & Co, James Scott & Co, & Peter McDougall & Co, merchants (New York City), to my trusty & loving friend Mr. Robert Muter, merchant (Wilmington, NC); power of attorney to receive money due to me or "detained from me by any manner" by Messrs. Mallets, Brice & Co merchants (of Wilmington, NC). (signed) Alexr Riddell, for Riddell Colquhoun & Co, for Jas Scott & Co, & for Peter McDougall & Co; (witness) W Claypool & John Telfair; wit. oath Jan. 1792 by Jno Telfair [or Felfair]; Mar. 12, 1792 recorded; book K p. 65.

2695. Aug. 1, 1791 John Bradley, executor of estate of John Howell esq deceased, to Arthur Mabson esq; for £220 paid by Col. John A Campbell sold to Mabson 2 Negro wenches Matty & Pleasant. (signed) John Bradley, exor of Howell's estate; (witness) Joshua "Bradey" [only one witness]; wit. oath Oct. 1791 by Jos Bradey; Mar. 13, 1792 recorded; book K p. 66.

2696. Apr. 10, 1790 James Walker esq & wife Magdaline Margeret, Jean DuBois widow, & James "Dubois" gentleman (all of Wilmington, NC) to Samuel Lowder, merchant (same); for £300 NC money sold part of lot #27 on old plan & #2 on new plan in Wilmington on N side of Market Street; border: between Front Street & Second Street, joined on W by ground & tenement of said Jean DuBois, on E by land lately owned by Jacob Friot, 20 feet on Market Street, & runs N 132 feet to Henry Toomer's Alley. (signed) James Walker, Jean "Dubois", James "DuBois", & Magdn. Margt. Walker; (witness) Daniel McNeill [only one witness]; [note at end indicates Lowder paid grantors £300]; wit. oath Feb. 1792 by Daniel NcNeill; Mar. 22, 1792 recorded; book K p. 66.

2697. Mar. 20, 1789 Thomas Devane jr, planter (New Hanover Co) to Charles Cogdell, planter (same); for £60 sold 212 ac on E side of Black R; border: begins at a pine on Fennel's line on E side of Little Clear Run, joins Thomas Bloodworth's former line now Benjamin Robinson's, crosses Clear Run, & joins "late" survey of Timothy Bloodworth's now Benjamin Robinson's; granted Nov. 9, 1784 to Timothy Bloodworth who sold to Thomas Devane jr. (signed) Thomas Devane; (witness) Nicholas "Fennell" & W "Sharples"; Jan. 1792 acknowledged; Mar. 23, 1792 recorded; book K p. 68.

2698. Dec. 4, 1790 Charles Cogdell (New Hanover Co) to William Wright (same); for £150 NC money sold a Negro man Will. (signed) Chs. Cogdell; (witness) John Maclellan & Bartholomew Byrns; [not at end indicates Wright paid Cogdell £150 Dec. 4, 1790]; wit. oath Jan. 1792 by John Maclellan; Mar. 23, 1792 recorded; book K p. 70.

2699. Jun. 22, 1790 Thomas Neale sr esq (Brunswick Co, NC) to Alfred Moore esq (Orange Co, NC); for £360 "secured to be paid" sold following Negroes: Peggy & her children Chloe, Lango [or Zango], Sarjoe, & Toney. (signed) Thos Neale sr; (witness) (witness) John Porter Grange [only one witness]; (Wilmington "District", NC) wit. oath Mar. 7, 1792 by John Porter Grange before Spruce McCay, JSCLE; Mar. 24, 1792 recorded; book K p. 70.

2700. Feb. 19, 179 John Kinneair [or Kinear] (New Hanover Co) to Isaac Lamb, planter (same); for £48 NC money sold 111 ac on [blank] Branch on W side of Long Cr; border: begins at a pine on Wm Braxton's line & joins Robert Lamb. (signed) John Kinneair; (witness) Benja "Unott" & William Walker; wit. oath Jan. 1792 by Wm Walker; Mar. 23, 1792 recorded; book K p. 71.

2701. Nov. 19, 1791 John Moore esq (New Hanover Co), acting executor of will of George Moore esq deceased (late of New Hanover Co), and George Moore esq (same), son & heir of George Moore deceased, to George Davis attorney at law (Brunswick Co, NC); for £300 NC money paid by Davis to John Moore & for £10 NC money paid by Davis to George Moore, the son, sold 2 adjoining tracts: (a) 220 ac or residue owned by George Moore deceased in grant to Roger Moore, his father, for 520 ac on W side of NE Cape Fear R; border: begins at a cypress on the river side & joins Long Cr; known as "the" cow pens; part or 300 ac was sold in his lifetime & on Aug. 9, 1777 George Moore sold to his daughter Mary Davis, wife of Thomas Davis esq (late of New Hanover Co & now of Brunswick Co); & (b) on S side of Long Cr; border: begins at Timothy Bloodworth's lower corner cypress & joins the cow pens line; granted Apr. 17, 1765 to George Moore; on Mar. 22, 1778 George Moore wrote his will and devised "sundry" tracts in North Carolina to "sundry" persons and directed his other land, which included land inherited from his father Roger and lots in Brunswick & Wilmington, to be divided between his wife Sarah Moore, all his "son", and his daughters Sarah Jones, margarett Moore, & Martha Moore OR land was to be sold for cash or young Negroes; George Moore appointed said John Moore executor; "afterward" George died without altering the will; John Moore proved the will in "proper" court & became executor and decided with George Moore's son George to sell above 2 tracts. (signed) Jno "B" Moore & George Moore; (witness) Thomas Ashe, Roger Davis, & Thomas Jones; wit. oath Jan. 1792 by Thos Ashe; Mar. 26, 1792 recorded; book K p. 72.

2702. May 4, 1791 Alexander McCulloch (New Hanover Co) to Samuel Lowder; for £70.10 sold a Negro girl Judy about 15 years old. (signed) Alexr McCulloch; (witness) Wm Nutt [only one witness]; wit. oath Feb. 22, 1792 by Wm Nutt; Mar. 26, 1792 recorded; book K p. 76.

2703. Nov. [blank], 1790 Henry Toomer to Samuel Lowder (Wilmington, NC); for £30 sold for use of an alley 12 feet wide from lot owned by me running from Front Street to Second Street for convenience of Lowder having a "back outset" from his lot he purchased from Jane DuBois [similar to book I p. 327]. (signed) Henry Toomer; (witness) Jonth Huntington [only one witness]; Feb. 1792 acknowledged; Mar. 27, 1792 recorded; book K p. 77.

2704. Aug. 15, 1791 Benjamin Leverett, merchant, & wife Comfort (Portsmouth, Rockingham Co, New Hampshire) to our trusty friend John Maclellan (Wilmington, NC); power of attorney to receive form anyone the money & merchandise owed to me and to enter 106 ac on Lewis' Cr, a branch of NE Cape Fear R; border: begins at a maple tree at mouth of Old Field Br, joins Reas Evans, & a small branch; "lately" owned by Capt. William Marshall deceased (late of said Portsmouth) & prosecute anyone on the land. (signed) Benjn. Leverett & Comfort Leverett; (witness) Jeremiah Hill & Danl Humphreys; (New Hampshire) Aug. 15, 1791 Daniel Humphreys, notary public living in Portsmouth, certifies he was witness to power of attorney & also saw Jeremiah Hill (of Portsmouth) sign as witness (signed) Danl Humphreys, NP; (Portsmouth, New Hampshire) Aug. 15, 1791 Saml Haven, clerk, certifies William Marshall & Margaret Marshall were married and unto them was born in wedlock Comfort their second daughter now lawful wife of Benjamin Leverett, William & Margt. Marshall were married by me who also baptized their daughter Comfort & married her to Benjamin Leverett (signed) Saml Haven, clerk; (New Hampshire) Aug. 15, 1791 Daniel Humphreys, notary public, certifies "Doctor" Samuel Haven is clerk and person & "settled officiating" parish minister of South Parish in Portsmouth (signed) Danl Humphreys; (New Hampshire) Nov. 12, 1791 Josiah Bartlett, governor or "president" of the state, certifies "Reverend" Samuel Haven Doctor of Divinity was clerk & officiating parish minister in Portsmouth and Daniel Humphreys es is notary public (signed) Josiah Bartlett & Joseph Pearson, Secretary; (New Hanover Co) Jan. 1792 power of attorney ordered registered (signed) Thos Maclaine, clerk; Mar. 29, 1792 recorded; book K p. 77.

2705. De. 12, 1791 Gabriel Kingsbury (New Hanover Co) to my beloved daughter Sarah Kingsbury; for natural love & affection gave a Negro fellow Bacchus and house & lot #5B in Wilmington on Market Street. (signed) Gabriel Kingsbury; (witness) Alexr Carmichael & John Mercer Gabie; wit. oath Jan. 1792 by Alexr Carmichael; Mar. 29, 1792 recorded; book K p. 80.

2706. May 20, 1791 George Hooper (New Hanover Co) to John Cogdell, George Smith, Josiah Smith, Daniel Deraussure, & Edward Darrell (Charleston, SC); on May 10, 1791 Nathan Crocker (of "said" town & state) sold to George Hooper part of lot #72, houses, & improvements in Wilmington on E side of Front Street; border: between Orange Street & Ann Street, begins at lot formerly owned by Robt Walker (of Wilmington), runs N 33 feet on Front Street, E 165 feet, S 33 feet, & W 165 feet; sale was conditioned on payment of 1493.14.8 by Jun. 1, 1793 by Crocker to Hooper; failure to make payment would mean Hooper would own the lot; SO for £0.5 sold, subject to foregoing deed, above part of lot #72 in Wilmington. (signed) G Hooper; (witness) Thomas Anderson [only one witness]; [note at end indicates Hooper received £0.5; Jan. 1792 acknowledged; Mara. 30, 1792 recorded; book K p. 81.

2707. Aug. 14, 1791 Nathan Byrd [or Bird] & wife Easter (Dobbs Co, NC) to John Miller, son of Richard Miller (New Hanover Co); for £40 specie sold 100 ac on E side of Long Cr; border: begins at upper corner hickory, joins an old line, & a branch below a field; part of 640 ac granted Feb. 16, 1737 to Joseph Portevint who sold to Thomas Hutchings who sold to Richard Miller who sold to Nathan Bird. (signed) Nathan Byrd & Easter Byrd; (witness) James Parrish & William Houston; wit. oath Jan. 1792 by William Houston; Mar. 31, 1792 recorded; book K p. 83.

2708. Dec. 12, 1791 Gabriel Kingsbury (New Hanover Co) to my beloved daughter Elizabeth Kingsbury; for natural love & affection gave a house & lot [number blank] in Brunswick town on [blank] street, Brunswick Co, NC; sold (no date) by Solomon Hammer to said Kingsbury. (signed) Gabriel Kingsbury; (witness) Alexr Carmichael & Jno Mercer Gabie; wit. oath Jan. 1792 by Alexr Carmichael; Mar. 31, 1792 recorded; book K p. 85.

2709. Apr. 13, 1780 Gov. Richard Caswell (Kingston, NC) to Alexander Nelson; grant #15; for £0.50 per 100 ac granted 247 ac on Keith Swamp, a branch of Long Cr & Stoney Run; border: begins at a pine on N side of Stoney Run, joins his own line, crosses Stoney Run through low end of an old rice field, crosses Long Cr, & joins Marsden. (signed) Richd Caswell & Wm Sheppard, D Sec; Apr. 1, 1792 recorded; book K p. 86.

2710. Dec. 12, 1791 Gabriel Kingsbury (New Hanover Co) to my beloved daughter Jane Hannah Kingsbury; for natural love & affection gave 2 tracts in Brunswick Co on upper side of Orton Cr, a branch of Cape Fear R; being patents #131 & 170. (signed) Gabriel Kingsbury; (witness) Alexr Carmichael & Jno Mercer Gabie; wit. oath Jan. 1792 by Alexr Carmichael; Apr. 2, 1792 recorded; book K p. 87.

2711. Oct. 29, 1787 Gov. Richard Caswell (Kinston, NC) to Alexander Nelson; grant #238; for £0.50 per 100 ac granted 118 ac on E side of Buck Br; border: begins at George Moore's corner large pine & joins Josiah Lamb. (signed) Rd Caswell & Wm Williams, D Secretary; Apr. 3, 1792 recorded; book K p. 88.

2712. Dec. 20, 1791 Gov. Alexander Martin (New Bern, NC) to Benjamin Smith; grant #299; for £10 per 100 ac granted 420 ac between NW River & NE River; border: begins at lower corner stake of Rowan's patent at mouth of Black R, joins James Moore's back line of his Fishing Creek survey and Blenning's now Benjamin Smith's line. (signed) Alex Martin & J Glasgow, Secretary; Apr. 3, 1792 recorded; book K p. 88.

2713. Dec. 20, 1791 Gov. Alexander Martin (New Bern, NC) to Benjamin Smith; grant #300; for £10 per 100 ac granted 100.5 ac "in" Black R opposite Hedden Bluff; border: joins Black R on W side and the thorofare that makes "round said" island on E side [no more description]. (signed) Alex Martin & J Glasgow,

Secretary; Apr. 4, 1792 recorded; book K p. 89.

2714. Dec. 20, 1791 Gov. Alexander Martin (New Bern, NC) to Benjamin Smith; grant #301; for £10 per 100 ac granted 11 ac being an island in Black [R] opposite said Benjamin Smith's Appleby "plantation"; border: begins at lowermost post of the island, runs "nearly" W 20 chains with the river to uppermost point of the island, N20W 4 chains round the point, N40E to a small creek or thorofare, & down the thorofare 20 chains to first station. (signed) Alex Martin & J Glasgow, Secretary; Apr. 5, 1792 recorded; book K p. 90.

2715. Dec. 20, 1791 Gov. Alexander Martin (New Bern, NC) to Benjamin Smith; grant #302; for £10 per 100 ac granted 240 ac on NE side of Black R; border: begins at a large pine by a large bay in James Colson's now said Smith's upper line, joins Hewet, & Black R "or" the thorofare by the island. (signed) Alex Martin & J Glasgow, Secretary; Apr. 6, 1792 recorded; book K p. 91.

2716. Dec. 20, 1791 Gov. Alexander Martin (New Bern, NC) to Benjamin Smith; grant #303; for £10 per 100 ac granted 100 ac on SW of Black R; border: begins at Stewart's lower corner on the river & joins a large bay. (signed) Alex Martin & J Glasgow, Secretary; Apr. 7, 1792 recorded; book K p. 92.

2717. Dec. 20, 1791 Gov. Alexander Martin (New Bern, NC) to Benjamin Smith; grant #304; for £10 per 100 ac granted 270 ac between NW River & NE River; border: begins at a stake & maple tree on NW river being "Blanning's" now said Benjamin Smith's lower corner, joins James Moore's Fishing Creek survey, mouth of Fishing Cr at NE River, & upper corner of Catfish or Negro head Point survey. (signed) Alex Martin & J Glasgow, Secretary; Apr. 8, 1792 recorded; book K p. 93.

2718. Dec. 20, 1791 Gov. Alexander Martin (New Bern, NC) to Benjamin Smith; grant #305; for £10 per 100 ac granted 100 ac on SW side of Black R; border: begins at a stake on the river that divides this [tract] from his upper survey, "below" his other 100 ac tract on the river, & joins Burdeaux. (signed) Alex Martin & J Glasgow, Secretary; Apr. 9, 1792 recorded; book K p. 94.

2719. Mar. 7, 1791 Jonathan Robeson (Wilmington, NC) to William Moseley, planter (same); Moseley agreed to sold to Robeson a house & lot & "vacant" lot [number blank] joining the same in Wilmington on Dock Street; border: between lot now owned by Henry Halsey & lot lately owned by John Brown deceased; SO for £0.10 NC money paid by Moseley now, for £217.15.4 NC money paid by Moseley on "first" arrival of Capt. Amhert Bartlet in port of Wilmington or "previous to his subsequent departure" thereafter in "paper medium of said state or gold & silver at relative value" and for Moseley's written obligation for £1,000 conditioned on payment of judgment & cost that may be awarded against Robeson due to suit now in Wilmington Dist. Equity Court by Jonathan Robeson complainant and Cochran & William "Macline" (of Charleston [SC]) defendants provided judgment & cost don't exceed £282.4.8 NC money or total of £510 & balance due in judgment Robeson promises to "make an indefeatable" title to the house, lot, & adjoining vacant lot upon payment of £217.15.4 and Moseley's bond for judgment; Robeson & Moseley agree to a bond of £2,000 to fulfill these conditions. (signed) Jno Robeson & William Moseley; (witness) Henry Tucker & James Grange; wit. oath Jan. 5, 1792 by Henry Tucker before Saml Ashe, JSCLE; [note at end indicates Moseley, by hands of Henry Tucker, paid Robeson £111.15.9 on Mar. 16, 1791 and paid £75.10 on Mar. 21, 1791 and Jan. 5, 1792 Henry Tucker before Saml Ashe, JSCLE, swears he saw Robeson sign both receipts];

Mar. 28, 1791 received of William Moseley, by hands of Henry Tucker, on account of Jonathan Robeson $36 and 2 pieces of gold "joes" one weighing 8 dwt [penny weight] 3 gains & other 8 dwt 14 grains and reduced to paper money at £0.12 per dollar amounts to £30.9.6 NC money (signed) Joshua Potts; Jan. 5, 1792 Henry Tucker before Saml Ashe, JSCLE swears he saw Joshua Potts, agent of Jona. Robeson, sign the receipt; book K p. 94.

2720. Jan. 4, 1792 James McAlester & Daniel Mallett to William Nichols; for 1100 cash in hand sold a Negro boy Nace about 14 years old. (signed) James McAlester & D Mallett; (witness) Dens. Reardan [only one witness]; Jan. 1792 acknowledged; Apr. 11, 1792 recorded; book K p. 97.

2721. Jan. [blank], 1792 David Jones jr (New Hanover Co) to John S S Ashford (same); for £100 sold 150 ac on S side of Rockfish [Cr]; border: begins at mouth of Docos [or Doeos] Br on bank of Rockfish [Cr], crosses the branch, near Fussel, joins "the" main road, & foot of Rockfish Bridge. (signed) D Jones jr; [no witness]; Jan. 1792 acknowledged; Apr. 12, 1792 recorded; book K p. 97.

2722. Apr. 6, 1790 Mrs. Mary Geekie before Jno Baptista Moore, JP (New Hanover Co) & swore: she heard Mr. Alexander Hostler say before he died that he gave a boy, who he was then binding to Mr. James Stephens ship carpenter, to John Mercer Gabie his son-in-law; and it was not "owing" to his gift to Gabie that he would have sold him for his faults before he bound him. (signed) Jno B Moore, JP [Mary doesn't sign]; Jul. 1790 exhibited in court & ordered recorded (signed) Tho Maclaine, clerk; Apr. 23, 1792 recorded; book K p. 99.

2723. Apr. 8, 1790 Mary Hostler before J B Moore, JP (New Hanover Co) & swore: Mary frequently heard Alexander Hostler (late of Wilmington, NC) in his lifetime say he gave a Negro boy Hestor to Mercer Gabie, Mary Hostler's son; in lifetime of Alexander Hostler, Hector was called property of Mercer "Gaibbie" and bound by A Hostler to a ship carpenter called Stephens as property of Mercer "Gaibie"; Mary Geekie was called & deposed on oath that above circumstances are, today, fresh in her memory & consistent with [Mary's statement]. (signed) Mary Hostler, Mary Geekie, & J B Moore, JP; Apr. 1790 exhibited in court & ordered recorded (signed) Tho Maclaine, clerk; Apr. 23, 1792 recorded; book K p. 99.

2724. Apr. 9, 1790 Mrs. Sarah Robeson before J B Moore, JP (New Hanover Co) & swore: Sarah frequently heard Alexander Hostler (late of Wilmington, NC) say, in his lifetime, he had given a Negro boy Hector to Mercer Gabie, son of Mary Hostler; the boy was considered property of Mercer Gabie; he had put him with Stephens, chip carpenter, in Wilmington to learn the trade for the "emolument" [profit] of said Gabie. (signed) S Robeson & J B Moore, JP; Apr. 1790 exhibited in court & ordered recorded (signed) Tho Maclaine, clerk; [note at end:] due to not having reced. this & within papers from Mr. Hooper in whose hands they fell after death of Mr. Maclaine, it was Apr. 21, 1792 before they were sent to the register's (signed) Geo Gibbs, D clerk; Apr. 23, 1792 recorded; book K p. 100.

2725. Nov. 26, 1789 Gov. Samuel Johnston (Fayetteville, NC) to Simon Molpus; grant #266; for £10 per 100 ac granted 150 ac on E side of widow Moore's Cr; between Jesse Kook, John Jones, & William Jones; border: begins at a water oak on run of said creek near said Kook's line & joins Simon Hogen. (signed) Sam Johnston & J Glasgow, Secretary; May 8, 1792 recorded; book K p. 100.

2726. May 17, 1792 Elizabeth Rogers (New Hanover Co) to my son James Rogers; for love & affection gave a Negro girl Peg. (signed) Elizabeth Rogers; (witness) Chs. Cogdell & Thomas Rogers; wit. oath May 1792 by Charles Cogdell; (witness) May 22, 1792; book K p. 102.

2727. Jan. 9, 1787 James Sikes & wife Drusiley (New Hanover Co) to George Bannerman; for £60 sold a Negro girl Mary Ann 3 years old. (signed) James Sikes & Drusiley's mark "+"; (witness) John Corbett & Jno Hawes; wit. oath May 1792 by John Corbett; May 22, 1792 recorded; book K p. 102.

2728. Sept. 14, 1789 John Anders sr (Bladen Co, NC) to George Bannerman (New Hanover Co); for £5 specie sold 25 ac; border: begins at said Bannerman's upper corner pine near the river bank and joins a dividing line between said "Andres" & Bannerman. (signed) John Anders sr; (witness) James "Andres" & Robert Bannerman; wit. oath May 21, 1792 by Robt Bannerman; May 23, 1792 recorded; book K p. 103.

2729. Oct. 22, 1788 James Sikes & wife "Drueseley" (New Hanover Co) to George Bannerman; for £50 "spacia" sold a Negro boy Quass about 2 years old. (signed) James Sikes & Drueseley's mark [a wiggly "+"]; (witness) John Corbett & Robt Bannerman; wit. oath May 1792 by Jno Corbett; May 23, 1792 recorded; book K p. 104.

2730. Feb. 23, 1792 John Rholan (Duplin Co, NC) to John Sears, chair maker (New Hanover Co); for £25 NC money sold 100 ac on "the" sound; border: begins at a pine in Mr. McKenzie's line & joins back line of Masonborough survey. (signed) John Rholan; (witness) Elizabeth Blyth, "Lovieth" Everatt, & Ed Russell; [note at end indicates Sears paid Rholan £25]; wit. oath May 1792 by Edward

Russell; May 23, 1792 recorded; book K p. 104.

2731. Feb. 4, 1773 Simon Parker (New Hanover Co) to John Harrod (same); for £30 proclamation money sold 100 ac; border: begins at a red oak in fork of a branch, joins South R, & above Bennit Smith; surveyed in 1768 for Simon Parker. (signed) Simon Parker's mark [backward "S"] & "Margett" Parker's mark "M" (sic); (witness) Ralph Mcgee [or Megee] & William Boon; wit. oath May 1792 by William Boon; May 24, 1792 recorded; book K p. 107.

2732. Dec. 6, 1791 Thomas Lewis, farmer (New Hanover Co) to my loving brother-in-law William McGufford (same); for love, good will, & affection gave200 ac; border: begins at a stake & joins run of a branch; known as "the White Oack". (signed) Thos Lewis; (witness) S Buxton & Margrett McGufford; wit. oath May 1792 by Saml Buxton; May 24, 1792 recorded; book K p. 108.

2733. Jan. 28, 1789 John B Moore (New Hanover Co) to Daniel Burdeaux (same); for £120 sold a Negro Harry [or Hany]. (signed) Jno B Moore; [no witness]; May 1792 acknowledged; May 24, 1792 recorded; book K p. 109.

2734. May 22, 1792 John Hill to Daniel Burdeaux; for £100 sold a Negro girl Monimia. (signed) John Hill; [no witness]; May 1792 acknowledged; May 24, 1792 recorded; book K p. 109.

2735. Feb. 28, 1787 Peter Mallett, for self and Malletts & Mumford, to William Ewans & Thomas Henderson; for £400 proclamation money sold lot in Wilmington. (signed) P Mallett; (witness) Richard Nixon [only one witness]; May 1792 acknowledged; [note at end:] deed on which above assignment was on back of was from John Molten & wife to Patrick Brennan recorded Mar. 15, 1786 in book H p. 346 [written above 385] by John Bradley, register; May 25, 1792 recorded; book K p. 110.

2736. Nov. 26, 1789 Gov. Samuel Johnston (Fayetteville, NC) to John Hening [or Herring]; grant #265 [see shuck #2179 in New Hanover Co in Secretary's grant files]; for £10 per 100 ac granted 135 ac on W side of Black R; border: begins at a "long" spruce pine on S side of Reedy Br on McKalip's line, joins lower end of Hawes' Marsh, S side of Kieth's Br at head of Dead fall Pecoson, & Hezekiah Doan. (signed) Saml Johnston & J Glasgow, Secretary; May 26, 1792 recorded; book K p. 110.

2737. May 25, 1792 A Macnaughton to John Bradley; Macnaughton received "full payment" of bond dated Jun. 15, 1790 for which Bradley's property was mortgaged to Macnaughton Jun. 16, 1790 & recorded in book I p. 255 & 256 [p. 194 in copy of book I]. (signed) A Macnaughton; (witness) Jno Mercer Gabie; wit. oath May 1792 by Jno Mercer Gabie; May 26, 1792 recorded; book K p. 111.

2738. Mar. 4, 1789 W H Hill to George Davis; today Hill bought Negro boy Scipio from Davis for £80; Hill agrees that if Davis "chuses" within 2 years, Davis can buy back Scipio for £80 "equal to £80 at this day with interest". (signed) W H Hill; (witness) T Hill;

Feb. 12, 1791 George Davis esq paid "the sum & interest mentioned within" to me, so I sell Scipio to him. (signed) W H Hill; (witness) R Quince; May 1792 acknowledged; May 26, 1792 recorded; book K p. 112.

2739. Mar. 21, 1792 John Huske to James Hogg, surviving executor of Robt Hogg; for £50 sold my interest in entry for 1,000 ac; entered in my name in [John] Armstrong's office; border: joins entry for same quantity in name of said James [Hogg] & both located at or near mouth of Wolf R on N side of Mississippi [R]; but I understand there was a prior entry there, so I empowered Col. James Robertson (of Nashville [TN]) to remove the location to wherever he thought proper; so as soon as the location is fixed & survey completed, I bind myself to make said James [Hogg] further conveyance that may be necessary for James Hogg to have my right & claim to the premises. (signed) John Huske; (witness) G Hooper & Geo Gibbs; wit. oath May 1792 by Geo Gibbs; May 26, 1792 recorded;

[closest match is warrant #2291 for 1,000 ac entered May 25, 1784 by James Hogg and sold (no date) by James Hogg to John Huske (sic) and used by John Huit to obtain grant in Middle Dist, TN; see warrant in John Armstrong's office and item #2901 in part 2 of book on entries & surveys due to entries in John Armstrong's office; competing claim was probably entry #382 by John Rice which was granted to Rice Apr. 25, 1789 and later sold by his heirs to Andrew Jackson, John Overton, & James Winchester and used to form town of Memphis]; book K p. 112.

2740. Mar. 1, 1792 John Huske to James Hogg; for £340 sold a Negro wench Carolina & her 4 children: Alexr, Cyrus, Betsey, & Judy. (signed) John Huske; (witness) G Hooper & Geo Gibbs; wit. oath May 1792 by G Gibbs; May 28, 1792 recorded; book K p. 113.

2741. Jan. 11, 1792 Woodhs. Rhodes & Thos Johnston, executors of Col. "Henery" Rhodes deceased, to John Nichols; £194 NC money sold at public vendue a Negro man Isaac. (signed) Woodhs. Rhodes & Thos Johnston; (witness) Elijah St. George [only one witness]; "May term" by Elijah St. George; May 29, 1792 recorded; book K p. 113.

2742. Oct. 7, 1788 George Mackenzie (Brunswick Co, NC) to Alexander Hostler; for £415 NC money sold 6 Negroes: Martin a fellow about 45 to 50 years old, Present a wench about 45 years old, Chloe a wench about 40 years old, Milley a wench about 20 years old, Princess a wench about 16 years old, & Peggy a girl about 14 years old & their increase. (signed) G Mackenzie; (witness) Tho Craike [only one witness]; [note at end indicates Hostler paid Mackenzie £415 Oct. 7, 1788]; wit. oath Jun. 16, 1689 by Thos Craike before Saml Ashe, JSCLE; May 29, 1792 recorded; book K p. 114.

2743. Mar. 26, 1792 Michael Blanchau & wife Ruth (New Hanover Co) to James Bloodworth (same); for £50 sold 100 ac on W side of Long Cr; granted (no date) to "Michal" Blanshau & where he lives [no more description, reference made to patent for metes & bounds]. (signed) Michal Blanchau's mark "+" & Ruth Blanchau's mark "X"; (witness) Timothy Bloodworth sr & Timothy Bloodworth jr; wit. oath May 1792 by Timothy Bloodworth jr; May 30, 1792 recorded; book K p. 115.

2744. Apr. 12, 1791 Sophia Gibbs to John Burgwin (Wilmington, NC); for £150 sold a Negro fellow Jack who has been in his possession for "some time past". (signed) Sophia Gibbs; (witness) Geo Gibbs [only one witness]; wit. oath mar. 9, 1792 by Geo Gibbs before Saml Spencer, JSCLE; May 31, 1792 recorded; book K p. 116.

2745. Apr. 12, 1791 John Gibbs to John Burgwin; for £150 "indorsed of his defeizance of a mortgage by me to him" & is in full consideration for a Negro fellow [no name]. (signed) book K p. 117.

2746. Mar. 10, 1792 John Gibbs, planter (Bladen Co, NC) to John Burgwin, merchant (Wilmington, NC); for £110 sold a Negro boy Sampson who I promise to deliver to Burgwin in 10 days from today. (signed) J Gibbs; (witness) William Hy. Beatty [only one witness]; [note at end indicates Burgwin paid Gibbs £110]; wit. oath May 1792 by William Hy Beatty; May 31, 1792 recorded; book K p. 117.

2747. Jun. [blank], 1784 "Skinking" Moore & wife Mary and Nathaniel Moore to William Ewans, merchant; for £400 NC money sold 2 tracts: (a) 420 ac in Bath Co now Brunswick Co on SW side of Lockwoods Folly [R] & upper side of Mr. Lane's land; border: begins at an ash on a creek; & (b) [blank] ac known as Beaver Dam "supposed" about 4 miles from above place [no more description]. (signed) Schenckk. Moore, Mary Moore, & Nath. Moore; (witness) David Flowers, Dunc. MacAuslan, & John Beck; (Fayetteville, NC) wit. oath May 4, 1792 by Duncan "MacCluslan" before Jno Williams, JSCLE; May 31, 1792 recorded; book K p. 118.

2748. Jul. 23, 1791 Thomas Wright, sheriff (New Hanover Co) to John Ablin Campbell esq (same); for £500 sold 8 tracts: (a) 200 ac on Island Cr; border: begins at corner gum tree of John Porter's patent on the creek side, below Sill's house, joins side of a bay pond, & a "branch or vally"; sold (no date) by John Porter to James Smallwood who sold to Roland Crocker & sold by his brother & heir Samuel Crocker to Frederick Gregg; (b) 455 ac on said creek; border: begins at John Porter's corner pine; granted (no date) to John Marshall who sold to Charles Harrison who sold to Frederick Gregg; (c) 149 ac; border: begins at NE corner pine of last mentioned tract, joins land bought by said Gregg of Roland Crocker, & another survey of said Gregg's; granted in 1769 to Frederick Gregg;

(d) 400 ac on a branch of Island Cr; border: begins at a pine on S side of a branch & joins N side of the branch; granted (no date) by Richard Earle who sold to James Smallwood who sold to "Rowland" Crocker and sold by his brother & heir Samuel Crocker to Frederick Gregg; (e) 200 ac; border: begins at corner pine of land formerly owned by Charles Harrison on W side of Middle Br & on "the" high land, joins S side of main branch near the fork, & Harrison's "other" survey; (f) 320 ac on a branch of said creek; border: begins at a bay tree on a branch near the creek being corner of Charles Harrison's "other" tract, crosses the creek swamp, & crosses "the" swamp; last 2 tracts granted (no date) to Charles Harrison who sold to Thomas Cunningham who sold to Rowland Crocker and sold by his brother & heir Samuel Crocker to Frederick Gregg; (g) 320 ac on said creek; border: begins at said Gregg's corner pine; & (h) 320 ac; border: begins at a pine in line of land said Gregg bought of Charles Harrison; last 2 tracts granted (no dates) to Frederick Gregg; sold (date blank) due to a "decretal" order from Wilmington Dist. Superior Court on the equity side returnable to court [date blank] against Frederick Gregg. (signed) Thos Wright, sheriff; (witness) John Bradley & "Nickson" Chester; [note at end indicates Wright received £500 "paid to William Campbell esq" Jul. 23, 1791]; wit. oath May 1792 by John Bradley; Jun. 1, 1792 recorded; book K p. 120.

2749. May 7, 1792 John London, attorney for Thomas Cobham, to James Bloodworth esq; for £150 sold all Doctor Thomas Cobham's interest in "sundry" tracts on Long Cr formerly in copartnership between said Thomas Cobham & Thomas Bloodworth. (signed) John London, atty. for Thos Cobham; (witness) Hy Hoskins & Timothy Bloodworth jr; wit. oath May 1792 by Henry Hoskins; Jun. 2, 1792 recorded; book K p. 125.
2750. Feb. 5, 1791 Bryan Buxton & William Buxton (New Hanover Co) to Fenla Murphy; for £70 NC money sold 100 ac on W side of widow Moore's Cr; border: begins at a white oak on S side of Pinsley's Br on Ward's line & joins "main water" of "said" creek; known as Pinsley's Ford; being a moiety of 200 ac granted Jun. 27, 1772 by Gov. Josiah Martin to Bryan Buxton. (signed) Bryan Buxton's mark "B" & William Buxton; (witness) S Buxton & William "Laing"; wit. oath May 1792 by Saml Buxton; Jun. 2, 1792 recorded; book K p. 126.

2751. Sept. 11, 1787 Mary Bland & James Bland (Duplin Co, NC) to John Fellow ("Wayn" Co, NC); for £270 specie sold 500 ac part in New Hanover & part in Duplin Co on both sides of "Bultale" Swamp, a branch of Rockfish Cr; border: begins at a sweet gum in the fork of Bull tale Swamp & Doctors Cr, joins Joshua Lee, Joseph Blake, & James Bland; granted Nov. 2, 1765 to James Bland. (signed) Mary Bland's mark "+" & James Bland; (witness) Aaron Williams, Maurice Fennell, & William James; wit. oath May 1792 by "Morris" Fennell; Jun. 4, 1792 recorded; book K p. 127.

2752. Sept. 12, 1787 Samuel Portevint (New Hanover Co) to John Fellow (Wayne Co, NC); for £150 sold 2 tracts: (a) 200 ac on "Booltail" [Br], a branch of Rockfish [Cr], border: begins at a white oan on S side of the branch & joins NE side of

Boltale Br; & (b) 300 ac; border: begins at a pine, joins Bland, & "Dowplin" [County] line. (signed) Samuel Portevint; (witness) Thomas Devane & Maurice Fennell; wit. oath May 1792 by "Morris" Fennell; Jun. 4, 1792 recorded; book K p. 129.

2753. Oct. 14, 1774 Elizabeth Maclaine, with consent of her husband Archibald Maclaine attorney at law (Wilmington, NC) signified by his signing, to Alexander Hostler, merchant (same); Mathew Rowan esq deceased (late of New Hanover Co) willed to Frederick Gregg esq & Richard Lyon esq now deceased, in trust for his daughter-in-law Elizabeth Maclaine, a yearly annuity "or rent" of £26.13.4 proclamation money for her separate use for her natural life from his estate; this has been done on Apr. 20 every year since death of Mathew Rowan; SO for £186 proclamation money sold said yearly annuity of £26.13.4 from Frederick Gregg, surviving trustee of said Rowan. (signed) Elizabeth Maclaine & A Maclaine; (witness) Jerom Maclaine & Thos Maclaine; wit. oath May 1792 by Thomas Maclaine; Jun. 5, 1792 recorded; book K p. 131.

2754. [blank], 1786 John Wilson (Wilmington, New Hanover Co) to Alexander Hostler (same); for £15 NC money sold 200 ac in Cumberland Co, NC on Horse Pen Br, lower side of Sandy Run, & E of Black R; border: begins at Wm Carver's SE corner stake near said branch. (signed) John Wilson; (witness) Richd Rundle & Henry Clarke; wit. oath May 1792 by George Rundle who recognized hand writing of Richard Rundle; Jun. 6, 1792; book K p. 133.

2755. Oct. 1, 1791 John Simmons, planter (New Hanover Co) to Joseph Serewes [or Sereves], farmer (same); for £30 NC money sold 150 ac; border: begins on N side of Cow head Br waters of Angolow [Br], near Buckhorn [Br ?}, & crosses Cowhead Br; granted in 1784 to me. (signed) John Simmons' mark [script "J" or "9"]; (witness) R Watson & Moses Fox; wit. oath "May term" by Moses Fox; Jun. 6, 1792 recorded; book K p. 135.

2756. Feb. 1, 1791 Isaac Brinson to Jacob Sheppard (New Hanover Co); for £40 NC money sold 400 ac on Moore Cr and in the fork of the creek on the run where the 2 prongs part; border: begins at a "popolaw", joins E prong of the creek, & crosses NE prong of Moores Cr; granted Apr. 20, 1768 by Gov. William Tryon to Isaac Brinson; and for £20 sold within mentioned 400 ac on NE prong of Moore Cr (sic). (signed) Isaac Brinson; (witness) Joshua Lutlow [or Lerttow] & Moses Fox; [note at end indicates Brinson received "within sum" Feb. 1, 1791]; wit. oath May 1792 by Moses Fox; Jun. 7, 1792 recorded; book K p. 136.

2757. Nov. 20, 1788 Ethenton Rochel (New Hanover Co) to Joseph Screws (same); for £21 NC money sold 150 ac on both sides of Buck horn [Br], a branch of "Angolan" [Br[; border: begins at a stake near Simmons' corner on W side of the branch, near head of a prong of Buck horn [Br], crosses Buck horn [Br], & near "Deuplin" [County] line. (signed) Ethenton Rochel's mark "+"; (witness) Jas Fentress, Joshua James, & "Mial" Walls; May 1792 acknowledged; Jun. 8, 1792 recorded; book K p. 139.

2758. Mar. 1, 1792 Thomas Rogers (New Hanover Co) to James Rogers (same); for £100 NC money sold 2 tracts: (a) 100 ac on E side of Black R; border: begins at a large pine by "the" river; part of 320 ac granted (no date) to John Andres [or Anches]; & (b) Thomas Rogers' half of a saw mill which is across Wile cat Cr [no more description]. (signed) Thomas Rogers; (witness) Fredk Simpson & Charles Simpson; wit. oath "May term" by Fredk Simpson; Jun. 8, 1792 recorded; book K p. 140.

2759. Nov. 26, 1789 Gov. Samuel Johnston (Fayetteville, NC) to William Wright; grant #271; for £10 per 100 ac granted 200 ac; border: begins at a spruce pine on S side of Sells Cr "a little" above Henry Wells' old field on side of a swamp & joins Thomas Gidings. (signed) Sam Johnston & J Glasgow, Secretary; Jun. 9, 1792 recorded; book K p. 142.

2760. Feb. 4, 1792 James Standley, planter (New Hanover Co) to James Bloodworth, planter (same); for £26 sold 30 ac on E side of Long Cr; border: begins at a cypress tree, joins Jenkins, & the creek. (signed) James "Staindley"; (witness) John Wright & Timothy Bloodworth; wit. oath Feb. 1792 by John Wright; Jun. 10, 1792 recorded; book K p. 143.

2761. Feb. 4, 1792 Richard Miller, planter (New Hanover Co) to James Bloodworth, planter (same); for £15 sold 50 ac on both sides of Long Cr; border: begins at Michael Blanchard's lower corner cypress on W side of the creek, joins Charles Bazen, a cypress on the creek 80 yards above Standley's Ford, joins Standley's corner, & Richard Miller. (signed) Richard Miller; (witness) Daniel Morgan & Timothy Bloodworth; wit. oath Feb.1792 by Daniel Morgan; Jun. 11, 1792 recorded; book K p. 144.

2762. Jul. 30, 1791 William Green, planter, & wife Mary (New Hanover Co) to Armand John DeRosset, doctor of phisic (Wilmington, NC); for £100 NC money sold back half of lot #55 in Wilmington on N side of Market Street; border: begins 132 feet from NW corner of Market Street & Third Street, runs N 66 feet on Third Street, W 165 feet parallel to market Street, S 66 feet [parallel to] Third Street, & E [parallel to] Market Street to first station; reference made to plan by act of Assembly Mar. 1745. (signed) William Green & Mary Green; (witness) John Bradley & Robert Muter; [note at end indicates DeRosset paid Green £100]; May 1792 acknowledged; Jun. 12, 1792 recorded; book K p. 146.

2763. May 19, 1792 John Erwin, planter (New Hanover Co) to Samuel Bunting, planter (same); for £22 NC money sold 28.5 ac at White oak Swamp on W side of said Samuel's land; border: begins at fourth corner lightwood stake of grant for 300 ac to Joseph Johnston, joins back line of Johnston's grant, a division corner, & Samuel Bunting's deed. (signed) John Erwin; (witness) Daniel Taylor & Benjamin Morgan; [note at end indicates Bunting paid Erwin £22 May 19, 1792]; May 1792 acknowledged; Jun. 14, 1792 recorded; book K p. 148.

2764. Jan. 17, 1791 John Hill, William Henry Hill, & Nathaniel Moore Hill to Thomas Hill; for £1,200 sold 400 ac on W side of NE Cape Fear R; known as Force putt; sold Apr. 21, 1778 by Roger Moore & wife Mary to William Hill esq deceased & recorded in New Hanover Co book G p. 497 (sic) [reference made to that deed for metes & bounds]. (signed) John Hill, W H Hill, & "N" Hill; (witness) Geo Davis & Thos Callender; [note at end indicates grantors received £1,200]; wit. oath May 1792 by Geo Davis; Jun. 14, 1792 recorded; book K p. 149.

2765. Nov. 29, 1785 Thomas Younger, merchant (Wilmington, NC) to James Walker, merchant (same); a bond for £5,000 sterling; a marriage is intended shortly between Thomas Younger & Anna Jean Dubois, daughter of John Dubois esq deceased & Mrs. Jean Dubois (of Wilmington); Anna owns, in her own right, 2 Negroes: a girl Sydney & female child Lavenia and, at death of her mother, Anna is entitled to lots & buildings in Wilmington due to will of her father to my beloved wife Jean the house, lot, & improvements where I live and adjoining "lot" for her widowhood & at end of that term to my daughter Anna Jean; it is intended by Jean Dubois, Anna J Dubois, & Thomas Younger that Sydney & Lavenia and said lots are to be sold in trust to James Walker with profits arising therefrom for use of Anna Jean for her life & after that to issue by said marriage; Anna's property won't be sold by Younger or liable for his debts; if there is no issue from marriage alive at Anna's death, then property goes to survivor of Thomas Younger & Anna J Dubois; bond is void if Younger sells or secures to be sold to Walker the above property. (signed) Thomas Younger; (witness) Robert McFarlane & John Huske; May 1792 acknowledged; Jun. 15, 1792 recorded; book K p. 151.

2766. Jul. 9, 1791 John Willkings to Marshall Robert Willkings (New Hanover Co); for £80 "mortgage" a Negro girl Hannah; Hannah to remain in possession of M R Willings until £80 borrowed is repaid; if Hannah dies or absent herself before money is repaid, I promise to make good all such deficiency. (signed) John Willkings; (witness) Thos Wright [only one witness]; wit. oath Feb. 1792 by Thos Wright; Jun. 16, 1792 recorded; book K p. 153.

2767. Oct. 26, 1765 Samuel Swann esq (New Hanover Co), surviving executor of will of Ann Montgomery deceased (late of Chowan Co, NC), to Parker Quince, merchant (Brunswick Co, NC); for £60 proclamation money sold 640 ac on W side of head of Elizabeth R [in Brunswick Co]; border: begins at a gum; granted Sept. 13, 1737 by King George II to Ann Montgomery who willed it Aug. 8, 1744 to be sold. (signed) Saml Swann; (witness) James Robeson & Will Mouat; [note at end indicates Quince paid Swann £60]; Oct. 26, 1765 acknowledged before Robt Howe; Jun. 18, 1792 recorded; book K p. 153.

2768. Jun. 3, 1789 Charles Jewkes & wife Ann (Wilmington, NC) to James McKay Stephens, ship carpenter (same); for £650 NC money sold part of lot #27B in Wilmington; border: 26 feet in front on Front Street, runs E 50 feet back, joined on N by house formerly owned by William Shiver, & on S by ground & house owned by estate of Jno Lyon. (signed) Charles Jewkes & Ann Jewkes; (witness) G Wright & C Young; [note at end indicates Stephens paid Jewkes £50]; dower renounced May 29, 1792 at New Hanover Co Pleas & Quarter Sessions Court by Mrs. "Anne" Jewkes before Ed Jones, JP; wit. oath May 1792 by Joshua G Wright & Edd. Jones esq appointed to obtain dower renouncement of Mrs. Jewkes (signed) Geo Gibbs, D clerk; Jun. 18, 1792 recorded; book K p. 155.

2769. Sept. 28, 1789 David Jones (New Hanover Co) to William Jones (same); for £50 sold 78 ac on S side of Rockfish [Cr] above the bridge; border: begins at a spruce pine on "the" bank, joins "the" main road, & the creek. (signed) D Jones "jr"; (witness) Wm Wright & Francis Savage; wit. oath Jul. 1791 by William Wright; Jun. 19, 1792 recorded; book K p. 158.

2770. Apr. 24, 1792 John Snow to John Fergus; for £80 sold a Negro girl Pheebe. (signed) John Snow; (witness) J Fergus; wit. oath May 1792 by James Fergus esq; Jun. 19, 1792 recorded; book K p. 159.

2771. Nov. 21, 1769 [10th year of reign of George III] Reverend John Watts (Turnbridge Wells, Kent Co [England]), one of sons of James Watts (Batcombe, Somerset Co), to Edward Bridgen, merchant (Pater Master Row, London); for £0.5 Great Britain money leased for a year John Watts' undivided half of 2 equal parts "to be paid into all" of 960 ac on New Topsail Sound in Bath Co (sic), NC; border: begins at mouth of a creek opposite Barren Inlet which creek divides said land from Job Howe's land & runs 240 poles on the sound; yearly quit rent is 1 pepper corn, if demanded. (signed) John Watts; (witness) George Clark & Rd Welch; [wit. oath at end of next deed]; book K p. 160.

2772. Dec. 19, 1774 Edward Bridgen, merchant (London) to Elizabeth Catharine DeRossett ("Chinese Temple", Wilmington, NC); for £0.5 sold undivided half of 960 ac on New Topsail Sound; border: begins at mouth of a creek "nearly" opposite Barren Inlet wich creek divides said land from Job Howe's land [no more description]; sold Nov. 21 & 22, 1769 by Reverend John Watts, clerk (Turnbridge Wells, Kent Co), one of sons of James Watts, gentleman (Batcombe, Somerset Co) to Edward Bridgen. (signed) Edward Bridgen; (witness) George Clark [only one witness]; Dec. 19, 1774 John Wilkes, lord mayor of city of London, due to act of Parliament passed in fifth year of reign of George II to make it easy to recover debts in the colonies in America, certifies George Clark, well known & worthy of good credit, swore "the several matters mentioned" [in this deed] are true (signed) "Rix"; Dec. 19, 1774 George Clark (Coffee House, Ludgate Hill, London) says he was present & saw Rev. Watts sign the deed to Bridgen and Richard Welch was also present and Clark saw Bridgen sign deed to E C DeRossett (signed) John Clark & John Wilkes, mayor; (New Hanover Co) May 1792 produced in open court & ordered registered; Jun. 20, 1792 recorded; book K p. 161.

2773. Nov. 22, 1769 [10th year of reign of George III] Reverend John Watts, clerk

(Tunbridge Wells, Kent Co), son of James Watts (Batcombe, Somerset Co), to Edward Bridgen, merchant (Pater Master Row, London); for £67.10 sold his half of 960 ac on New Topsail Sound in Bath Co (sic); border: begins at mouth of a creek "near" opposite Barron Inlet which creek divided the land from Job Howe's land & runs 240 poles on the sound; sold Dec. 22 & 23, 1763 by James Watts, the elder, to his sons John Watts & James Watts, the younger. (signed) John Watts; (witness) George Clark & Richd Welch; [note at end indicates Bridgen paid Walls £67.10]; Apr. 8, 1783 registered in office of Benjamin Hammatt, notary public in Birchin Lane London folio 365-367; (New Hanover Co) May 1792 produced in open court & ordered registered (signed) Geo Gibbs, D Clerk; Jun. 23, 1792 recorded; book K p. 164.

2774. Oct. 26, 1778 Herald Blackmore & wife "Nacy" (New Hanover Co) to Parker Quince, merchant (same); for £2,500 proclamation money sold part of lot #6B in Wilmington; border: begins 14 feet 2 inches from SW corner of Benjamin Stone's lower house on a "right line" with the house, runs N 28 feet 6 inches on right line with Front Street to John Quince's lot, W along his lot to the river, 28 feet 6 inches down the river, & E to first station; "with" free use & occupation jointly with Benjamin Stone & Thomas Henderson "of the passage or alley" 4 feet 6 inches wide on S side of said lot 6 from the river to Front Street. (signed) "Herall" Blackmore & Nacy Blackmore; (witness) John Gordon & Joseph Titley; [note at end indicates Quince paid Blackmore £2,500 Oct. 29, 1778 (sic) (witness) John Gordon & Dd Flowers]; wit. oath May 1792 Thomas Callender, executor of D Quince & Francis Brice (sic), swears he recognizes hand writing of John Gordon, Joseph Titley, & "Herall" Blackmore, he believes Blackmore & wife and Gordon are dead and Titley is out of state and William Nutt swears he recognized handwriting of Titley; Jul. 20, 1792 recorded; book K p. 169.

2775. Feb. 14, 1789 John "Bewford" & his daughter Mary Bewford to Elizabeth Moore; for £60 sold a Negro wench Lucy 12 years old. (signed) Mary Bewford's mark "X" & John Bewford's mark "X"; (witness) John Batt, David "Borker", Jno F Blake, & Sam Lane; wit. oath Jan. 1791 by John Batt; Aug. 8, 1792 recorded; book K p. 171.

2776. Nov. 26, 1789 Gov. Samuel Johnston (Fayetteville, NC) to John Gerrard; grant #263; for 110 per 100 ac granted 340 ac; border: begins at John Gerrard's line on main "rodd", joins the sea, & Lords Cr. (signed) Sam Johnston & J Glasgow, Secretary; Aug. 21, 1792 recorded; book K p. 172.

2777. Jul. 2, 1792 John Thompson (New Hanover Co) to my beloved daughter Sarah Thompson (same); for natural love & affection gave a Negro girl Hanna. (signed) John Thompson; (witness) William McVenrich & J "Fergias" jr; wit. oath Aug. 1792 by John Fergus; Aug. 21, 1792 recorded; book K p. 173.

2778. Jul. 10, 1792 John Thompson (New Hanover Co) to my beloved daughter Jane Thompson (same); for natural love & affection gave a dark bay mare called

Queen's Delight and all my household furniture except my wearing "apperal" & my wife's wearing apperal. (signed) John Thompson; (witness) William "MacVenrich" & J Fergus jr; wit. oath Aug. 1792 by John Fergus; Aug. 21, 1792 recorded; book K p. 174.

2779. Aug. 2, 1792 John Thompson (New Hanover Co) to my beloved daughter Mary Thompson (same); for natural love & affection gave a Negro boy James. (signed) John Thompson; (witness) William MacVenrich & J Fergus jr; wit. oath Aug. 1792 by John Fergus; Aug. 21, 1792 recorded; book K p. 174.

2780. Apr. 13, 1780 Gov. Richard Caswell (Kingston, NC) to Abner Stephens [or Stevens]; grant #79; for £0.50 per 100 ac granted 130 ac on W side of Black R; border: begins at a white oak on the river bank & joins Heron. (signed) Rd Caswell & Wm Sheppard, D Secretary; Aug. 22, 1792 recorded; book K p. 175.

2781. Aug. 17, 1792 Thomas Corbett, James Corbett, & William Corbett, planters (New Hanover Co) to John Corbett, planter (same); for love, good will, & affection gave our part of 100 ac on E side of Black R; border: begins at a large pine near said Thomas Corbett's line, joins "the" sand hills, & crosses Rooty Br; granted (no date) to Thomas Corbett deceased. (signed) Thos Corbett, James Corbett, & William Corbett; (witness) John Devane & John Devane jr; wit. oath Aug. 1792 by Jno Devane sr & Jno Devane jr; Aug. 22, 1792 recorded; book K p. 176.

2782. [no date] Thomas Craike to General Thomas Clark; for 500 Spanish milled dollars "lent & paid in hand to" Craike mortgaged, as security of loan of same amount by Clark, 7 Negroes: a fellow Joss lately owned by Mrs. Sarah Jones but now owned by said Craike by purchase, Rose a woman and Sam & Amelia her children, Barbary & Ben "her children", Tom a boy; all Negroes were owned by estate of Edmund Corbin deceased & sold to pay "sundry" executions against said estate; sale void if Craike pays Clark 500 Spanish milled dollars [no deadline mentioned]; otherwise Clark owns the "eight" Negroes. (signed) Thomas Craike [only one witness]; wit. oath Aug. 1792 by Thomas Davis; Aug. 23, 1792 recorded; book K p. 177.

2783. Apr. 14, 1792 Thomas Moore, gentleman (New Hanover Co) to General Thomas Clark (Brunswick Co, NC); for £115 sold a Negro man Meshach. (signed) Thomas Moore; (witness) Geo Davis [only one witness]; [note at end indicates Moore received £115 (witness) John Maclellan]; wit. oath Aug. 1792 by George Davis; Aug. 23, 1792 recorded; book K p. 178.

2784. Jul. 2, 1791 Alexander Rouse (New Hanover Co) to Alexander McCulloch (same); for £150 NC money sold 200 ac; border: begins at Calep Grainger's "eastmous" corner on John Howe's back line, joins Cow [or Con] Br, James "Mor's" westmost back line, & John Loper. (signed) A Rouse; (witness) B McCulloch & Wm Simpson; wit. oath Aug. 1792 by Wm Simpson; Aug. 24, 1792 recorded; book K p. 179.

2785. Jul. 2, 1792 Alexr Rouse, "laboure" (New Hanover Co) to to Alexr McCulloch (same); for £50 [150--lined out] "spacy" sold 100 ac; border: begins at Coors Br on Newbern "Rode" & joins Mathew Johnston; half of grant Oct. 24, 1767 to Alexr Rouse; being the part of the grant on W side of "Nuborn" Rode. (signed) A Rouse; (witness) B McCulloch & Wm Simpson; wit. oath Aug. 1792 by Wm Simpson; Aug. 24, 1792 recorded; book K p. 180.

2786. Nov. 1, 1791 Luke White sr (Sampson Co, NC) to Stephen Williamson (same); for £200 sold 2 tracts: (a) 150 ac; border: begins at mouth of Crabs Br; West "angle" or half of grant May 28, 1773 to said Luke White; & (b) 179 ac; border: begins at a small pine. (signed) Luke White's mark ["L" laying on its side]; (witness) "Anthoney" Williamson & Stephen Costin; wit. oath Aug. 1792 by Stephen Costin; Aug. 25, 1792 recorded; book K p. 181.

2787. Oct. 3, 1791 Luke White (Sampson Co, NC) to Josiah Register (New Hanover Co); for £100 "specia" sold 150 ac; border: begins at mouth of Crabs Br & joins a new line; W "angle" or half of grant May 28, 1773 to said Luke White & divided by a diagonal line. (signed) Luke White's mark ["L" laying on its side]; (witness) Stephen Williamson & Stephen Costin; wit. oath Aug. 1792 by Stephen Costin; Aug. 25, 1792; book K p. 183.

2788. Dec. 2, 1791 Samuel Ashe to James Howard, planter (New Hanover Co); for £100 NC money sold 100 ac on New Topsail Sound & SW side of Whitehouses Cr; border: begins at John Ashe's corner on said creek, joins fork of the creek, round the point to "the" Bridge Landing, up Mullot Run, mount of a branch, & John Ashe's head line. (signed) Saml Ashe & James Moore (sic); (witness) Peter Batson, Amos Atkinson, & Jas Howard (sic); wit. oath Aug. 1792 by James Howard jr; Aug. 27, 1792 recorded; book K p. 184.

2789. Sept. 27, 1788 Morris Fennel, planter (New Hanover Co) to Jacob Johnston, planter (same); for £50 "spice" sold 100 ac on W side of Black R & head of Devanes Marsh and between Devane's & Lyon's lines; border: begins at a pine near Griffins Br & joins "the" low ground. (signed) Morris Fennel; (witness) Chs. Cogdell, Isaac Portevint, & Nicholas Fennel; wit. oath Aug. 1792 by Isaac Portevint; Aug. 27, 1792; book K p. 185.

2790. Aug. 18, 1792 Jacob "Johnson" (Sampson Co, NC) to Ezekiel Hawes (same); for £60 "specia" sold 100 ac on W side of Black R and between Devane's & Lyon's lines on head of Devane's Marsh; border: begins at a pine near Griffin's Br & joins "the" low ground; granted Apr. 13, 1786 to Maurice Fennel. (signed) Jacob Johnson; (witness) Isaac Portevint & William Johnson; wit. oath Aug. 1792 by Isaac Portevint; Aug. 28, 1792; book K p. 186.

2791. Dec. 2, 1792 James Malpass (New Hanover Co) to John Herron,   planter (same); for £60 NC money sold 100 ac on S side of widow Moores Cr; border: begins at a stake near Swanns Br in line of said 200 ac [grant] and near Samuel "Ash"; being back half of 200 ac granted Dec. 20, 1768 by Gov. William Tryon to Rowan Roe who sold to David Mason who sold to Samuel Herron who sold to Arthur Stuckey who sold to James Malpass. (signed) James Malpass; (witness) Wm Wright & Jacob Dubose; Aug. 1792 acknowledged; Aug. 28, 1792 recorded; book K p. 187.

2792. Mar. 16, 1792 Samuel Lowder (New Hanover Co) to William Nichols; for £90 sold a Negro boy Harry about 11 or 12 years old. (signed) Saml Lowder; (witness) H Campbell [only one witness]; Aug. 1792 acknowledged; Aug. 29, 1792 recorded; book K p. 188.

2793. Jun. 22, 1790 Frederick Ward (NC) to Fenla Murphy (New Hanover Co); for £40 sold 100 ac on W side of widow Moores Cr; border: begins at a red oak on S side of Red Bank Br & joins a swamp. (signed) Fred. Ward; (witness) William "Laing" & Wm "Henney"; wit. oath Aug. 1792 by Wm Hennesy; Aug. 29, 1792 recorded; book K p. 189.

2794. Mar. 31, 1791 Thomas James (Duplin Co, NC) to William New (New Hanover Co); for £80 specie sold 160 ac on W side of NE River & on a branch of Rockfish Cr; border: begins at a black oak on S side of the branch about 0.5 miles above "the" house. (signed) Thos James; (witness) John "S S" Ashford & Benjamin Fussell; wit. oath Oct. 1791 by Benjamin Fussell; Aug. 30, 1792 recorded; book K p. 190.

2795. Dec. 26, 1791 Peter Mallett (New Hanover Co) to Daniel Mallett (same); for £70 NC money sold 6 ac; border: begins at E side of a high bluff on SW side of NE River 19 poles above Mrs. Margarett Hill deceased's line on the river, joins a stake near a pine on a sand hill 4 poles S of said Daniel Mallett's house "on top of said hill", & joins line of deed Mar. 7, 1787 by said Peter Mallett & wife Sarah to said Daniel Mallett; part of land sold Jun. 24, 1777 by Roger Moore deceased to said Peter Mallett & Arthur Magill recorded in book H p. 59 & 60. (signed) P Mallett; (witness) James Mumford [only one witness]; [note at end indicates Daniel paid Peter £70]; Jan. 1792 acknowledged by Peter Mallett; Aug. 30, 1792 recorded; book K p. 192.

2796. Feb. 14, 1789 William Patterson & Spines Standly [or Spirces Standley] (NC) to Daniel Mallett (NC); for £100 NC money sold a Negro Bridget about 14 years old. (signed) William Patterson & Spines Standly; (witness) Richard Nixon [only one witness]; wit. oath Jan. 1790 by R Nixon; Aug. 31, 1792 recorded; book K p. 193.

2797. Jan. 10, 1789 Mary Mabson widow and Arthur Mabson & wife Mary (New Hanover Co) to Daniel Mallett (same); for £800 NC money sold 100 ac of tide swamp land on E side of NE Cape Fear R about 4 miles above Wilmington;

border: begins at mouth of Nesses Cr, runs up NE River to "the" point, round the point to a small creek that leads thro' the swamp to Nesses Cr, joins land Arthur Mabson sold to Jehu Davis; part of Nesses Creek "plantation" left to Mary Mabson & her son Arthur Mabson by Arthur Mabson deceased. (signed) Mary Mabson, Arthur Mabson, & Mary Mabson; (witness) Frances Farmer & Richard Nixon; [note at end indicates Mallet paid Mary & A Mabson £800]; wit. oath Jan. 1790 by Richard Nixon; Sept. 1, 1792; book K p. 194.

2798. Feb. 13, 1792 John Bowden & wife Elizabeth and Susanna Nelson (New Hanover Co), heirs of Alexander Nelson deceased, to James Bloodworth (same); for £250 paid to Alexander Nelson in his life time & due to bond of £500 given by said Nelson compelling his heirs to execute a title sold 320 ac on E side of Long Cr; border: begins at a gum in the swamp by "the" run side & joins Mr. Hatchin; granted in 1756 to Peter Dravilland who sold in 1758 to Alexander Nelson deceased. (signed) John "bowden", Elizabeth Bowden, & Susanna Nelson; (witness) Thomas Bloodworth jr & Timothy Bloodworth jr; wit. oath May 1792 by Timothy Bloodworth jr; Sept. 1, 1792 recorded; book K p. 196.

2799. Feb. 15, 1792 John Bowden & wife Elizabeth and Susanna Nelson (New Hanover Co), heirs of Alexander Nelson deceased, to James Bloodworth (same); for £100 paid to Alexander Nelson in his life time & due to bond of £500 given by said Nelson compelling his heirs to execute a title sold 125 ac on E side of Long Cr; border: begins at a sweet gum on his own line on the swamp side, joins Peter Lamb, Arthur "Mobson", & Blanchard Pharis. (signed) John Bowden, Elizabeth Bowden, & Susanna Nelson; (witness) Thomas Bloodworth jr & Timothy Bloodworth [jr]; wit. oath May 1792 by Timothy Bloodworth jr; Sept. 1, 1792 recorded; book K p. 197.

2800. Aug. 15, 1792 John Nutt, cabinet & chair maker (Wilmington, NC) to Armand John DeRossett, physician (same); for £700 NC money sold lot #17A in old plan & 30A in new plan in Wilmington on E side of Front Street between Market Street & "Prince's" Street; border: begins at SW corner of lot owned by late John Slingsby deceased, runs E 75 feet to lot owned by said John Nutt, S 30 feet along Nutt's land to a 3 foot alley which is agreed to be kept open, W 75 feet along the alley that joins lot owned by William Campbell to Front Street, & N 30 feet on Front Street to first station; sold (no date) by late John Forster (of Wilmington) to John Nutt; it agreed that the said 3 foot alley formerly owned by John Nutt shall be kept open for mutual benefit of "both" parties. (signed) John Nutt & A J DeRossett; (witness) Richd Bradley [only one witness]; [note at end indicates Nutt received £700]; wit. oath Aug. 1792 by Richd Bradley; Sept. 2, 1792 recorded; book K p. 199.

2801. Aug. 23, 1792 Henry Toomer, merchant, & wife Magdalen Mary (Wilmington, NC) Armand John DeRossett, doctor of physic (same); for £150 sold [part of a lot (no number)] on N side of Market Street & W side of Third Street in Wilmington; border: begins at corner of Market Street & Third Street, runs W 30 feet down Market Street, N 132 feet parallel to Third Street, E 30 feet parallel with Market Street, & S 132 feet on Third Street to beginning; sold May 1, 1754 by Caleb Grainger & wife Mary to John Campbell who willed it to Mary Hanson then his wife Mary Campbell and his daughters Mary Campbell & Rachel Campbell who sold Jul. 7, 1788 to Henry Toomer. (signed) Henry Toomer & M M Toomer; (witness) Wm Nutt [only one witness]; [note at end indicates DeRossett paid Toomer £150]; wit. oath Aug. 1792 by William Nutt; Sept. 2, 1792 recorded; book K p. 201.

2802. Jan. 8, 1791 Thomas Craike, planter (New Hanover Co) to John Nutt, cabinet maker (Wilmington, New Hanover Co); for 1200 NC money sold part of lot #206B in Wilmington on N side of Coney Street; border: between Surry Street & Front Street, joined on W by Surry Street, on S by Coney Street, E by Front Street, N by lot owned by said John Nutt, 66 feet on Surry Street, 330 feet on Coney Street, & 66 feet on Front Street; sold May 10, 1737 by James Wimble to James Shirley deceased and sold Nov. 18, 1738 by Ann Shirley, devisee of James Shirley, to Roger Moore esq deceased who willed it to George & William Moore and sold by Frederick Jones the younger & John Moore, executors of George Moore esq deceased & Roger Moore deceased (sic) heir of William Moore esq deceased, to Thomas Craike. (signed) Thos Craike; (witness) Ths. Maclaine; [note at end indicates Nutt paid Craike £200 (witness) Wm Nutt]; wit. oath Aug. 1792 by William Nutt who recognized hand writing of Thomas Craike & Thomas Maclaine; book K p. 203.

2803. Feb. 1, 1785 Maurice Ward to William Ewans; for £100 NC money sold 500 ac on both sides of main road from Wilmington to Newbern and between 6 & 8 miles from Wilmington; border: begins at a pine in Job Howe's line on E side of the road & joins Caleb Gainger; formerly sold (no date) by Isaac Ogden to Mathew Johnston. (signed) Maurice Ward; (witness) Dun. MacAuslan & John Allan; wit. oath "Aug. term" by John Allan; Sept. 3, 1792 recorded; book K p. 206.

2804. Feb. 27, 1789 John Wilkinson to Aulay McNaughton & Company; for £250 sold a Negro fellow Sancho. (signed) John Wilkinson; (witness) John Macauslan; [note at end:] Feb. 27, 1789 for £250 we assign Negro "boy" Sancho to John Martin, cooper (of Wilmington, NC) (signed) A "MacNaughton" & Co (witness) Joseph Milne [only one witness]; wit. oath Aug. 1792 by John Macauslan & John Milne; Sept. 4, 1792 recorded; book K p. 207.

2805. Aug. 16, 1788 A MacNaughton & Company, merchants (Wilmington, NC) to John Martin; for £200 sold a mulatto boy Hardy. (signed) A MacNaughton & Co; (witness) John Milne [only one witness]; wit. oath Aug. 1792 by Joseph Milne; Sept. 4, 1792 recorded; book K p. 208.

2806. May 24, 1788 Ann Smith (Wilmington, NC) to James White; for £125 NC money sold a Negro wench Mary. (signed) Ann Smith; (witness) Wm Nutt [only one witness]; wit. oath Aug. 1792 by Wm Nutt; Sept. 5, 1792 recorded; book K p. 209.

2807. Apr. 23, 1789 John Huske to John Martin; for £150 sold a Negro fellow Bristol about 20 years old. (signed) John Huske; (witness) G Duncan [only one witness]; wit. oath Aug. 1792 by Geo Duncan; Sept. 5, 1792 recorded; book K p. 209.

2808. Jul. 4, 1792 David Barlow James White; for £185 sold a Negro wench Nancy & her 2 children [no names]. (signed) David Barlow; (witness) Wm Nutt [only one witness]; wit. oath Aug. 1792 by William Nutt; Sept. 6, 1792 recorded; book K p. 209.

2809. Jul. 8, 1789 John Fergus to James White; for 1150 sold a Negro fellow London. (signed) Jno Fergus; [no witness]; Jul. 1789 acknowledged; Sept. 7, 1792 recorded; book K p. 210.

2810. Apr. 4, 1789 John Mackenzie to John Huske, attorney of executors of Robert Hogg; for 1120 sold 3 Negroes: Betty & her 2 children Ialand [or Inland] & Phillis. (signed) John Mackenzie; (witness) J Fergus; wit. oath Aug. 1792 by John Fergus; Sept. 7, 1792 recorded; book K p. 210.

2811. Sept. 5, 1791 Hiram Jeremiah Richards to John Bleakley, Henry Tucker, & Richard Watson (New Hanover Co); on Jun. 4, 1785 Richards "lawfully" married Elizabeth Rowan, only daughter of late Robert Rowan by his wife Ester; now Richards is about to leave the state; to secure Elizabeth for her life time & after her death heirs of her body "begotten by me" to my real & personal estate due to my marriage AND for £25 sold in trust my interest in any real or personal estate. (signed) Hiram J Richards; (witness) Jona Robeson & Thomas Robeson; wit. oath Aug. 1792 by Jonathan Robeson; Sept. 8, 1792 recorded; book K p. 211.

2812. Aug. 2, 1790 Daniel O'Hara to Edward Jones (Wilmington, NC); appoint Jones attorney at law for me to liquidate "within mentioned demand with" Mr. Stephen Cabarrus and give him good receipts. (signed) Daniel O'Hara; (witness) Rt. Howe [only one witness]; wit. oath Jan. 1791 by Robert Howe; Sept. 17, 1792 recorded; book K p. 212.

2813. Jul. 7, 1791 Moses Treadaway (New Hanover Co) to Isaac Bourdeaux (same); for £80 NC money sold 190 ac on NE side of Buckle Swamp; border: begins at a sweet gum on S side of an island in the swamp, joins a small meddow, & two other swamps; granted Apr. 13, 1780 by Gov. Richard Caswell to Samuel Herring. (signed) Moses Treadaway; (witness) John G Scull [only one witness]; [note at end indicates Treadaway received £80 Jul. 7, 1792 (sic)]; wit. oath Aug. 1792 by John G Scull; Sept. 18, 1792 recorded; book K p. 212.

2814. Mar. 17, 1791 Gabriel Kingsbury (Wilmington, NC) Mathew Johnston (same); John Kingsbury deceased (late of Wilmington) owned at his death "diverse" houses & lots and other estate in said town and willed that it should be sold; John appointed his brothers Demellion Kingsbury & said Gabriel Kingsbury executors; the will was proved; SO for £1,075 sold lot #1 in Wilmington on S side of Market Street; border: 26 feet 10 inches on Market Street, runs back S 71 feet; being one of lots directed to be sold in John Kingsbury will; includes a brick tenement theron & other improvements. (signed) Gabriel Kingsbury, executor of John Kingsbury; (witness) Mar. R Willkings [only one witness]; [note at end indicates Kingsbury received £1,075]; Aug. 1792 acknowledged; Sept. 19, 1792 recorded; book K p. 214.

2815. Oct. 8, 1790 Joshua Grainger Wright esq (New Hanover Co) to Nathaniel Moore Hill, "phisician" (same); for £1,955 sold 195 ac of rice swamp land on NE Cape Fear R; border: between land now owned by John Hill on N & William Henry Hill on S, begins at mouth of Wrays Cr "so called" on NE Cape Fear R, & runs through a swamp & across the main road from Wilmington to Northeast Bridge "so called"; [part of] 640 ac by "old patent" (no date). (signed) Jos G Wright; (witness) James Moore & W H Hill; [note at end indicates Doctor Nathaniel Hill paid Wright £1,955]; Oct. 1790 acknowledged; Sept. 20, 1792 recorded; book K p. 216.

2816. Jun. 20, 1790 Edward Jones, attorney at law (Wilmington, New Hanover Co) to George Hooper merchant and Joshua Wright & George Davis esquires (same); a bond for £5,000 NC money to be paid to Hooper, Wright, & Davis by Aug. 1 next; "by grace of God" a marriage is intended between Edwrd Jones & Mary Elizabeth Mallett, spinster & daughter of Peter Mallett planter; to secure estate of M E Mallett due to will of James Emmitt deceased (formerly of Fayetteville, NC) which at present is in a settlement by "said parties" limited by E Jones on Aug. 1 next (sic) as follows: all the property M E Mallett has claim to in hands of Hooper, Wright, & Davis; property to be used for M E Mallett's sole sue & benefit and not liable to control of E Jones; bond is void if Jones makes settlement agreeable to Hooper, Wright, & Davis. (signed) Edwd Jones; (witness) Dan Carthy & Thom. Anderson; wit. oath Jan. 1791 by Thomas Anderson; Oct. 1, 1792 recorded; book K p. 217.

2817. Aug. 1, 1790 Edward Jones, attorney at law (Wilmington, NC) George Hooper merchant and Joshua Wright & George Davis esquires (same); a marriage is contemplated between Edward Jones & Mary Elizabeth Mallett; the marriage has happened (sic); by bond Jun. 20, 1790 for £5,000 Jones promised to make settlement to Hooper, Wright, & Davis, trustees by Aug. 1, 1790; settlement was to secure M E Mallett's real & personal property to her sole use; property was to come from her father & guardian or any other manner including will of James "Emmett"; SO for £0.10 sold in trust his interest, due to marriage, in M E Mallett's property. (signed) Edwd Jones; (witness) John Blakeley & J B Gautier; May 1792 acknowledged; Oct. 2, 1792 recorded; book K p. 219.

2818. Nov. 21, 1789 Jacob Lewis, planter (New Hanover Co) to my beloved brother Richard Lewis, now a minor or "at least under age"; for natural love & affection gave upper "part" of 200 ac on "& includes" Pursleys Br of widow Moores Cr; border: begins at a pine by a pond; upper part is "agreeable" to running of said [widow] Moores Cr or said Pursleys Br. (signed) Jacob Lewis; (witness) Saml Buxton [or Burston] & James Smith; wit. oath Jul. 1791 by J Smith; Oct. 3, 1792 recorded; book K p. 222.

2819. May 20, 1790 Alexander Riddell [or Riddle], merchant (New York City) to William Campbell, merchant (Wilmington, NC); for £150 sterling sold [blank] ac an undivided half of land with a distillery lately destroyed by fire; border: joins upper part of Wilmington; formerly sold Jun. 1, 1784 by William Campbell to Lewis McPherson who sold Apr. 8, 1786 to Peter Maxwell who sold Mar. 7, 1789 to Alexander Riddell. (signed) Alexr Riddell; (witness) J Mackenzie & Geo Duncan; [note at end indicates Riddell received £150 sterling]; wit. oath Jan. 1791 by John Mackenzie; Oct. 3, 1792 recorded; book K p. 223.

2820. Apr. 1, 1791 William Taylor, planter (New Hanover Co) to James McGufford, planter (same); for £225 sold 494 ac in 4 tracts: (a) 200 ac on head of Bear Br of Long Cr; border: begins at a pine by a pond; granted (no date) to John Taylor; (b) 100 ac on E side of Long Cr; border: begins in his old line 23 poles from his NW corner, joins a savanna on N side of a branch, & joins John Taylor; granted (no date) to said William Taylor; (c) 100 ac on head of Bear Br of Long Cr; border: begins at John Taylor's corner on side of a prong of Bear Br, joins Arthur Mabson, John Stokeley, & a savanna; granted (no date) to said William Taylor; & (d) 94 ac; border: begins at a large pine in his own line near head of Taylors Br, joins a bay pond, John Stokeley, Walker, & John Taylor; granted (no date) to said William Taylor. (signed) William Taylor; (witness) James Gufford jr & Sweeting Bond; Jul. 1791 acknowledged; Oct. 5, 1792 recorded; book K p. 224.

2821. Mar. 9, 1790 Thomas Wright, sheriff (New Hanover Co) to William Campbell (same); for £462 sold lot (no number) in Wilmington; border: 33 feet in front on Front Street, joins lot & house now owned by Henry Toomer, runs back to Second Street, & 33 feet on Second Street; sold due to writ of fieri facias from New Hanover Co Pleas & Quarter Sessions Court returnable to court first Monday in Oct. 1789 against John Foster, in hands of Thomas Craike his attorney, for £1,080 & £5.14.11 costs due to suit by Samuel Donaldson, surviving partner of William Gibson & Company. (signed) Thomas Wright, sheriff; (witness) Mar. R Willkings [only one witness]; [note at end indicates Wright received £462]; Jan. 1791 acknowledged; Oct. 6, 1792 recorded; book K p. 226.

2822. Feb. 20, 1790 Colin McLennan, mariner (NC) to James Ramsay & William Keddie, shipwrights & copartners (Wilmington, NC); for £275 NC money sold a boat or petiagua, in which McLennan has a good & "indefeasable" right, & all appurtenances. (signed) Colin McLennan; (witness) Robt Harley; [note at end indicates Ramsay & Keddie paid McLennan £270]; wit. oath Apr. 1790 by R Harley [or Hailey]; Oct. 6, 1792 recorded; book K p. 228.

2823. Jun. 15, 1790 James Hogg (Orange Co, NC) to Marshall Robert Willkings (Wilmington, New Hanover Co); for £120 sold a Negro fellow Daniel; "lately" sold by James Flowers, administrator of estate of David Flowers deceased (of Brunswick Co, NC) to James Hogg. (signed) James Hogg; (witness) Wm Bingham [only one witness]; wit. oath Jul. 1790 by Wm Bingham; Oct. 6, 1792 recorded; book K p. 229.

2824. Sept. 15, 1791 John Andres sr (Bladen Co, NC) to Thomas Devane jr (New Hanover Co); for £250 sold 640 ac on W side of Black R, below the path from Stephen Andres' to John Hawes', & on "the maind" road; border: begins at a pine in Mr. "Mapson's" line; granted Apr. 23, 1762 to John Andres. (signed) John "Anders"; (witness) Pr. Portevint & E Andres; wit. oath "Jan. term" by Peter Portevint; Oct. 10, 1792 recorded; book K p. 230.

2825. Jul. 5, 1791 Frederick Ward (Brunswick Co, NC) to David Smith (New Hanover Co); for £40 NC money sold 320 ac; being all of the grant on E side of widow Moores Cr & includes mouth of Clayfield Br; border: begins at a white oak by James Larkins' upper corner now Boneham's [or Bonham], joins lower side of Clayfield Br, "main waters" of widow Moores Cr, upper line of said Ward's land, & crosses the creek; half of 640 ac on both sides of widow Moores Cr granted Dec. 11, 1770 by Gov. William Tryon to Anthony Ward, father of said Frederick, and at death of Anthony Ward fell to Frederick Ward, his elder son. (signed) Fredk. Ward; (witness) Bargun Hoff, Richard Proby, & John Harvey; wit. oath Oct. 1791 by Richard Proby; Oct. 10, 1792 recorded; book K p. 231.

2826. Feb. 6, 1790 John Marshall & wife Mary (New Hanover Co) to John Rowe; for £80 sold 100 ac on or near Clifts Br; border: begins at back of said survey, joins Simpson, & "advancing forward" [no more description]; part of survey where John & Mary Marshall live when "said bargained first commenced" by bond Aug. 23, 1774; except timber suitable for sawing for a saw mill's use. (signed) John Marshall & Mary Marshall; (witness) Saml Buxton & John Mashall jr; wit. oath Oct. 1791 by Saml Buxton; Oct. 11, 1792 recorded; book K p. 233.

2827. Nov. 15, 1791 Samuel Lowder, merchant (Wilmington, NC) William Campbell esq (same); for £400 sold part of lot (no number) in Wilmington; border: begins at S corner of Forster's now said Campbell's line on Second Street, runs 50 feet down Forster's now Campbell's line, S 27 feet, E 50 feet to Second Street, & up the street to first station. (signed) Saml Lowder; (witness) Rob Harley & Isaac Golding; [note at end indicates Campbell paid Lowder £400]; wit. oath Jan. 1792 by Rob Harley; Oct. 12, 1792 recorded; book K p. 234.

2828. May 17, 1791 James Walker, merchant (Wilmington, NC) to Thomas Murray, planter (New Hanover Co); for £100 NC money sold 640 ac; border:

begins at a pine on NE Cape Fear R in Patrick Boiling's line & joins Nathaniel Johns; granted Apr. 7, 1752 to Ann Walker and at her death willed to James Walker. (signed) James Walker; (witness) Thomas Younger & James Walker jr; Oct. 1791 acknowledged; Oct. 13, 1792 recorded; book K p. 236.

2829. Jul. 5, 1791 Frederick Ward (Brunswick Co, NC) to Charles Russel (New Hanover Co); for £40 sold 320 ac or all the grant on W side of widow Moores Cr; border: begins at David Smith's orner on "main water" of widow Moores Cr & joins other half of the grant sold by Frederick Ward to David Smith; half of 640 ac granted Dec. 11, 1770 by Gov. William Tryon to "Anthoney" Ward, father of said Frederick, and at his death fell to Frederick Ward, his "eldest" son. (signed) Fred. Ward; (witness) Bargun Hoff, Richard Proby, & John Harvey; wit. oath Oct. 1791 by Richard Proby; Oct. 20, 1792 recorded; book K p. 238.

2830. Oct. 6, 1790 Nathan Crocker the elder, mariner (New Hanover Co) to his sons Nathan Crocker the younger & Lemuel Crocker; for "great" love & affection and for £5 NC money sold part of lot #12 in old plan or #72 in new plan in Wilmington on E side of Front Street; border: between Orange Street & Ann Street, begins at lot formerly owned by late Robert Walker, runs N 33 feet on Front Street, E 165 feet, S 33 feet, & W 165 feet to first station; "lately" owned by late John Gardner (of Rhode Island) who sold in 1773 to Peter Mallett who with wife Sarah sold to Nathan Crocker. (signed) Nathan Crocker; (witness) J Jennings & Robt Hailey [or Harley]; [note at end indicates Nathan the younger & Lemuel paid Nathan the elder £5]; wit. oath Oct. 1790 by Robt Hailey; Oct. 20, 1792 recorded; book K p. 239.

2831. Mar. 3, 1790 William Jones before John James, JP (New Hanover Co), swears: he was present and "was knowing to" his father Evan Jones making a deed to Patrick Boylan for 640 ac now owned by John Boylan & joins David Bloodworth. (signed) Wm Jones & Jno James, JP;
Mar. 3, 1790 "and" there is "just reason" to suppose above deed is lost or mislaid, so William Jones quit claims land to John Boylan (signed) Wm Jones (witness) Jno James & William Ramsey; wit. oath Apr. 1790 by Jno James; Oct. 22, 1792 recorded; book K p. 241.

2832. Dec. 17, 1789 James "Ffoyle" to William Nichols (New Hanover Co); for £130 specie sold a Negro woman Oris [or Orois]. (signed) James Ffoyl; (witness) "Elijath" St. George; wit. oath Apr. 1790 by Elijah St. George; Oct. 23, 1792 recorded; book K p. 242.

2833. Mar. 12, 1790 Richard Quince, administrator of will of Richard Quince sr deceased, to William Cutlar, merchant (Wilmington, NC); for £120 sold a Negro man Isaac. (signed) Richd Quince; (witness) Geo Davis [only one witness]; wit. oath Apr. 1790 by George Davis; Oct. 24, 1792 recorded; book K p. 242.

2834. Apr. 10, 1790 Michl Sampson (New Hanover Co) to William Hall (Orange

Co, NC); for £125 sold a Negro woman Lucy. (signed) Michl Sampson; (witness) William Cutlar [only one witness]; wit. oath Apr. 1790 by Will Cutlar; Oct. 25, 1792 recorded; book K p. 243.

2835. Oct. 22, 1788 George Blyth, "sylver" smith (New Hanover Co) to John Hill esq (same); for £250 sold 213 1/3 ac on "the" sound; border: begins at Fredk Gregg's corner black oak, joins a dividing line between this deed & Samuel Green deceased's land, & on N side of Fredk Gregg; sold Jun. 20, 1768 by Edward Spearman to Doctor Samuel Green deceased recorded in New Hanover Co register's office book F p. 39. (signed) George Blyth; (witness) W H Hill & T Hill; [note at end indicates Hill paid Blyth £250]; wit. oath Apr. 1789 by "W" Hill; Oct. 26, 1792 recorded; book K p. 243.

2836. [blank], 1789 Thomas Wright, sheriff (New Hanover Co) first part, William Campbell esq (Wilmington, NC) second part, & Benjamin Smith esq (Brunswick Co, NC) third part; for £[blank] sold 640 ac on E side of Cape Fear R & both sides of Mottes Cr; border: begins at a cedar post opposite lower end of James' or the big island "said to be" upper corner of Alexander Nesbit's land, runs 400 poles up the river to a pine "supposed" to be in line of late Maurice Moore, & joins Arthur Ireland; sold [blank], 1784 at Wilmington due to writ of fieri facias from New Hanover Co Pleas & Quarter Sessions Court returnable to court first Monday in Oct. 1784 against Robert Ellis deceased, in hands of Robt Shaw administrator, for £150.8.10 & £3.1.3 costs due to suit by William Hooper, James Hogg, & James Burges, executors of will of Robert Hogg deceased; land sold to Jonathan Dunbiben, agent of Benjamin Smith & transferred to W Campbell for £0.5 paid by Campbell to Wright, so Campbell owns the land. (signed) Thos Wright, shff, & Benja Smith; (witness) Mar. R Willkings [only one witness]; [note at end indicates Smith paid Wright (blank) pounds]; wit. oath Apr. 1792 by M R Willkings; Oct. 27, 1792 recorded; book K p. 245.

2837. Feb. 15, 1790 Alexander Rouse (New Hanover Co) to Anthony Millar (Duplin Co, NC); for £400 NC money sold 300 ac on "Topsale" Sound; border: begins at Ludly Cassd [or Cattd] on the sound, runs 105 poles on the sound, & joins mouth of a small branch; granted in 1725 to Samuel Swann "a sqr". (signed) Alexr Rouse; (witness) William Hubbard & Silas Page; Oct. 1790 acknowledged; Oct. 28, 1792 recorded; book K p. 249.

2838. Feb. 15, 1790 Nicholas Fennell [or Fennal], planter (New Hanover Co) to James Devane, planter (same); for [amount blank] sold 89 ac on E side of Black R between James Robinson & Bryant Lee; border: begins at a pine on the river swamp in Robinson's line, near "his" field, & "near" Bryant Lee; granted Nov. 5, 1764 to Jobe Hurson(?) who sold to Thomas Devane who sold to Nicholas Fennell. (signed) Nicholas Fennell's mark "N"; (witness) Thos Devane jr, Thos Devane (sic), & Nicholas Fennell jr; wit. oath Oct. 1790 by Thos Devane; Oct. 29, 1792 recorded; book K p. 250.

2839. Mar. 18, 1790 Jasper Fitzgerald ("Halyfax" Co, NC) to James Brennan (Wilmington, NC); for £120 NC money sold a Negro boy Myles. (signed) Jasper Fitzgerald; (witness) John Campbell & James Brennan (sic); wit. oath Jul. 1790 by J Brennan; Oct. 30, 1792; book K p. 252.

2840. May 29, 1790 Malatiah Hamilton & wife Ann (New Hanover Co) to William Cutlar, merchant (same); for £10 NC money sold a square 0.25 ac on NE Cape Fear R; at Welch tract; border: begins about 40 yards from W corner of land laid out for town of [South] Washington & 50 feet from land of estate of Robert Bloodworth deceased; part of land will be on each side of "the" main road; we agree to keep 50 feet open as a street; includes the houses said Cutlar is now building & "privileges" of timber for improvement of the lot to be taken off said Hamilton's land. (signed) Malatiah Hamilton & Ann Hamilton's mark [backward "P" and "V" OR "V" with loop on left]; (witness) Thos Wright & Benjn Liddon; [note at end indicates Hamilton received £10 May 29, 1792 (sic)]; wit. oath Jul. 1790 by Thos Wright; Oct. 31, 1792 recorded; book K p. 252.

2841. Mar. [blank], 1791 Thomas Jones & wife Mary to John Hill; for £50 sold 2 adjoining tracts: (a) [omitted] ac in Bladen Co; called Black Rock; formerly owned by Berringer Moore deceased; & (b) [omitted] ac in Bladen Co; formerly owned by Berringer Moore who willed it to "said John & one John Davis". (signed) Thomas Jones & Mary Jones; (witness) Arthur Howe & Nathl Hill; wit. oath Apr. 1791 by N Hill; Nov. 1, 1792 recorded; book K p. 254.

2842. Nov. 8, 1791 Thomas Cunningham (New Hanover Co), son & heir of Thomas Cunningham deceased, to Joshua Potts (Wilmington, NC); for $1 (sic) sold house & lot (No number) that I presently occupy on W side of Front Street; where the collector's office is now kept by "him" and was formerly leased to said Potts for 10 years by my father T Cunningham deceased; includes all buildings now erected or to be erected by Potts within the term of the lease; lot to remain in Potts' possession for a year after termination of the 10 year lease from Jan. 1 1800 to Jan. 1, 1801; Potts agrees to build an additional room or chamber on the house for a lodging room & adjoining the second story. (signed) Tho. Cunningham & Joshua Potts; (witness) John Allan [only one witness]; wit. oath "May term" by John Allan; Nov. 2, 1792 recorded; book K p. 255.

2843. Mar. 17, 1792 James Patterson, John Borritz, & Joshua Potts, 3 of copartners formerly of firm of Borritz & Company established in Wilmington Feb. 1, 1785 as per articles of copartnership, to William Borritz, partner of said firm residing in Edenton [NC]; for £1,000 sold their shares of water lot #96 in new plan with a wharf, houses, & improvement in Wilmington; border: joins Cape Far R on W & Front Street on E; being second full lot on S side of "Annes" Street joining corner lot purchased by Robert Wills of John Burgwin; sold Jul. 26, 1785 by James Bradley & wife Anna to firm of Borritz & Company. (signed) J "Paterson", Jno Borritz, & Joshua Potts; (witness) Severin Erickson & L A(?) Dorsey; wit. oath May 1792 by Severin Erickson; Nov. 3, 1792 recorded; book K

p. 256.

2844. Aug. 30, 1792 Archibald McNaughtan, brewer (Glasgow, Scotland), John NcNaughtan, potmaker (Dumbarton, Scotland) & Walter Ewing Maclae, merchant (Glasgow, Scotland) to James Ritchie, merchant (Fayetteville, NC); power of attorney; Auly McNaughtan, merchant (late of Wilmington, NC) died in June last intestate with wife, child, or parent; at time of his death, Auly was copartner in trade with Messrs Colquhoun & Ritchie, merchants (of Glasgow, Scotland); in the copartnership, Auly was managing partner of firm Auly McNaughtan & Company in North Carolina; all real & personal estate that belonged to Colquhoun & Ritchie were, by order of Scotland Court of Sessions Nov. 17, 1791, sequestered due to act of Parliament passes in 23rd year of reign of "the" king called an act for rendering to creditors more equal & expeditious payment in the part of Great Britain called Scotland; Walter Ewing Maclae was appointed by creditors of Colquhoun & Ritchie trustee of the sequestered estate & selection was confirmed by court; SO Archibald McNaughtan & John McNaughtan, "brothers German" of Auly McNaughtan, and Walter E Maclae trustee give power of attorney to James Ritchie to appear in North Carolina Court of Ordinary to procure letters of administration on Auly McNaughtan's estate; James Ritchie to settle the estate with anyone in North Carolina related to company of Colquhoun & Ritchie or Auly McNaughtan company or Auly McNaughtan deceased; attorney can sue or levy to collect money due or take possession of Negroes owned; attorney can sell property if he thinks fit; attorney can hire other attorneys to help; attorney is bound to pay money collected to grantors. (signed) Archd "McNaughton", John McNaughton, & Walter Ewing Maclae; (witness) James Paterson & John Fleming; (Glasgow, Lanoch Co, Scotland) Aug. 30, 1792 James Paterson, attorney at law, before James McDowall, lord provost & chief magistrate of the city, swears: Paterson & John Fleming, attorney at law, saw Archibald "MacNaughton", John MacNaughton, & William E Maclae sign the power of attorney (signed) James Paterson & James McDowall; (Glasgow, Scotland) Aug. 30, 1792 James McDowall, lord provost, certifies James Paterson made above affidavit before me & I know him to be a man of good credit (signed) James McDowall; Aug. 30, 1792 John Lang, notary public (Glasgow, Scotland) certifies James McDowall is lord provost (signed) John Lang, NP; [New Hanover Co] (no date) ordered registered (signed) Saml Ashe, JSCLE; Nov. 19, 1792 recorded; book K p. 258.

2845. May 19, 1773 Alexander McDougal to William Robinson (New Hanover Co); for £30 proclamation money sold 200 ac on E side of Black R; border: begins at a large white oak in the river swamp joining Thomas Land & joins Doanes Br; granted Oct. 3, 1755 to John Roe. (signed) Alexr McDougal; (witness) William Cromerty & John Sillars; [note at end indicates McDougal received £12 part payment May 19, 1773 and £16.8 "in full" Mar. 20]; wit. oath "Nov. term" by William Cromerty; book K p. 265.

2846. May 17, 1773 Alexander McDougal (New Hanover Co) to Duncan Sillers (same); for £100 proclamation money sold 200 ac on E side of Black R about 4 miles below John Andres; border: begins at a hickory near his house; granted in 1752 to Robt Knowles. (signed) Alexr McDougal & Hannah McDougal (sic); (witness) Archd "Sillirs", Thos Corbett, & Ephraim Doane; wit. oath Nov. 1792 by Archibald Sellars; Nov. 26, 1792 recorded; book K p. 267.

2847. Aug. 20, 1791 Thomas Beesly (New Hanover Co) to Jacob Moore (same); for £42 NC money sold 80 ac on E side of Long Cr between Anthony Bourdeaux & James Portevint; border: begins at a pine by the creek swamp & joins James Portevint; granted Feb. 3, 1754 by Gov. Matthew Rowan to Peter Lamb who sold to John Williams who sold to Mr. Swann who sold to Bourdeaux who sold to Baker Bowden [or Bozoden] who sold to Thomas "Beesley". (signed) Thomas Beesly's mark "+"; (witness) Richard Proby, Joshua Penny, & Jas Gufford jr; wit. oath Nov. 1792 by Richd Proby; Nov. 27, 1792 recorded; book K p. 268.

2848. May 23, 1792 Abraham Beesly sr to Richard Proby (New Hanover Co); a bond for £400; bond void if Beesly, before his death, makes a good deed to Proby for 80 ac where said Proby lives and Beesly agrees for Proby to occupy the land as Beesly might do in tending, cutting, clearing, & making use of the land. (signed) Abraham "Beesley"; (witness) Saml Buxton, Wm Marshall, & Henry Holley; wit. oath Nov. 1792 by Henry Holley; Nov. 27, 1792 recorded; book K p. 270.

2849. [blank], 1786 Thomas Devane "minor", planter (New Hanover Co) to James Lee, planter (same); for £30 sold 150 ac on W side of Black R, S side of Devane Mill Br, & on Rattlesnake Br of "said" creek; border: begins at a pine in center of 3 "marked" on E side of Rattlesnake Br, crosses the branch twice, & joins W side of the mill branch. (signed) Thos Devane; (witness) John Devane jr & Isaac "Portivent"; Nov. 1792 acknowledged; Nov. 28, 1792 recorded; book K p. 270.

2850. Oct. 2, 1792 Elizabeth Gurley, spinster (New Hanover Co) to John Futch (same); for £0.5 yearly rent leased for 31 years from today 100 ac at head of Colonel Moore's land on Topsail [Sound]; border: begins at a pine by a gallberry near Benjamin Gurley's house & joins Topsail Road; granted (no date) to Benjamin Gurley and at his death descended to his daughter Elizabeth Gurley; Elizabeth reserves right of cutting & carrying away wood or timber she may want during the lease. (signed) Elizabeth Gurley's mark "X"; (witness) Richard Nichols, Jesse Jones, & Wm Blake; wit. oath Nov. 1792 by Richd Nichols; Nov. 28, 1792 recorded; book K p. 271.

2851. Feb. 3, 1775 Francis Waffers, planter (New Hanover Co) to Arthur Gornto (same); for £23 proclamation money sold 100 ac on SW side of Causeway Br & NW side of John Ashe's land; border: begins at a black gum in run of Causeway Br near said Ashe's line, near Ezekiel Alexander, between Merrick & Alexander, & Bishop Dudley; granted Dec. 22, 1768 to Francis Waffers. (signed) Francis

"Wafers"; (witness) Bishop Dudley, A Haskins [or Maskins], & James Towning; [note at end indicates Gornto paid Wafers £23 Feb. 23, 1775]; wit. oath Nov. 1792 by James Towning; Nov. 28, 1792 recorded; book K p. 273.

2852. Dec. 23, 1791 William Larkins, planter (New Hanover Co) to Sweeting Bond (same); for £12 specie sold 25 ac on E side of Long Cr & W side of James McGufford's Br; border: begins at a black gum in James McGufford's Br, runs S85W "so far as necessary" to make up the complement, crosses "the" back line, runs N85E down the back line to a sweet gum in head of James McGufford's Br, & down the branch to first station; part of 640 ac granted Apr. 25, 1767 to Wm Larkins. (signed) Willm Larkins; (witness) James Larkins & Abel Morgan; wit. oath Nov. 1792 by James Larkins; Nov. 29, 1792 recorded; book K p. 275.

2853. Dec. 20, 1791 Gov. Alexander Martin (New Bern, NC) to Peter Portevint; grant #335; for £10 per 100 ac granted 230 ac on W side of Black R between "Mumpford" Marsh & Enoch Hening's [or Herring] land formerly John Lyon's; border: begins at Enoch Hening's corner pine marked "E H", joins the river, Richard Hening, a bay, & head of E prong of Rooty Br. (signed) Alex Martin & J Glasgow, Secretary; Nov. 29, 1792 recorded; book K p. 276.

2854. Dec. 20, 1791 Gov. Alexander Martin (New Bern, NC) to Ezekiel Hawes; grant #328; for £0.50 per 100 ac granted 100 ac on W side of Black R; border: begins at a sweet gum on the river bank near his lower corner & joins Enoch Herring; includes part of Sugar loaf Hills. (signed) Alex Martin & J Glasgow, Secretary; Nov. 30, 1792 recorded; book K p. 277.

2855. Oct. 1, 1792 Hugh Waddell & John Burgwin Waddell, surviving sons & heirs of late General Hugh Waddell deceased (formerly of Bladen Co, NC), to John Burgwin, merchant (Wilmington, NC); for release & discharge Burgwin from any action or suit of money in law or equity that either of us has against partnership of John Brugwin & General Hugh Waddell under firm of John Burgwin & company or any other firm and any claim against Burgwin as executor of our father or mother or as our guardian from "the beginning of the world to today"; except the money Burgwin, as executor, received for us and whatever Burgwin, as surviving partner of Richard Lyon & company, may collect as debts from Richard Lyon & company due to John Burgiwn & company; excepted money belongs to Hugh & John B Waddell. (signed) Hu Waddell & John B Waddell; (witness) Geo Gibbs [only one witness]; wit. oath Nov. 1792 by George Gibbs; Dec. 1, 1792 recorded; book K p. 278.

2856. Oct. 1, 1792 John Burgwin Waddell, gentleman (Bladen Co, NC) to John Burgwin, merchant (Wilmington, NC); for £1,380 NC money sold a Negro man Hamblet, his wife Celia, their children Hagar, Romeo, & Betty, Negro Violet, Bachus, Newry, a man Jack & wife Armanda, their children Mary, John, Demar, Primus, Sukey, & Cator, a Negro Quaco & Cecile, their children Antra, Dido, Mary, & Clarissa [all ?] now in possession of John Burgwin. (signed) John B

Waddell; (witness) Geo Gibbs [only one witness]; wit. oath Nov. 1792 by George Gibbs; Dec. 2, 1792 recorded; book K p. 279.

2857. Sept. 3, 1792 Hugh Waddell & John B Waddell, sons & heirs of General Hugh Waddell deceased (of Bladen Co, NC) to John Burgwin (Wilmington, NC); for £1,000 NC money sold lot (no number) in Wilmington between Market Street & Second Street; border: 100 feet in front on Market Street & runs back to Mr. Toomer's line; formerly occupied by Mrs. Lord & now in possession of Lawrence Dowey; said lot & buildings were willed by General Hugh Waddell to his eldest son Haynes Waddell who died without issue and it descended to Hugh & John B Waddell his brothers. (signed) Hu Waddell & John B Waddell; (witness) Geo Gibbs & Wm Browne; wit. oath Nov. 1792 by Geo Gibbs; Dec. 4, 1792 recorded; book K p. 280.

2858. Aug. 25, 1792 Rebecca Bloodworth & D Jones jr, acting executors of estate of Robert Bloodworth deceased (New Hanover Co), to William Jones (same); for £5 paid to Robert Bloodworth before his death sold lot #50 in South Washington on NW side of Second Street & NW side of Walnut Street [no more description]. (signed) Rebecca Bloodworth & D Jones jr; (witness) Thomas Finlow & Timothy Wilson; wit. oath Nov. 1792 by Thos Finlow; Dec. 5, 1792 recorded; book K p. 282.

2859. Apr. 2, 1792 Sarah Jones, relict of Wm Jones deceased (New Hanover Co) to David Jones esq (same); for rents & covenants mentioned leased for 30 years beginning today 128 ac on Topsail Sound; known at Porters Creek (sic); border: begins at John Meher [or Mohoe] jr's, Benjamin Mott's, & Thomas Loper's corner pine and joins the creek; part of land owned by heirs of James Watts; with liberty of taking & making use of timber on the land joining said premises as much as necessary to keep the same under a "awful" fence; yearly rent is £0.5; at end of lease, David Jones to leave the land; during the lease David has quiet possession of the land. (signed) Sarah Jones; (witness) Jeremiah Ward [or Hard] & Thomas Finlow; wit. oath Nov. 1792 by Thomas Finlow; Dec. 19, 1792 recorded; book K p. 283.

2860. [blank], 1792 Rebeccah Bloodworth, relict of Robert Bloodworth deceased, to David Jones esq; for £25 NC money sold half of 250 ac on Topsail Sound & head of Samuel Bridgen's line; border: begins at a pine; granted Apr. 20, 1745 by Gov. [Gabriel] Johnston to Thomas Morris. (signed) "Rebecah" Bloodworth; (witness) Timothy Wilson & Maltiah Hamilton; [note at end indicates Jones paid Rebeccah £25 Apr. 2, 1792]; wit. oath Nov. 1792 by Maltiah Hamilton; Jan. 1, 1793; book K p. 285.

2861. Oct. 29, 1773 [13th year of reign of George III] Charles Jewkes, merchant & wife Ann (Wilmington, NC) to John Cheeseborough, planter (Brunswick Co, NC); for £250 proclamation money sold lot #[blank] in Wilmington; border: 20 feet fronting on Market Street, runs 132 feet back, & joins house & lot of Alexander Ross. (signed) Charles Jewkes & Ann Jewkes; (witness) Henry Young [only one witness]; wit. oath Nov. 1792 by Henry Young; Jan. 7, 1793; book K p. 286.

2862. Nov. 4, 1773 [13th year of reign of George III] John Cheeseborough, planter (Brunswick Co, NC) to Charles Jewkes (Wilmington, NC); for £255 proclamation money sold lot #[blank] in Wilmington; border: 25 feet fronting on Market Street, runs back 132 feet, & joins house & lot of Alexander Ross. (signed) John "Cheesborough"; (witness) Henry Young [only one witness]; wit. oath Nov. 1792 by Henry Young; Jan. 8, 1793 recorded; book K p. 288.

2863. Jan. 10, 1778 John Edwards to Charles Jewkes, by hands of Mr. Cornelius Harnet Grainger; for £2,500 sold land & houses; known as home of Purviance's tar House in Wilmington [no more description]. (signed) John Edwards; [no witness]; wit. oath Nov. 1792 by Geo Hooper who recognized hand writing of John Edwards; Jan. 8, 1793 recorded; book K p. 289.

2864. May 23, 1792 John George, George Gibbs, & Robert Gibbs (Bladen Co, NC) to John Gambier Scull (New Hanover Co); for £60 NC money sold in 100 ac New Hanover, formerly Brunswick, Co on S side of Black R; border: begins at upper end of first mentioned bluff near Isaac Hayes' line & joins a dividing line to "the" back line, & "the" line on the river [no more description]; being a moiety of land granted May 12, 1753 by Gov. Mathew Rowan to George Gibbs esq deceased; grant begins at a pine at upper end of a bluff & joins a cove making out of Black R at another bluff. (signed) J Gibbs, Geo Gibbs, & Robt Gibbs; (witness) S Buxton, Wm H Beatty, & Wm Huffham; [note at end indicates Scull paid grantors "within mentioned sum" May 23, 1792]; Nov. 1792 acknowledged by Geo Gibbs (sic); Jan. 8, 1793 recorded; book K p. 290.

2865. Nov. 20, 1773 William Huffham (New Hanover Co) to Edward Spearman (same); for £40 proclamation money sold [omitted] ac on E side of South R; border: begins at a sweet gum in line of John Andrews jr & "Isack Johne's" land on South R, joins a pine above a marsh, & mouth of Thomhawke Br. (signed) William Huffham's mark "M" (sic); (witness) Chas Bannerman & Jacob Warren; wit. oath Nov. 1792 by Jacob Warren; Jan. 8, 1792 recorded; book K p. 291.

2866. Sept. 20, 1773 Joshua Sikes & wife Emery (New Hanover Co) to Edward Spearman (same); for £100 proclamation money sold 400 ac on E side of South R opposite his "other" survey and between Solomo. Huffham & Henry Skibbow; border: begins at Solomon Huffham's lower corner cypress on the river bank & joins Skibbow; granted Sept. 26, 1766 by Gov. William Tryon to Joshua Sikes. (signed) Joshua Sikes & "Amry" Sikes' mark "A"; (witness) John Murphey, Jonathan Sikes, Jacob Warren, & William Lee; [note at end indicates Spearman paid Sikes £100 Sept. 27, 1773]; [another note:] (no date) Edward Spearman obliges himself to pay quit rents from date of the patent on within land (signed) Edward Spearman's mark "E" (witness) John Murphey & Jonathan Sikes; wit. oath Nov. 1792 by Jacob Warren; Jan. 8, 1793 recorded; book K p. 293.

2867. Jan. 5, 1784 Mildred Lyon, executrix, and Samuel Swann & Archibald Maclaine, executors of will of John Lyon esq deceased (late of New Hanover Co), to Archibald Kelso, planter (New Hanover Co); for £13.18.9, being remaining of consideration money with interest, & to fulfil John Lyon's intentions sold 80 ac on E side of South R "a little" above John Huffham's corner; granted Oct. 28, 1765 to Solomon Huffman sr who with wife Mary sold Apr. 22, 1769 to (John Lyon ?); "about" Jun. 9, 1774 John Lyon sold the land to Archibald Kelso for £20 of which £9.3.9 was paid; in his will, Lyon empowered his [executors] to sell his real & personal estate for purposes mentioned in the will; John Lyon appointed as executors Mildred Lyon, Samuel Swann, & Archibald Maclaine with George Seamen Inman, who is in "foreign" parts. (signed) A Maclaine, Mildred Lyon, & Saml Swann; (witness) Edward Spearman & Alexander Hostler "to Saml Swann signing"; [note at end indicates Kelso paid grantors £13.18.9]; wit. oath Nov. 1792 by Ewd Spearman; Jan. 9, 1793 recorded; book K p. 295.

2868. Jun. 1, 1791 John Marshall sr, planter (New Hanover Co) to John G Scull (same); for £100 NC money sold [omitted] ac about 4 miles above widow Moore's old "plantation" on E side of Black R; border: begins at a cypress on the river about 17 poles above the marked stooping birch. (signed) John Marshall; (witness) Ephraim Doane [only one witness]; [note at end indicates Marshall received £100]; Nov. 1792 acknowledged; Jan. 9, 1793 recorded; book K p. 297.

2869. Jul. 27, 1791 George Hooper, merchant, & Catherine (New Hanover Co), devisees of all real & personal estate and will May 22, 1790 of Archibald Maclaine esq deceased, to John Abraham Gasser, house carpenter (same); due to a bond for £400 dated Jun. 4 "last mentioned year", Archibald Maclaine obligated himself to execute to Gasser a deed for part of a lot in Wilmington when Gasser produced to Maclaine a "writing" under hand of George Hooper, party to this deed, that carpenter's work amounting to £200, consideration money agreed on by them, had been performed for Hooper by J A Gasser; since death of Maclaine, Gasser has performed carpenter's work amounting to l200 for Hooper and he is "fully contented & paid"; SO for £200 sold half of lot #73B in Wilmington on E side of Second Street "or" however it is known; border: joins S side of lot where house now occupied by Michael Kenan & John McItheney presently stands, 66 feet on the street, & runs E 165 feet. (signed) G Hooper & "Catharine" Hooper; (witness) Tho Maclaine & William Simpson; [note at end indicates Gasser paid Hooper £200]; dower renounced Nov. 10, 1791 by Catharine Hooper before Ed Jones, JP; wit. oath Oct. 1791 by Thomas Maclaine; Jan. 10, 1793 recorded; book K p. 298.

2870. Mar. 20, 1791 Penelepy Lewis & Jacob Lewis, planters (New Hanover Co) to James Smyth; for £200 sold 100 ac; includes Pursleys Br; border: begins at a pine by a pond & "to ingross" S side of Pursley's Br; being moiety of 200 ac grant. (signed) Penelepy Lewis' mark "9" [or backward "P"] & Jacob Lewis; (witness)

S Buxton & Hapcebeth [or Hapabeth] Lewis; wit. oath May 1792 by Sam Buxton; Jan. 10, 1793 recorded; book K p. 301.

2871. Feb. 12, 1791 John Reardan, merchant (Fayetteville, NC) to Robert Scott, planter (Bladen Co, NC); for £100 specie sold a Negro wench Molly, now in possession of John Reardan at Fayetteville & to be delivered to said Scott whenever he demands her. (signed) John Reardan; Mar R Willkings [only one witness]; wit. oath Nov. 1792 by Mar R Willkings; Jan. 11, 1793 recorded; book K p. 302.

2872. Nov. 23, 1792 William Campbell, merchant (New Hanover Co) to Elijah St. George, planter (same); for £400 NC money sold 2 tracts: (a) 150 ac on New Topsail Sound near Rich Inlet; border: begins at a small cedar at point on NE side of a little gut or marshy cove on NE side of Rush Watts' line, joins SW "or other" side of the same cove, S side of Thomas Morris' "plantation" now owned by his grand daughter Rebecca Bloodworth, head of a branch that comes from said marshy cove; part of a larger tract; & (b) 150 ac; border: begins at NE corner black oak on head of marshy cove on "side" line of "within" mentioned tract, joins John Hodgson's side line now owned by James & David Greer, near an old road, head line of the grant, line of land formerly sold by Charles Harrison to Thomas & James Morris, E side of land formerly owned by Frederick Gregg, Rush Watts, & Clem's Point on the sound. (signed) Wm Campbell; (witness) John Bradley & Dd Jones jr; [note at end indicates Campbell received £400]; wit. oath Nov. 1792 by John Bradley; Jan. 11, 1793 recorded; book K p. 302.

2873. Feb. 23, 1792 Frederick Ward to Marshall Robert Willkings (Wilmington, NC), attorney for my sister Hannah Ward; for £90 sold a Negro wench Patt, formerly owned by my late father Anthony Ward and sold at public vendue by New Hanover Co sheriff due to execution against goods & chattels of Anthony Ward's estate; Patt sold to Hannah Ward & delivered to her attorney. (signed) Fred Ward; (witness) Jos G Wright [only one witness]; wit. oath Nov. 1792 by Saml R Jocelin who recognized hand writing of J G Wright; Jan. 11, 1793 recorded; book K p. 305.

2874. Aug. 4, 1792 Benjamin Larkins, planter (New Hanover Co) to James Larkins; for £50 specie sold 200 ac on both sides of Rileys Cr; half of 400 ac granted in 1778 to James & Benjamin Larkins [reference to grant for metes & bounds]. (signed) Bn. Larkins; (witness) Thos Larkins [only one witness]; Nov. 1793 recorded; Jan. 11, 1793 recorded; book K p. 305.

2875. Jul. 4, 1792 David Barlow (Shatford, Fairfield Co, Connecticut, but now of Wilmington, New Hanover Co) and Silvanus Dickson (Milford, Fairfield Co, Connecticut), copartners, to James Walker, nephew of Major John Walker (Wilmington, NC); for 256 Spanish milled dollars sold 4 Negroes: a man Frank, a woman Hannah, a boy Bilitha, & female child Sally. (signed) David Barlow, for self & Silvanus Dickson; (witness) Wm Nutt & Thos Walker; [note at end indicates Walker paid Barlow 256 Spanish milled dollars]; wit. oath Nov. 1792 by Wm Nutt; Jan. 12, 1793 recorded; book K p. 306.

2876. Sept. 10, 1792 Caleb Nichols (Wilmington, NC) to Thomas Loper, planter (NC); for £0.20 per year leased for natural life of said Loper "about" 600 ac on Topsail Sound; border: joins Ozwell "Scill" [no more description]; includes all Negroes, horses, cattle, & all implements of husbandry. (signed) Caleb Nicholls' (sic) mark "CN" [or "N" with big loop in front]; (witness) Alexr Carmichael, John Nichols jr, & J Lucy; wit. oath Nov. 1792 by John Nichols jr; Jan. 12, 1793 recorded; book K p. 307.

2877. Feb. 9, 1792 Edward Russell, planter (New Hanover Co) to George Logan (same); for £80 sold four-sevenths of 200 ac on "the" sound; border: begins at a lightwood post on SE drain of Ways Pond, joins "the" mouth, head of a branch, head of Moloney's Swamp, a line between Joseph Watson & Thos Cunningham, "the" big hammock on the sound; knows as Tally House; includes the improvements thereon; land was "vested" in heirs of Samuel Marshall, at "that time" he was "of" the American war with Great Britain "enimical" to the American cause & land was confiscated by New Hanover Co court; "some time after" the cause was "relayed" by said court & they reinvested the former rights to said heirs; granted (no date) to John Watson who sold to Jonathan Watson and sold again by John Watson as executor of will of his brother Jonathan to Samuel Marshall and his heirs sold to Edward "Russel". (signed) Edward Russell; (witness) Alexr Carmichael [only one witness]; [note at end indicates Logan paid Russell £80 Jan. 9, 1792; wit. oath May 1792 by Alex Carmichael; Jan. 21, 1793; book K p. 308.

2878. Dec. 20, 1791 Gov. Alexander Martin (New Bern, NC) to James Paggett; grant #314; for £0.50 per 100 ac granted 179 ac on W side of NE Cape Fear R; border: begins at Plenny Fuller's upper corner water oak on the river bank, joins John Allan, & Edward Dickson. (signed) Alex Martin & J Glasgow, Secretary; Jan. 26, 1793 recorded; book K p. 310.

2879. Apr. 10, 1792 Gov. Alexander Martin (Hillsborough, NC) to Plenny [or Plenney] Fuller; grant #339; for £0.30 per 100 ac granted 75 ac on W side of Cape Fear R; border: begins at Fuller's own corner white oak on the river bank & joins Frederick "Gragg". (signed) Alex Martin & J Glasgow, Secretary; Jan. 26, 1793 recorded; book K p. 311.

2880. Oct. 14, 1786 Thomas Wright, sheriff (New Hanover Co) to Matthew Johnson (same); for £60 "spacey" sold lot #231 in Wilmington; border: 66 feet fronting on W side of Front Street, runs W between South Street & Coney Street to a new street called "Surray" Street, 66 feet "from" W side of Surray Street to the low water mark [of the river]; lot is one of "sundry" lots purchased jointly by Bernard & said Majr John Walker from Solomon Ogdin; sold due to act of North Carolina Assembly in ninth year of independence [maybe 1783] allowing sheriffs to sell land to pay debts after 1776 and sold due to writ of fieri facias from Wilmington Dist. Court returnable to court [no date mentioned] against Daniel Benard (of NC) for "eighty odd" pounds "spacey" damages & [blank] costs due to suit by "Mag" John "Waker a sqr". (signed) Thos Wright, shff; (witness) Wm Robinson & Abel Leach; Jun. 17, 1788 acknowledged before Sam Ashe, JSCLE; Feb. 20, 1793 recorded; book K p. 311.

2881. Jun. 25, 1792 Samuel Ashe esq & wife Sarah (New Hanover Co) to William Moseley esq (same); for £200 sold [blank] ac; border: divided from Mr. Maclaine's land by mouth of Hickory Ridge Br, runs up the branch to its fork, straight line to low water mark of the sea, up the sea shore to Cabbage Inlet, up the inlet to the sound, up the sound to its head, down sound to John Guerrard's line, with Guerrard's line to day's Cr, along the creek to "the" river, & down the river to first station; Thomas Musick in his will bequeathed to his daughters Sarah, wife of Samuel Ashe, & Dorothy above land to be equally divided between them; division was done by court order & Sarah owned half; Dorothy "settled" her half on herself & her heirs by marriage "article" with James Augustus Tabb; Dorothy died without heirs & without will, so Sarah became owner of all the land. (signed) Saml Ashe & Sarah Ashe; (witness) Jno B Moore & Henry Tucker; [note at end indicates "Mosely" paid Ashe £200]; dower renounced (no date) by Sarah Ashe before Jno B Moore JP, due to order of court; wit. oath Aug. 1792 by Henry Tucker; Feb. 21, 1793 recorded; book K p. 313.

2882. Jan. 6, 1786 James Bloodworth (New Hanover Co) to Alexander Hostler (same); a bond for £100; bond void if Bloodworth makes Hostler a good title to 400 ac on "Hors" Br of Long Cr. (signed) Jas Bloodworth; (witness) Timothy Bloodworth & Hugh Campbell; wit. oath Feb. 1793 by Hugh Campbell; Feb. 26, 1793 recorded; book K p. 316.

2883. Oct. 31, 1788 Maurice Fennel to James Devane; for £75 sold 89 ac on E side of Black R; border: begins at a pine beside of the river swamp on Robinson's line, near his field, & joins Bryant Lee; granted May 16, 1763 to Job Hudson. (signed) Maurice Fennel; (witness) Thos Devane jr & Samuel Portevint; wit. oath Jan 1790 by Thos Devane; Feb. 27, 1793 recorded; book K p. 316.

2884. Feb. 18, 1789 Margrett Jones (New Hanover Co) to my son Isaac Portevint (same); for love & affection gave 320 ac; border: begins at David Lee's beginning corner pine on E side of Black R; willed to me by John Gardner "squire" deceased. (signed) Margrett Jones; (witness) Chs. Cogdell & W Jones; wit. oath Jul. 1792 by Willm. Jones; Feb. 27, 1793 recorded; book K p. 318.

2885. Feb. 16, 1793 Peter Portevint (New Hanover Co) to Enoch Hening (same); for £15 "spacia" sold 230 ac on W side of Black R and between Mumford's Marsh & Enoch Hening's line formerly John Lyon's; border: begins at Enoch Hening's corner pine marked "E H", joins the river, Richard Hening, Rooty Br, head of E prong of Rooty Br; granted Dec. 20, 1791 to Peter Portevint. (signed) Peter

Portevint; (witness) Benja Robinson & James Devane; [note at end indicates Hening paid Portevint £15 Feb. 16, 1793]; wit. oath Feb. 1793 by Benja "Robison"; Feb. 27, 1793 recorded; book K p. 318.

2886. Oct. 28, 1790 Robert Bannerman & wife Frances (Wilmington, New Hanover Co) to Rev. Colin Lindsay (late of "North Britain" but now New Hanover Co); for £200 NC money sold 200 ac in fork of Black R; border: begins at an oak on the river; granted Sept. 30, 1771 to Solomon Huffham and formerly owned by Benjamin Robinson who sold to said Bannerman. (signed) Rt Bannerman & Frances Bannerman; (witness) John Johnston & Danl Densey [or Dursey]; [note at end indicates Lindsay paid Bannerman £200 Oct. 28, 1790]; wit. oath Jan. 1791 by John Johnston; Feb. 27, 1793 recorded; book K p. 320.

2887. Dec. 17, 1792 William Mosely & wife Margaret (New Hanover Co) to Simon Sellers (Brunswick Co, NC); for £300 sold 320 ac on E side of Cape Fear R; border: begins at a stake at low water mark on "the strand" of Atlantic Ocean, joined on E by Atlantic Ocean, on S by land owned by said William Mosely, on W by Cape Fear R at place known as lower Turpentine Landing "or" Alley Landing where "the" foot path comes down to the landing, on N by land owned by Peter Robeson, Deep water Point above Fort Johnston on W side of the river, & a stake near a branch that divides Hooper's land from said Mosely's; except tax due by law. (signed) William "Moseley" & Margaret Moseley; (witness) Jesse Atkins & Edwd Newton; [note at end:] plat of within premises is annexed to original deed as specified in the deed; Feb. 1793 acknowledged; Feb. 27, 1793 recorded; book K p. 322.

2888. Nov. 9, 1784 Gov. Alexander Martin (New Bern, NC) to John Hawes; grant #204; for £0.50 per 100 ac granted 333 ac on W side of Black R; border: begins at Edmund Hawes' corner white oak, joins edge of a marsh, a "loblolley" bay in a "bad" swamp, McCalep's new corner, & the river. (signed) Alex Martin & J Glasgow, Secretary; Feb. 28, 1793 recorded; book K p. 324.

2889. Feb. 16, 1793 John Erwin, planter (New Hanover Co) to Daniel Taylor, planter (same); for £350 sold 3 tracts: (a) 267 ac on Derby's Br of Turkey Cr; border: begins at David James deceased's & said John Erwin's corner ash [in] the dividing line at said branch, joins Morgan's line near an old tar kiln bed, & head of the branch; part of 640 ac granted Feb. 20, 1735 to Edmund "Rourks"; (b) 89.5 ac in White oak Swamp; border: begins at fourth corner lightwood stake of the patent & joins Samuel Bunting; being westermost part of grant (no date) to Joseph Johnson; & (c) 42 ac between David James' new survey & land he purchased of Thomas James; border: begins at David James' corner water oak & ashe on Derby's Br by "the" main road, joins White oak Swamp, his own corner, Samuel Bunting, & Rourk's upper corner on Derby's Br; granted Dec. 26, 1789 to [omitted]. (signed) John Erwin; (witness) Samuel Bunting & James Fentress; [note at end indicates Taylor paid Erwin £350]; Feb. 1793 acknowledged; Feb. 28, 1793 recorded; book K p. 325.

2890. Mar. 10, 1790 John Hawes (New Hanover Co) to Edmund Hawes jr (same); for £50 NC money sold 333 ac on W side of Black R; border: begins at a dogwood near where Edmund Hawes sr's corner white oak stood, joins edge of a marsh, a loblolly bay in a "bad" swamp, McCaleb, & the river. (signed) John Hawes; (witness) Thomas "Ayrs" & Edmund Hawes (sic); Feb. 1793 acknowledged; Mar. 1, 1793 recorded; book K p. 327.

2891. Aug. 6, 1792 Jeremiah Doane (Bladen Co, NC) to John Hawes (New Hanover Co); for £35 sold 150 ac on E side of Black R; border: begins at a pine at mouth of a small branch at the bluff, joins a pocoson, & the round about on the river; at place called Nelson's Bluff, but through mistake at surveying land is called Five mile Board Bluff; agreeable to a copy [of grant ?] from Secretary's office dated Apr. 25, 1767. (signed) Jeremiah Doane; (witness) Edmund Hawes & John Kirkwood; wit. oath Feb. 1792 by Edmund Hawes; Mar. 1, 1793 recorded; book K p. 328.

2892. Dec. 19, 1791 John Kirkwood to Edmund Hawes; for £120 sold a Negro man Toney about 21 years old. (signed) John Kirkwood; (witness) John "Haves" & James Hendry; wit. oath May 1792 by John Hawes; Mar. 1, 1793 recorded; book K p. 330.

2893. Feb. 27, 1793 John Blakeley, merchant (Wilmington, New Hanover Co) to John Martin, cooper; for £90 NC money sold part of lot 22A in old plan or 31 in new plan in Wilmington on S side of Princess Street and between Front street & Second Street; border: begins at NE corner of John Martin's lot, runs E 13.5 feet on Princess Street, S66 feet on part of lot sold today by said John Blakeley to John Nutt, W 13.5 feet along lot owned & occupied by John Nutt, N 66 feet along back of lots owned by John Blakeley & John Martin "or however it is called"; sold Jul. 30, 1791 by John Hall & wife Elizabeth to John Blakeley recorded in book K p. 60 & 61. (signed) John Blakeley; (witness) John "Macauslan" & Thos Callender; [note at end indicates Martin part Blakeley £90]; wit. oath Feb. 1793 by John Macauslan; Mar. 2, 1793 recorded; book K p. 330.

2894. Feb. 27, 1793 John Blakeley, merchant (Wilmington, NC) John Nutt, cabinet maker & riding chair maker (same); for £90 sold part of lot #22A in old plan in Wilmington on S side of Princess Street and between Front Street & Second Street; border: begins at NE corner of part of lot sold today to John Martin, runs E 13.5 feet on Princess Street, S 66 feet along said John Nutt's lot, W 13.5 feet along lot owned & occupied by said John Nutt, N 66 feet along said of lot sold to John Martin to first station; sold Jul. 30, 1791 by John Hall & wife Elizabeth to John Blakeley recorded in book K p. 60 & 61. (signed) John Blakeley; (witness) John Macauslan & Thos Callender; [note at end indicates Nutt paid Blakeley £90]; wit. oath Feb. 1793 by John Macauslan; Mar. 3, 1793 recorded; book K p. 332.

2895. Mar. 1, 1792 Matthew Sellers & wife Ann (Brunswick Co, NC) to Nehemiah Harris (Wilmington, NC); for £110 NC money sold a Negro man London. (signed) Matthew Sellers & Ann Sellers' mark "X"; (witness) I Bernard [only one witness]; wit. oath Feb. 1793 by Isaac Bernard; Mar. 3, 1793 recorded; book K p. 334.

2896. Jul. 4, 1792 David Barlow to Nehemiah Harris; for $238 sold 2 Negroes Levi & Flora. (signed) David Barlow; (witness) Wm Nutt [only one witness]; wit. oath Feb. 1793 by William Nutt; Mar. 3, 1793; book K p. 334.

2897. Sept. 10, 1792 Thomas Loper, planter (New Hanover Co) to Caleb Nichols (Wilmington, NC); for £200 NC money sold 2 Negroes: a man Will & a woman Fanny. (signed) Thomas Loper's mark ["A" with vertical line through it]; (witness) Alexr Carmichael, John Nichols, & Jacob Levey; wit. oath Nov. 1792 by John Nichols; Mar. 4, 1793 recorded; book K p. 335.

2898. Sept. 10, 1792 Thomas Loper (New Hanover Co) to my well beloved daughter Unity Nichols (Wilmington, NC); for natural affection & parental love gave a Negro woman Tener now in possession of Caleb Nichols. (signed) Thomas Loper's mark "X" (sic); (witness) Alexr Carmichael, Jacob Levey, & John Nichols jr (sic); wit. oath Nov. 1793 by John Nichols; Mar. 4, 1793 recorded; book K p. 335.

2899. Sept. 10, 1792 Thomas Loper (New Hanover Co) to my well beloved daughter Unity Nichols, wife of Caleb Nichols (Wilmington, NC) for natural affection & parental love gave (a) 600 ac on Topsail Sound; border: joins Ozwell Sill's "plantation"; where I live [no more description]; & (b) a Negro wench Phillis. (signed) Thomas Loper's mark "H" (sic); (witness) Alexr Carmichael, John Nichols jr, & Jacob Levey; wit. oath Nov. 1792 by Jno Nichols jr; Mar. 4, 1793 recorded; book K p. 336.

2900. Sept. 10, 1792 Thomas Loper (New Hanover Co) to Caleb Nichols (same); for £100 sold all my horses, hogs, cattle, & sheep now ranging on my "plantation" in New Hanover Co and all my farming & plantation tools now on said plantation. (signed) Thomas Loper's mark "X"; (witness) Alexr Carmichael, John Nichols jr, & Jacob Levey; wit. oath Nov. 1792 by Jno Nichols (sic); Mar. 4, 1793 recorded; book K p. 337.

2901. Oct. 25, 1783 Solomon Ogden, planter (New Hanover Co) to John Walker & Daniel Bernard (both of Wilmington, NC); for £15 NC money sold 4 whole lots & half of a lot in lowermost part of Wilmington between Front Street & Second Street: #226, 231, half of #236 all being water lots & 2 lots behind said 2 whole water lots #227 & 232 as in Joshua Grainger's plan; the water lots run from Front Street to low water mark "or as much farther as said lots generally run. (signed) Solomon Ogden; (witness) Charles Jewkes & James Walker; [note at end indicates Walker & Bernard paid Ogden £15]; wit. oath Sept. 14, 1792 by James

Walker esq before John Williams, JSCLE; May 23, 1793 recorded; book K p. 338.

2902. Jul. 7, 1785 Thomas Brown & John London to Henry Toomer, James Walker, & Alexr Hostler, "Dunbibon's" executors; Thomas Brown (of Wilmington, NC) obtained judgment in New Hanover Co court Jan. "last" against Jonathan Dunbibon deceased & John James for £278.2.6 and against Jonathan Dunbibon for £15.12.6 which with costs amounts to £288.15.10 with interest; immediately after Jan. term on Jan. [blank], Dunbibon mortgaged "divers" land to John London to secure payment of "about" £1,600 or upwards with interest & "soon afterwards" he died; in his will, Dunbibon appointed James Walker, Henry Toomer, Alexr Hostler, & "others" executors; Walker, Toomer, & Hostler proved the will & took up execution of it; when he died, Dunbibon was "considerably" indebt to several other persons; executors want to dispose of the estate to satisfy the creditors, if possible; SO it is agreed by Brown & London and the executors that Brown's executions will issue against goods, chattels, & land of Dunbibon and be divided & sold on 12 months credit with purchasers paying interest; sufficient security to be taken for the purchase money; sale price to be used to pay Brown & London; any remaining money to be used to pay other debts. (signed) Thomas Brown, John London, Henry Toomer, James Walker, & Alexr Hostler; May 22, 1793 acknowledged by James Walker, J London, & Henry Toomer and M R Willkings swears he recognized hand writing of Alexr Hostler and William Bunten recognized hand writing of Thos Brown before Jno Williams, JSCLE; May 22, 1793 recorded; book K p. 340.

2903. Apr. 28, 1787 Thomas Wright, sheriff (New Hanover Co) to Jonathan Dennet Tomkins, merchant (same); for £1,155 sold part of a lot (no number) in Wilmington on S side of Market Street; border: begins at house lately owned by Jonathan Dunbibin deceased now Thomas Brown's property, runs along the street from Thomas Brown's house to low water mark, includes the wharf which is "said to contain" 87 feet, runs 33 feet back from the street to lot owned by estate of John Quince deceased; taken by execution from New Hanover Co Pleas & Quarter Sessions Court held first Monday in [blank] & returnable to succeeding court due to "sundry" writs of fieri facias against Jonathan Dunbibin deceased due to suits by Thomas Brown, Thomas "Handerson", Charles Jewkes, Peter Mallet, Archibald Maclaine, & "others". (signed) Thos Wright; (witness) Mar. R Willkings & Robert Scott; [note at end indicates Tomkins paid Wright £1,155]; wit. oath May 22, 1793 by Mar R "Wilkings" before Jno Williams, JSCLE; May 23, 1793 recorded; book K p. 342.

2904. Oct. 29, 1778 Peter Mallett esq (Campbelton, Cumberland Co, NC) to Charles Jewkes, merchant (Wilmington, NC); for £1,500 NC money sold water lot #71B or #11 in Wimble's plan in Wilmington between Orange Street & Ann Street [no more description]; part of estate of Robert Walker esq deceased and sold Jan. 19, 1778 by Lewis Henry Derosset esq & wife Margaret, daughter & one of legatees of R Walker, to Peter Mallet. (signed) Peter Mallett; (witness) A Maclaine & Alexander Spiers; [note at end indicates Jewkes paid Mallett £1,500];

wit. oath Aug. 1792 by A Maclaine; May 22, 1793 recorded; book K p. 344.

2905. May 21, 1793 Charles Jewkes to Joshua "Granger" Wright; for £300 NC money sold 3 female Negroes: Peg, Foey, & Cloey. (signed) Charles Jewkes; (witness) Mar. R Willkings & Jno Scott; May 22, 1793 acknowledged before Judge Williams; May 22, 1793 recorded; book K p. 347.

2906. May 21, 1793 Charles Jewkes, merchant (Wilmington, New Hanover Co) to Joshua Grainger Wirght, attorney at law (Wilmington, NC); for £1,000 sold water lot #71B or #11 in Wimble's plan in Wilmington between Orange Street & Ann Street [no more description]; part of estate of Robert Walker esq deceased and sold Jan. 19, 1778 by Lewis Henry Derosset esq & wife Margaret, daughter & one of legatees of R Walker to Peter Mallett recorded in New Hanover Co book I p. 343-345 [original copy of book I] and sold Oct. 29, 1780 by Peter Mallett to Charles Jewkes. (signed) Charles Jewkes; (witness) Mar. R Willkings & Jno Scott; [note at end indicates Walker paid Jewkes £1,000]; May 22, 1793 (New Hanover Co) before J Williams, JSCLE; May 22, 1793 recorded; book K p. 348.

2907. [blank], 1787 Janet McAlister, spouse of "Daneld" McAlister deceased, to Charles McAlister (Bladen Co, NC); for £46 NC money sold 100 ac on E side of Black R; border: joins John Marshall's land on Colvins Cr [no more description]. (signed) book "Jennat" McAlister's mark "X"; (witness) Hugh Murphy & Robert Murphy; wit. oath Feb. 1792 by Robert Murphy; May 23, 1793 recorded; K p. 351.

2908. May 3, 1792 Thomas Wright, sheriff (New Hanover Co) & Henry Toomer, coroner (same) to John Bleakely; for £118 NC money sold part of lot #14 in Wilmington on Front Street; border: begins at N corner of Dubois' lot, runs 50 feet on W side of Front Street, W 138 feet to line of stores lately purchased by John Walker, S 50 feet on E end of said "store or stores", & E 138 feet to first station; and undisturbed & free use of passage or alley from Front Street to the line of said store or stores belonging to Jno Walker "as a common way" between N line of said lot & S line of lot or lots lately purchased by John Bradly; willed by Wm Wilkinson deceased to John Wilkinson and levied on due to 2 writs of execution against John Wilkinson due to 2 judgments against him for £418 or one judgment from Wilmington Dist. Superior Court Sept. term 1791 due to suit by executors of Caleb Grainger for £330 & interest and other judgment from New Hanover Co court Jul. term 1791 due to suit by James Gardner for £88. (signed) Thos Wright & Henry Toomer; (witness) Saml R Jocelin [or Joulin] & Mar. R Wilkings; [note at end indicates Wright & Toomer received £141 "which with sum before this paid" is in full for £418 or full consideration for within (sic)]; wit. oath Feb. 1793 by S R Jocelin; May 24, 1793 recorded; book K p. 353.

2909. Sept. 13, 1792 Stephen Player, gentleman (Wilmington, NC) to James Walker, merchant & nephew of Major John Walker (same); for £40 sold 4,620 square feet or part of a lot (no number) in Wilmington; border: 28 feet front on N side of Market Street, begins 76 feet from corner [blank] of lot that belonged to William "McKensie" where Joshua Grainger formerly lived, runs N 165 feet at right angle to Market Street, E 28 feet to part of lot that belonged to Joseph Price, at right angle 165 feet to Market Street, & 28 feet on Market Street to beginning; sold Apr. 6, 1771 by James Crane to Richard Player who willed it Oct. 12, 1784 to Stephen Player. (signed) Stephen Player; (witness) Wm Nutt & F Brice; [note at end indicates Walker paid Player £40]; wit. oath Feb. 1793 by Francis Brice; May 24, 1793 recorded; book K p. 356.

2910. Nov. 30, 1792 Solomon Huffham, planter (Orange Co, NC) to George Bannerman, planter (New Hanover Co); for £35 NC money sold 100 ac on E side of South R opposite where Mary Striker formerly lived; border: begins at a water oak on the river bank; granted Oct. 28, 1765 to Solomon Huffham. (signed) Solomon Huffham's mark "H"; (witness) John Corbet & Robert Bannerman; wit. oath May 1793 by John Corbet; May 29, 1793 recorded; book K p. 357.

2911. Dec. 6, 1787 Aaron Moore (Cumberland Co, NC) to James Andres (Bladen Co, NC); for £50 specie sold 500 ac on E side of South R; border: begins at a gum, joins pocoson, Miry Br, & John Sikes; granted Mar. 4, 1774 to Aaron Moore. (signed) Aaron Moore; (witness) Samuel Andres & Elizabeth Andres; wit. oath Jan. 3, 1790 by Elizabeth Andres before Saml Ashe, JSCLE; May 29, 1793 recorded; book K p. 359.

2912. Apr. 7, 1790 William Gordon, sadler (Wilmington, NC) to John Allan, carpenter (same); for £26 NC money sold 528 square "or superficial" feet or part of lot (no number) in Wilmington; border: joined on E by John Allan's lot, on N by "Prices" Street, 8 feet in front on Princes Street, & runs N 66 feet; being part of lot sold (no date) by George Hooper to William Gordon; and "assign or annex" an alley on E part of said lot; alley is 3 feet wide from Princes Street & running 33 feet "North in same direction of the premises". (signed) Will Gordon; (witness) John Brown & Wm Ewans; wit. oath Apr. 190 by Will Ewans; May 29, 1793 recorded; book K p. 360.

2913. Dec. 1, 1785 John Patterson & wife Margaret (Cumberland Co, NC) to Joseph Bland (New Hanover Co); for £30 sold a third of lot in Wilmington on Front Street; border: begins 165 feet S of corner of Dock Street on W side of Front Street, runs S 33 feet on Front Street, W at right angle with Front Street to low water mark, N 33 feet parallel to Front Street, E to beginning on Front Street; John & Margaret Patterson own a third of lot because Margaret is one of 3 daughters & heirs of John Walker, carpenter deceased (late of Wilmington). (signed) John Patterson & Margaret Patterson; (witness) Daniel Patterson, Daniel MacDugald, John Buie, & James Bland; wit. oath Feb. 1793 by James Bland; May 30, 1793 recorded; book K p. 361.

2914. Feb. 18, 1793 James Hogg (Orange Co, NC), surviving brother, sole representative, & heir of Robert Hogg & John Hogg deceased (late of NC), to

George Whitfield & Robert Brown, merchants & copartners (Charleston, SC); for £4,000 Great Britain money sold lot #16A in Wilmington; border: 66 feet on Front Street, runs W same breadth to channel of NE Cape Fear R, joined on N by Mulberry Street, on S by lot owned by Spafford Drewry & Samuel Parish (of Wilmington); formerly owned by Gabriel Wayne; part of lot was sold Feb. 14, 1742 by Gabriel Wayne to Christian Campbell who married William Mackenzie and after his death sold it Jul. 23, 1785 to James Hogg; this part begins 20 feet above high water mark on line "then" called Cuthbert's now line of lot owned by Spafford Drewry & Samuel Parrish, 16 feet wide to the river; On Mar. 9, 1742 Gabriel Wayne also sold all the rest of the lot to Magnus Cowan who sold May 8, 1744 to James Campbell and at his death it fell to his son William Campbell (of Wilmington) who with wife Catherine sold Jun. 21, 1768 to Robert Hogg & John Hogg, late brothers of James Hogg who inherited it as their heir. (signed) James Hogg; (witness) J R Gautier, J L Kirkby, & Galvin Alves; wit. oath Feb. 1793 by Joseph R Gautier esq; May 30, 1793 recorded; book K p. 362.

2915. Aug. 10, 1775 Archibald Maclaine, attorney at law, & wife Elizabeth (Wilmington, NC) to Alexander Hostler, merchant (same); for £100 proclamation money sold lot #111B in Wilmington between Ann Street & Nun Street; border: runs from front Street down to the river, joined on S by lot of late Hugh Waddle esq formerly owned by Col. Edward Mosely deceased; lot was in estate of William Wimble deceased and sold by Arthur Benning, late New Hanover Co Sheriff, to A Maclaine due to suit in Wilmington Dist. Superior Court by Bridget Beatty, administratrix of Bunbury Dy deceased, against Richard Quince, administrator fo William Wimble. (signed) A Maclaine & Elizabeth Maclaine; (witness) Jerom Maclaine [only one witness]; [note at end indicates Hostler paid Maclaine £100]; wit. oath May 1793 by Jerom Maclaine; May 31, 1793 recorded; book K p. 367.

2916. Jan. 1, 1790 James Bourdeaux (New Hanover Co) to Daniel Bourdeaux (same); for £100 NC money sold 160 ac; border: begins at a pine, joins E side of Long Cr, & lower part of said tract; moiety of 320 ac granted Jun. 6, 1739 by Gov. Gabriel Johnston to Anthony Bourdeaux. (signed) James Bourdeaux; (witness) John G Scull & John Bourdeaux; wit. oath May 1793 by John Bourdeaux; May 31, 1793 recorded; book K p. 369.

2917. Nov. 1, 1791 John Wilkinson, gentleman, & wife Ann (Wilmington, NC) to John Blakeley, merchant (same); for £15 sold a "pew lot" #31 in "the" church of Wilmington. (signed) Jno Wilkinson & Ann Wilkinson; (witness) Jno Holdon [only one witness]; wit. oath May 1793 by Jno Holdon; May 31, 1793 recorded; book K p. 370.

2918. Dec. 2, 1785 James Gee & wife Mary (Cumberland Co, NC) to Joseph Bland (New Hanover Co); for £50 sold a third of lot in Wilmington on Front Street; border: begins 160 feet S of corner of Dock Street on W side of Front Street, runs S 33 feet along Front Street, W at right angle with Front Street to low water mark, N 33 feet parallel to Front Street, & E from low water mark to beginning on Front Street; James & Mary Gee own part of lot because Mary is one of 3 daughters & heirs of John Walker, ship wright deceased (late of Wilmington). (signed) James Gee & Mary Gee; (witness) N Campbell, Rt. Livingston, & James Bland; wit. oath Feb. 1793 by James Bland; May 22, 1793 recorded; book K p. 371.

2919. Jul. 7, 1792 John Hill, planter (New Hanover Co) to David & James Greer, "planter" (same); for £250 NC money sold 200 ac on New Topsail Sound; border: between land now owned by heirs of Samuel Green deceased & land formerly owned by Charles Harrison now William Campbell's land, begins at Charles "Harison's" now Wm "Campbel's" corner black oak near the sound side, & joins dividing line between this tract & land of heirs of Samuel Green; being a third of land bought by Comfort Davis who sold to Benjamin Mott; & being a third of land sold Aug. 20, 1738 by [omitted] to Joshua Johnston who sold Mar. 6, 1743 to George Bould who sold Aug. 4, 1744 to William Faris. (signed) John Hill; (witness) Thomas Callender & J Fergus jr; May 1793 acknowledged by John Hill esq; "May 1793" recorded; book K p. 373.

2920. May 18, 1793 Jacob Dubose (New Hanover Co) to Samuel Heron [or Herring], planter (same); for £200 sold 240 ac on W side of Long Cr; border: begins at beginning corner forked gum of the grant on Mill Br, joins an old line, & a stake in a large bay "the" giving line of the grant; includes "plantation" where said Samuel "Herron" lives; part of 640 ac granted Nov. 2, 1764 by Gov. Arthur Dobbs esq to Anthony "Debose" who devised it to his son Jacob Debose. (signed) Jacob Dubose; (witness) John Jones & Jane Reiley; wit. oath May 1793 by John Jones esq; book K p. 375.

2921. Mar. 22, 1793 William Ware (SC) to Mrs. Elizabeth Stephens (New Hanover Co); for £30 NC money sold 0.5 ac on SW side of NE River & "joins" town of Washington; border: begins in back line of town of Washington on E side of Market Street, runs S40W 210 feet parallel with Market Street to a sassafras stake, N50W 105 feet to a stake, & N40E to a stake to first station. (signed) William Ware; (witness) Thomas Dinkins & Jno Abm Gassar; wit. oath May 1793 by John McIthenny who recognized hand writing of J A "Gasser"; book K p. 377.

2922. Feb. 2, 1785 Henry Watters esq (Richfield, Brunswick Co, NC) to Benjamin Smith, gentleman (Blue Banks, Brunswick Co, NC); for £500 NC money sold 200 ac on NE side of NW River; border: begins at mouth of Black R at lower corner stake of land of estate of John Rowan esq deceased, joins Hugh Blanning, mouth of a small creek on NW River about 0.5 miles above Dalison's Landing; granted (no date) to Samuel Watters deceased who devised to his daughter Martha Watters who died under age without issue and land went to her surviving brother Saml Watters, as son & heir of original patentee, who sold to Henry Watters. (signed) Henry Watters; (witness) Thos Neal sr & Mary Rowan; [plat on bottom of p. 380 with same metes & bounds]; wit. oath Jun. 17, 1785 by Miss Mary Rowan before

Saml Spencer, JSCLE; book K p. 379.

2923. Mar. 30, 1792 James Price to John A Campbell; for £85 sold a Negro man Peter; lately owned by Richd Price. (signed) Jas price; (witness) Wm Fergus [only one witness]; May 1793 acknowledged; book K p. 381.

2924. Oct. 15, 1791 James Price to John A Campbell; for £100 sold a Negro boy Matt; lately owned by my brother Richard Price & now in possession of Barnaba Fuller and sold due to Campbell "taking up" my brother's mortgage from Jonathan Jennings for £100. (signed) J Price; [no witness]; May 1793 acknowledged; "May 1793" recorded; book K p. 381.

2925. Aug. 12, 1775 George Moore (New Hanover Co) to my son-in-law Thomas Hooper (same); for affection & for £10 sold 200 ac; border: begins at a gum beside a little creek that makes out of "the" thoroughfare being dividing corner between my land & Roger Moore's, joins "the" high land, & the thoroughfare; part of land in Mount misery Neck. (signed) George Moore; (witness) P Corbin, Maurice Jones, & Maurice Moore; [note at end indicates Moore received purchase money Aug. 12, 1775]; wit. oath May 1793 by James Moore who recognized hand writing of George Moore; book K p. 382.

2926. Sept. 11, 1792 Henry Toomer, merchant, & [wife] Magdalen Mary (Wilmington, NC) to Benjamin Smith, planter (Belvidere, Brunswick Co, NC); for £150 NC money sold part of lot [number blank] in Wilmington on NW corner of Dock Street & Second street; border: begins at said corner, runs W 40 feet on Dock Street to William Claypoole's lot, N 39 feet with his lot parallel to Second Street to land now "or lately" owned by estate of Andrew Ronaldson deceased, E 40 feet with said land & parallel with Dock Street to Second Street, 39 feet on Second Street to beginning; sold Nov. 5, 1790 by New Hanover Co Sheriff Thomas Wright, due to execution from New Hanover Co court against estate of Andrew Ronaldson, to Henry Toomer. (signed) Henry Toomer & M M Toomer; (witness) Jno W Burton; Sept. 11, 1792 acknowledged by Henry Toomer & wife Magdalen Mary & dower renounced by M M Toomer before John Williams, JSCLE; "May 1793" recorded; book K p. 383.

2927. Nov. 22, 1792 Ann Wain, widow (New Hanover Co) to my beloved children John, Margaret, Ann, William, & Thomas Wain; for natural love & affection & for £0.10 sold (a) all my household furniture, cattle, & stock; (b) 60 ac on the sound; sold (no date) by John MacKenzie "in my late husband" John Wain's lifetime, & (c) whatever property I possess. (signed) Ann Wain's mark "X"; (witness) John Erwin & James Robertson; [note at end indicates Ann received £0.10 Nov. 22]; wit. oath May 1793 by J Erwin; "May 1793" recorded; book K p. 385.

2928. Dec. 20, 1791 Gov. Alexander Martin (New Bern, NC) to Samuel Larkins; grant #299 [see shuck #2218 in New Hanover Co in Secretary's grant files]; for

£10 per 100 ac granted 100 ac on W side of Rileys Cr; border: begins at a water oak on the creek bank, joins his own line, & James Larkins. (signed) Alex Martin & J Glasgow, Secretary; "May 1793" recorded; book K p. 386.

2929. Apr. 20, 1793 Anne Hooper, relict of William Hooper lately deceased, & John J Clarke (both of Wilmington, NC) to John MacLellan (same); for 889 Spanish milled dollars "paid or secured to be paid" sold 0.5 ac in lot #7 in Wilmington on W side of Front Street; formerly owned by James Campbell who sold May 13, 1737 to James Murray [reference to New Hanover Co register] and by act of North Carolina General Assembly passes in 1783 land was confiscated & vested in Thomas Clarke lately deceased, John J Clarke, & Anne Hooper then wife of William Hooper "in satisfaction of a claim" they have as representatives of their father Thomas Clarke against estate of said Murray and John (sic) is heir of Thomas Clarke; (b) part of lot #8 in Wilmington; border: 26 feet wide, joins above lot, & being length of said lot from the river except 80 feet next to Front Street; (c) privilege of passage from said part of lot to the street 80 feet wide; sold Feb. 3, 1743 by Magnus Cowan to James Murray & became property of Anne Hooper & John Clarke due to said act of Assembly [confiscation act]. (signed) Anne Hooper & John J Clarke; (witness) Henry "D'herbe" & Geo Hooper; [note at end indicates MacLellan paid Anne & John 889 Spanish milled dollars]; wit. oath May 1793 by Henry D'herbe; book K p. 387.

2930. Jun. 1, 1785 Robert Bloodworth, planter, & wife Rebecca (New Hanover Co) to Edward Pearsall, planter (Duplin Co, NC); for £3 NC money sold 3 lots #47, 15, & 14 of 0.25 ac at Welch Tract on land laid out for building a town known as [South] Washington. (signed) Robert Bloodowrth & Rebecca Bloodworth; (witness) Jno James & William Ware; wit. oath May 1793 by John James esq; book K p. 389.

2931. Oct. 9, 1768 Frederick Door, taylor (New Hanover Co) to John Kelly, hatter (same); for £15 proclamation money sold 106 ac on Lewis Cr, a branch of NE Cape Fear R; border: begins at a may pole at mouth of Old field Br & joins Reas Evans. (signed) Frederick Door & Isabel Door's mark "X" (sic); (witness) Henry Hyrne & John Bourrous; wit. oath May 1793 by Henry Hyrne; "May 1793" recorded; book K p. 390.

2932. May 25, 1793 Robert Stoddard, merchant (New York) & Marshall Robert Willkings, merchant (NC) to Samuel Lowder; a bond for £1,000 NC money; before death of William Stoddard, brother of Robert, he was copartner with Isaac Golding since dead in firm Golding & "Stoddart"; the firm contracted "sundry" debts without the limits of this state; on closing the copartnership, there have been found sundry debts owed to the copartnership; Robert, claims as next of kin of his brother, William Stoddard's share of debts due Golding & Stoddard; Lowder has "bought in from" Robert, William Stoddard's share of the debts due; Robert promised indemnified Lowder for claims by anyone as next of kin & any share of the debts of the copartnership and any private debts of William Stoddard; SO bond void if Robert indemnifies Lower form "all consequences that may arise" from anyone claiming, as next of kin, William's share of Golding & Stoddard and any private debts of William. (signed) Rt Stoddard & Mar. R Willkings [Willkings not mentioned in body of bond]; (witness) John Allan & Robt Harley; [note at end indicates Stoddard received 866 Spanish milled dollars from Lowder Mar. 25, 1793 in full for Robert's share of William Stoddard's part of Golding & Stoddard & all debts of the firm]; wit. oath May 1793 by Mar. R Willkings (sic); book K p. 391.

2933. Jan. 26, 1793 Michael Lobar (New Hanover Co) to Lewis Hynes (same); for £150 NC money sold 150 ac in 2 tracts: (a) 75 ac near Rich Inlet; border: begins at Thomas Lobar's corner stake & small live oak on the sound & joins a landing on the sound; sold by Michael Lobar to Peter Lobar and fell by heirship from Peter Lobar deceased to Michael Lobar; & (b) 75 ac near Rich Inlet; border: begins at Michael Lobar's corner dead pine & stake on the sound, joins head line of "the" patent, & a stake on the sound between 2 guts; sold (no date) by Michael Lobar deceased to Thomas Lobar who sold to Peter Lobar deceased & fell from him to his son Michael Lobar by heirship. (signed) Michal. Lobar; (witness) Elijah St. George & Thomas Hughs; wit. oath Feb. 1792 by Elijah St. George; book K p. 393.

2934. Jan. 26, 1793 Francis Brice to Thomas Simmons; for $180 sold a Negro man Dick. (signed) F Brice; [no witness]; Feb. 1793 acknowledged; book K p. 394.

2935. Jan. 20, 1793 Michael Lobar (New Hanover Co) to Lewis Hynes (same); for £200 NC money sold 285 ac in 2 tracts: (a) 200 ac on New Topsail Sound; border: begins at a hickory, joins Samuel Swann, & head line of the patent; part of grant Mar. 17, 1736 to Henry Bishop & sold (no date) by Thomas Lobar to Michael Lobar; (b) 85 ac on Topsail Sound; border: begins at William Swann's NE corner large gum in a swamp or pond, joins land sold by Henry Bishop from "same tract" to Henry Cooper, & William Swann's land he bought of Thomas Cole; sold (no date) by William Mitchel to Thomas Fenney who sold to Danl Bennet who sold to Benjamin & Elizabeth Lane who sold to Peter Lobar and both tract fell by heirship from Peter Lobar to Michael Lobar. (signed) Michal. Lobar; (witness) Elijah St. George & Thomas Hughs; wit. oath Feb. 1793 by Elijah St. George; book K p. 394.

2936. Dec. 22, 1790 Joseph Tooke to John Ball; for "full satisfaction" sold a Negro Doll. (signed) Joseph Tooke; (witness) Stokeley Sidbuy [only one witness]; wit. oath Apr. 1791 by "Stokely" Sidbury; book K p. 396.

2937. Apr. 30, 1792 Thomas Giddeons [or Giddens] (New Hanover Co) to William Pigford (same); for £50 NC money sold 100 ac near head of Sells Cr; border: begins at a gum by main branch of said creek & joins a swamp; where Thomas Giddeons lives; granted Sept. 1, 1753 to Thomas Murphy who sold to

Benjamin Giddeons & fell by heirship to his son Thomas Giddeons. (signed) Thomas Giddeons' mark ["X" with horizontal line above it]; (witness) Wm Wright & Jacob Pigford; wit. oath May 1793 by William Wright esq; book K p. 396.

2938. Oct. 3, 1792 Thomas Wright, sheriff (New Hanover Co) to William Duffy, attorney at law (New Bern, Craven Co, NC); for £25 sold part of lot #1A in Wilmington on N side of market Street; border: 31 feet front on Market Street, runs back 66 feet from the street, joined on E by land lately owned by Thomas Maclaine now deceased, on N by lot formerly owned by Alexander Duncan, & on W by house & land of John Moran; presently occupied by John Mauger & Peter "Mangeon"; sold Aug. 25, 1783 by Joseph Eagles & wife Sarah to Marshall Robert Willkings who sold Nov. 6, 1784 to Jonathan Tomkins who sold in 2 deeds Dec. 9, 1785 & Apr. 11, 1789 to John Mauger with two-thirds sold in one deed & remaining third in other deed; sold Aug. 31, 1791 by Mar. R Willkings, deputy sheriff, due to writ of fieri facias from Wilmington Dist. Superior Court Mar. 1, 1791 returnable to court Sept. 1, 1791 against John Mauger, merchant (late of Wilmington, NC) for £3,184.3.2 damages & £8.17.8 costs due to suits by John Dearman & "others" and sold due to act of Assembly in such cases. (signed) Thos Wright, sheriff; (witness) Jos G Wright [only one witness]; [note at end indicates Duffy paid Wright £25]; May 17, 1793 acknowledged before Jno Williams, JSCLE; book K p. 398.

2939. Mar. 10, 1793 Charles Jewkes, merchant (Wilmington, NC) to John Burgwin, merchant (same); Jewkes signed a bond yesterday to Burgwin for £5,000 sterling Great Britain money conditioned on payment of £2,250 British sterling or "as much of any other monies" as will purchase good bills of exchange of London at the time specified; to secure payment & for £0.5 sterling sold (a) lot "or lots" in Wilmington; known as Jewkes' lots [wharf--lined out] between house & lot Jewkes purchased of Peter Mallett & lot now owned by Col. Thomas Brown on which said lots are brick buildings, warehouses occupied by Charles Jewkes with brick buildings, stores, out houses, & wharf erected on said lot; (b) a water lot 66 2/3 feet [wide ?] formerly owned by late William Purviance esq who mortgaged it to John Edwards & company (of Charleston {SC}) who sold to Charles Jewkes; (c) lot & store in Wilmington presently occupied by Jno MacLellan & in his possession; includes any buildings on any of the lots; sale void if Jewkes pays Burgwin £1,000 sterling Great Britain money by Jan. 1, 1795 with interest from Feb. 10 last and all other sums of the £2,250 that are due on Jan. 1, 1795 over said £1,000; until default, Jewkes can enjoy the premises & receive rent & profit from it. (signed) Charles Jewkes; (witness) Saml R Jocelin & Jno B Waddle; wit. oath May 27, 1793 by Jno B Waddle before Jno Williams, JSCLE: book K p. 402.

2940. Mar. 10, 1793 Charles Jewkes, merchant (Wilmington, NC) to John Burgwin, merchant (same); Jewkes signed a bond yesterday to Burgin for £5,000 sterling Great Britain money conditioned on payment of £2,250 British sterling or "as much of any other monies" as will purchase good bills of exchange of London at the time specified; to secure payment & for £0.5 sterling sold all his interest in 640 ac on W side of NW River in Bladen Co; known ad Porters Neck; sold (no date) by Bladen Co sheriff to late Col. Hugh Waddle who sold to Henry Graham and it descended to his eldest son & heir Faithfull Graham and sold by Bladen Co Sheriff William Smith to Charles Jewkes due to writ from [date & amount blank] Wilmington Dist. Superior Court due to suit against Faithfull Graham by John Burgwin, Henry Humphries, & Charles Jewkes, merchant & copartners ("formerly" of Wilmington); sale void if Jewkes pays Burgwin £1,000 sterling by Jan. 1, 1795 with interest from Jan. 10 last; until default, Jewkes can enjoy the premises & receive rent & profit from it. (signed) Charles Jewkes; (witness) Saml R "Jocelyn" & John B Waddle; wit. oath May 27, 1793 by Jno R Waddle before Jno Williams, JSCLE; book K p. 405.

2941. Nov. 26, 1789 Gov. Samuel Johnston (Fayetteville, NC) to James Anderson; grant #264; for £10 per 100 ac granted 200 ac on E side of South R; border: begins at Isaiah Sikes' corner oak on the river, near James Anderson, & Bannerman. (signed) Samuel Johnston & J Glasgow, Secretary; book K p. 408.

2942. Nov. 26, 1789 Gov. Samuel Johnston (Fayetteville, NC) to James Andres; grant #265 [see shuck 2178 New Hanover Co in Secretary's grant files]; for £10 per 100 ac granted 200 ac on E side of South R; border: begins at a pine beside Miry Branch Bay opposite Aaron Moore's survey, joins head of Stephen Andres Mill Cr, & swamp of Miry Br. (signed) Samuel Johnston & J Glasgow, Secretary; book K p. 409.

2943. Dec. 20, 1791 Gov. Alexander Martin (New Bern, NC) to Moses Ritter; grant #313 [see shuck #2232 in Secretary's grant files]; for £10 per 100 ac granted 100 ac on E side of widow Moores Cr and between Thos Lewis & Moses Ritter; border: begins at a pine on said Ritter's line, joins a meadow, & a stake "in the bay called" Cuffies Point. (signed) Alexander Martin & J Glasgow, Secretary; book K p. 410.

2944. Dec. 20, 1791 Gov. Alexander Martin (New Bern, NC) to Moses Ritter; grant #313 [sic, 312 see shuck #2231 in Secretary's grant files]; for £10 per 100 ac granted 100 ac on E side of widow Moores Cr and both sides of Poplar Br; border: begins at a pine on his own line. (signed) Alexander Martin & J Glasgow, Secretary; book K p. 411.

2945. Feb. 12, 1793 Fredk. Jones to John Jones esq; for £142 sold a Negro fellow Willey now in possession of said John Jones. (signed) Fredk, Jones; [no witness]; wit. oath May 1793 Jno Hill esq who recognized hand writing of Fredk. Jones esq; book K p. 412.

2946. Mar. 31, 1792 J R Gautier to William Campbell esq; for £1,101 sold & delivered to him following Negroes: old Quaw, young Quaw, Dick, Robbin, cooper Jim, Amey, Die, Bookey, Rose, Ned, Franky, Patience, Phillida & her child Tunah. (signed) J R Gautier; (witness) William Richardson [only one witness]; May 1793 acknowledged; book K p. 413.

2947. Jun. 1, 1793 George Davis esq to William Campbell esq; for £120 sold a Negro man Joe. (signed) Geo Davis; [no witness]; May 1793 acknowledged; book K p. 413.

2948. May 14, 1793 Thomas Woodward to John Erwin; for [amount omitted] sold a Negro man Cato. (signed) Thos Woodward; (witness) Elijah St. George [only one witness]; [note at end indicates Woodward received £85 May 14, 1793 for Negro man Cato]; wit. oath May 1793 by Elijah St. George; book K p. 413.

2949. Mar. 5, 1792 James Fleming, planter, & wife Christian (Bladen Co, NC) to Henry Toomer, merchant (New Hanover Co); for £40 NC money sold 1 ac on W side of NE Cape Fear R opposite Wilmington; border: joined on upper side by land formerly owned by Thomas Clarke, 6 "roods" in front on the river, & runs back "for the compliment"; sold Jun. 22, 1784 Brunswick Co Sheriff John Cains to James Fleming, due to writ of fieri facias from New Hanover Co Pleas & Quarter Sessions Court, & recorded in Brunswick Co register's office. (signed) Jas Fleming; (witness) Heny. Tucker "for James Fleming's signature" [only one witness]; [note at end indicates Toomer paid "Fleeming" £40]; Wit. oath Aug. 1792 by Henry Tucker; book K p. 414.

2950. Oct. 29, 1787 Gov. Richard Caswell (Kingston, NC) to Samuel Bunting; grant #252; for £0.50 per 100 ac granted 60 ac; border: begins at corner "maypole" of Fredk Jones' upper tract, joins Fredk Jones' lower tract, & a clear water branch. (signed) Rd Caswell & W Williams, D Secretary; book K p. 416.

2951. Jan. 19, 1790 Jonathan Robeson [or Robinson], gentleman, & wife Latitia Kitty (New Hanover Co) to William Henry Halsey & Ann Sophia Halsey (same); for £250 NC money sold part of a lot (no number) in Wilmington; border: begins at SW corner of Dock Street & Second Street, runs 36 feet on Dock Street, & 66 feet on Second Street "or howsoever otherwise" it is bounded. (signed) Jonathan Robeson & L Kitty Robeson; (witness) Robert Harley; [note at end indicates W H & S Halsey paid Robeson £250]; Apr. 1790 John Fergus esq appointed to obtain dower renouncement of L Kitty Robeson (signed) Thos Maclaine, clerk; dower renounced (no date) by Mrs. L Kitty Robeson before John Fergus JP; wit. oath May 1793 by Robert Harley & Fergus made return of dower renouncement; book K p. 417.

2952. May 14, 1793 Thomas Woodward to John Erwin; for [amount omitted] sold a Negro man Cato formerly owned by James Erwin. (signed) Thos "Woodard"; (witness) Elijah St. George [only one witness]; [note at end indicates Woodard received £85 or full consideration May 14, 1793 for Cato]; wit. oath May 1793 by E St. George; Jun. 8, 1793 recorded; [appears to be same as on p. 413]; book K p.

419.

2953. May 27, 1793 William Robinson (Sampson Co, NC) to Garrett Cumberford (Wilmington, NC); for £161 sold part of lot #6B in Wilmington on N side of Hendersons Alley and between Front street & the river; border: joined on E by John Bradley, begins in Hendersons Alley, runs N 28.5 feet a parallel line from Front Street along said Bradley's line & "thro" center of a stack of chimneys, W 25.5 feet, S 28.5 feet to Hendersons Alley, & 25.5 feet along the alley to beginning; except free use jointly with heirs of Thomas Henderson deceased & Parker Quince deceased of the alley 4.5 feet wide "of" S side of the part of a lot for passage from Front Street to the river; sold Nov. 17, 1785 by John Bradley to William Robinson the elder, father of grantor of this deed recorded in book H p. 432 [sic, 295]. (signed) William Robinson; (witness) Wm Nutt & John Brown; [note at end indicates Cumberford paid Robinson "full consideration" of £157 (sic) May 22, 1793]; wit. oath May 1793 by Wm Nutt; Jul. 12, 1793 recorded; book K p. 419.

2954. Mar. 20, 1790 William Robinson & Thomas Robinson (Sampson Co, NC) to Henry Rooks (New Hanover Co); for £25 NC money sold part of lot [number blank] in Wilmington on Blackmores Alley; border: 13 feet in front, runs back 21 feet, joined on one side by house & lot owned by Wm Robinson, & on other side by "one" owned by Henry Toomer. (signed) William Robinson & Thos Robinson; (witness) Matthew Johnson & Cornelius Hurste; [note at end indicates Robinsons received £25]; wit. oath May 1793 by C Hurste; Jul. 12, 1793 recorded; book K p. 421.

2955. May 8, 1793 John Abram Gasser, house carpenter (New Hanover Co) to Nehemiah Harris, black smith (same); for 350 Mexican dollars sold half of lot #73B [67—lined out] in Wilmington on E side of Second Street; border: joined on S by lot on which houses of Michl Keenon & John McIlhany presently stand, 66 feet on the street, & runs E 165 feet "or howsoever otherwise it may be distinguished"; sold Jul. 7, 1791 by George Hooper & wife Catherine to J A Gasser. (signed) Prudence Gasser's mark "X" (sic) & Jno Abrm Gasser; (witness) John McIlhany & Scedgick Springs; [note at end indicates Harris paid Gasser 350 Mexican dollars]; wit. oath May 1793 by J McIlhany; Jul. 12, 1793 recorded; book K p. 422.

2956. Sept. 21, 1786 John Bradley to Matthew Johnson; for £200 sold upper house I possess in Hendersons Alley; border: begins at SE corner of foundation of the house, runs E 14.5 feet "or more" to Thomas Henderson's corner, N up Henderson's line to said Matthew Johnson's house, W to NE corner of foundation of my house, & to beginning; with full & free use of an alley that runs from Front Street to the river. (signed) John Bradley; (witness) Jno Simpson [only one witness]; [note at end indicates on Sept. 21, 1786 Johnson paid Bradley a promissary note of Benjamin Robinson to William Taller endorsed by Toller for £200 payable Apr. 1 next]; Jan. 1790 acknowledged; Aug. 17, 1793 recorded;

book K p. 424.

2957. Dec. 17, 1791 Gov. Alexander Martin (New Bern, NC) to Plenny Fuller; [#306, see shuck #2225 in Secretary's grant files]; for £10 per 100 ac granted 100 ac; border: begins at a pine in his own line & joins Thomson; includes vacant land within his own lines. (signed) Alexr Miller & J Glasgow, Secretary; Aug. 26, 1793 recorded; book K p. 425.

2958. Sept. 11, 1787 Gov. Richard Caswell (Kingston, NC) to John Kingsborough; grant #260 [see shuck 2107 in New Hanover Co in Secretary's grant files]; for £5,050 specie "secured to be paid" granted part of lot #1 in Wilmington on N side of Market Street; border: 33 feet on the street, runs back 27 feet from the street, improved with a dwelling house 2 stories high; sold at public vendue to act of General Assembly for confiscation of property & confiscated as estate of Daniel Sutherlin. (signed) Rd Caswell & J Glasgow, Secretary; Apr. 1790 presented in court & ordered registered (signed) T Maclaine, clerk; book K p. 426.

2959. Oct. 2, 1792 John Bradley & James Fergus (both of Wilmington, NC) and David Lydig & John Thorne (New York City, NC), executors of Mary Harnett, to Caleb Nichols (Wilmington, NC); Mary Harnett deceased (formerly of Wilmington but lately of New York City) owned "diverse" lots in Wilmington; in her will Apr. 19, 1792, Mary empowered her executors to sell her real & personal estate; Mary's will was published & authenticated in New York City; SO for £415 sold part of lot [number blank] is Wilmington on N side of Market Street; border: begins at SE corner of lot purchased today by Joshua G Wright, runs E 15 feet on Market Street, N 33 feet to a 3 foot alley, W 15 feet along the alley to Joshua G Wright's line, & s 33 feet on said line to first station; sold (no date) by John Rutherford to Cornelius Harnett deceased (formerly of Wilmington) who devised to his wife Mary Harnett deceased. book John Bradley & J Fergus [Lydig & Thorn don't sign]; (witness) Richd Bradley & Thos Wright; [note at end indicates Fergus received £415]; wit. oath Aug. 1793 by T Wright esq; Aug. 29, 1793 recorded; K p. 427.

2960. Aug. 12, 1793 William Davis (New Hanover Co) to Caleb Nichols (same); for 140 Spanish milled dollars sold a Negro boy Albert between 10 & 11 years old. (signed) W Davis; (witness) Alexr Carmichael & Ja Walker; wit. oath Aug. 1793 by A Carmichael; Aug. 29, 1793 recorded; book K p. 429.

2961. Jul. 2, 1791 Thomas Clarke, gentleman (Brunswick Co, NC) to John Bradley; for £50 sold water lot #26 in Wilmington; being a corner lot on S side of Red Cross Street; border: 66 feet on Front Street & from Front Street to low water mark. (signed) T "Clark"; (witness) Thos Wright [only one witness]; wit. oath Aug. 1793 by T Wright; Sept. 1, 1793 recorded; book K p. 429.

2962. Jan. 11, 1792 William Campbell esq (New Hanover Co) to John Walker esq (same); on Jan. 24, 1777 Campbell signed a bond promising to deliver to Maurice Moore esq (of New Hanover Co) a good deed; in his will [date blank] Moore devised his right & property to the land to his son James Moore; about Mar. 14, 1782 James Moore sold the land to John Walker for £250 specie as endorsed on back of the bond; SO for bond to Maurice Moore & for £0.5 NC money sold 50 ac on E side of NE Cape Fear R 0.5 miles "or thereabouts" above Wilmington; border: begins at the river, runs past a large cypress 20 feet from the river "which" is the dividing line between Wm Campbell & John Walker, & joins Cornelius Harnett's now William Shell's line. (signed) Wm Campbell; (witness) Ja Walker & Jno Holden; [note at end indicates Walker paid Campbell £0.5]; wit. oath Aug. 1793 by J Walker; Sept. 1, 1793 recorded; book K p. 430.

2963. Apr. 12, 1793 David Johnson (Wilmington, NC) to John Walker esq (same); for 220 Spanish milled dollars sold a Negro boy Sam, a sadler, about 17 years; old formerly owned by Wm Gordan & afterwards by Henry Toomer who sold Dec. 5, 1792 to David Johnson. (signed) David Johnson; (witness) Ja Walker & Wm Routledge; [note at end indicates Walker paid Johnson 220 Spanish milled dollars Apr. 12, 1793]; wit. oath Aug. 1793 by J Walker; Sept. 1, 1793 recorded; book K p. 432.

2964. Jun. 15, 1793 Thos Callender & Rd Quince jr to William Henry Hill; for £97 sold a Negro boy March; lately owned by estate of Parker Quince deceased & purchased by said Hill at public vendue last month. (signed) Thos Callender, exor, & Rd Quince jr; (witness) J Fergus jr [only one witness]; wit. oath Aug. 1793 by J Fergus; Sept. 2, 1793 recorded; book K p. 433.

2965. Jul. 20, 1793 John Hamilton & wife Unity (New Hanover Co) to William Nichols (same); for £60 NC money sold 115 ac on branches of Harrisons Cr; border: begins at a white oak on S side of Godfreys Br about 80 poles above "the" bridge in the road from Henry Bishop's, joins a tar kiln, Middle Br, crosses Godfreys [Br] twice, joins a swamp, & Topsail Road; part of a grant Feb. 20, 1735 to Charles Harrison and part or about 480 ac was sold to William Morris who sold 115 ac to Wm Nichols and sold by John Nichols "William Nichols' heir as by will from William Nichols" to "his" son John Nichols who sold to Thomas Price who sold to Charles Morris and now owned by John Hamilton who married Unity Morris, daughter of Charles. (signed) John Hamilton's mark "X" & Unity Hamilton's mark "V"; (witness) John A Campbell & Robt Nichols; Aug. 1793 acknowledged; Sept. 3, 1793 recorded; book K p. 434.

2966. Jun. 28, 1793 Benjn. Liddon before Saml Ashe swears: "some time" last Fall or Winter in Wilmington, Mrs. James, widow of late David James, complained that John James had accused her with privately retaining some certificates that belonged to her late husband; I answered I thought the affair was at an end & I understood the certificates were found and asked her whether she had not hear anything of it; she said she had not & desired to know how I came by the "intelligence"; I said it was a matter that didn't concern me & did not give any particular attention or "charge my memory" as to any particulars; but I had heard something of the certificates being found; I had heard Mr. James himself mention he found some certificates or of some being found among his brother's papers; I could not tell what certificates; but either from something I had heard from other persons at other times or for some reason I knew not what, I supposed it was the certificates I had frequently heard were lost; she said it can't be no others than them he accused her with as there was no others lost; afterward, perhaps last February, being again in Wilmington Mrs. James asked whether Mr. James had not informed me he had found the lost certificates; I answered in same words or to the same purpose as formerly recited; since that, on discoursing with Mr. James on the subject, he informs me the certificates were found among his brother's papers were a few small ones that his brother's son Thomas found in looking for the large ones; the small ones he never knew of until they were found; I think these may very probably be the same certificates I heard him mention formerly as I think I formerly heard him mention his brother's son & the certificates some way or other connected in his discourse. Benjn Liddon & Sam Ashe, JSC; wit. oath Jun. 28, 1793 by Benjn Liddon before Sam Ashe; Sept. 4, 1793 recorded; book K p. 435.

2967. Apr. 9, 1793 Thomas Hooper (Stateburgh, SC) to Thomas Hogg Hooper (New Hanover Co); for £3,750 paid by William Hooper esq to John Gordon deceased "as b said Gordon's receipt" sold half of 96 ac below Wilmington; border: begins at upper corner small cypress of John Robeson & Thomas Owens on the river side, runs 80 poles up the river, & joins Eagles Cr; sold Aug. 25, [year blank] by Henry Toomer & wife (of Wilmington, NC) to George Hooper who sold to Thomas Hooper. (signed) Thos Hooper; (witness) Galvin Alves & Thos Anderson; wit. oath Aug. 1793 by T Anderson; Sept. 4, 1793 recorded; book K p. 436.

2968. Feb. 8, 1787 Bryant Buxton (New Hanover Co) to Moses Ritter (same); for £100 NC money sold 250 ac on Poplar Swamp of widow Moores Cr; border: begins at first corner pine of his own land granted to Thomas Moore, joins Jeremiah Malpass, Nathaniel McGufford, & Anthony Ward; includes "plantation" known as Clay Fields; granted Mar. 4, 1775 by Gov. Josiah Martin to James Larkins who sold Aug. 8, 1780 to Bryant Buxton. (signed) Bryant Buxton's mark "B"; (witness) John Jones, Jesse Rooks, & David Jones; wit. oath Apr. 1793 by J Jones; Nov. 1, 1793 recorded; book K p. 438.

2969. Jan. 7, 1786 Thomas Bloodworth (New Hanover Co) to Alexander Hostler (same); a bond for £1,500 NC money; bond void if Bloodworth makes a good deed to Hostler for half of land belonging to the "mills" on Long Cr build by said Thos Bloodworth. (signed) Thos Bloodworth; (witness) Hugh Campbell & John "Kenniear"; wit. oath Nov. 1793 by H Campbell; Nov. 25, 1793 recorded; book K p. 440.

2970. Jan. 6, 1786 Thomas Bloodworth (New Hanover Co) to Alexander Hostler (same); a bond for £160; bond void if Bloodworth makes a deed to Hostler for 640 ac on W side of NE [River] "against" South Washington. (signed) Thos Bloodworth; (witness) John Larkins sr & Hugh Campbell; wit. oath Nov. 1793 by H Campbell esq; Nov. 25, 1793 recorded; book K p. 441.

2971. Oct. 19, 1793 Elizabeth St. George (New Hanover Co) to Elizabeth Bowen; for [amount omitted] sold a dark bay mare branded "I M" & her yearling, a sorrell horse branded "E G", a cow & yearling, a hieffer, a feather bed & bedstead & furniture, an iron pot, a frying pan & skillet, a chest & table, a "barrel" of cotton, a tule [or feele], a water pail, bucket & bowl, 5 plates, 5 knives, 6 forks, 6 cups & saucers, 2 muggs, a sugar box, a pair of cotton cards, "some" leather, a hatchet. (signed) "Elisabeth" St. George's mark "X"; (witness) James Barwick & White Barwick; wit. oath Nov. 1793 by James Barwick; Nov. 27, 1793 recorded; book K p. 441.

2972. Oct. 12, 1793 Elizabeth Bowen (New Hanover Co) to my son David Bowen; for love & good will gave a bay mare, a saddle & bridle, 4 cows & calves, a bed & furniture, & pair of dog irons; but Elizabeth has the "care" of the property until David is 21; if Elizabeth dies, she appoints John Futch & Robert Nichols to take care of the property until David is 21. (signed) Elizabeth Bowen's mark "X"; (witness) Dd Jones & Jno Morris; wit. oath Nov. 1793 by D Jones esq; Nov. 30, 1793 recorded; book K p. 442.

2973. Oct. 12, 1793 "Elisabeth" Bowen (New Hanover Co) to my daughter Cumford Bowen; for love & good will gave a grey mare & colt, 4 cows & calves, a bed & furniture, a saddle & bridle, & all other property I have or may have at my death: Elisabeth to have "use, care, & management" of the property for her natural life; if Elisabeth dies before Cumford marries or is 21 years old, Robert Nichols & John Futch are appointed to care for the property until Cumford is "of age" [21--lined out] or marries. (signed) Elisabeth Bowen's mark "X"; (witness) Dd Jones & John Morris; wit. oath Nov. 1793 by D Jones esq; Nov. 30, 1793 recorded; book K p. 442.

2974. Aug. 23, 1777 John Lyon & Thomas Bloodworth to Alexander Hostler; a bond for £2,000 NC money; bond void if Lyon & Bloodworth pay Hostler £1,000 NC money or make a good deed for following 4 tracts: (a) 100 ac granted (no date) to James Larkins, (b) 350 ac which we bought of James Ratcliffe, (c) 295 ac which we entered in "the" land office opposite "the" mill, & (d) 320 ac "ditto" joins George Moore entered as aforesaid; all the land is on or joins Long Cr. (signed) Joh. Lyon & Thos Bloodworth; (witness) Charles Jewkes & W Sharples; [note at end:] if any of within patents fall short of the surveys mentioned by "running into other lines", it is understood the quantity sort shall be made up by Lyon & Bloodworth out of 640 ac they bought of Soloman Hewit & to begin on Long Cr & run agreeable to patent "in proportion to the quantity" (signed) John Lyon & Thos Bloodworth [same witnesses]; wit. oath Nov. 1793 by William "Sharpeles"; Nov. 30, 1793 recorded; book K p. 443.

2975. Nov. 1, 1793 Moses Tredaway (Bladen Co, NC) to Daniel Bourdeaux (New Hanover Co); for £256 NC money sold a Negro boy Sam valued at £100, a Negro wench Nelly valued at £40, 18 cattle with my mark valued at £54, 50 hogs with said mark valued at £30, 3 feather beds valued at £12 with furniture thereof, a white mare unbranded valued at £10, a chesnut sorrel horse branded "O" on off shoulder valued at £10. (signed) Moses "Treadaway"; (witness) W Sharples & Priscilla Bourdeaux; wit. oath Nov. 1793 by Wm Sharples; Nov. 30, 1793 recorded; book K p. 444.

2976. Sept. 30, 1793 William Mabson, planter (New Hanover Co) to Daniel Bourdeaux, planter (same); for 1100 NC money sold 160 ac on E side of Long Cr; border: begins at a white oak in Gibbs Lamb's line & joins Long Cr; being a moiety of grant in 1738 to Martin Jenkins. (signed) Wm Mabson; (witness) W Sharples & Jas Harper; wit. oath Nov. 1793 by Wm Sharples; Nov. 30, 1793 recorded; book K p. 445.

2977. Sept. 3, 1792 David Jones (New Hanover Co) to Arthur Savage (same); for £100 NC money sold 2 adjoining tracts: (a) 101 ac on Rockfish Cr; border: begins at mouth of Sills Cr & joins Rockfish Cr; & (b) 110 ac; border: begins at uppermost corner water oak of "said" land on Sills Cr in the creek swamp, joins James Blyth, & John Rivenbark. (signed) Dd Jones jr; (witness) F Blake & Wm Jones; wit. oath Nov. 1793 by Wm Jones; Nov. 30, 1793 recorded; book K p. 447.

2978. Feb. 7, 1793 Jacob Moore, planter (New Hanover Co) to Gibbs Lamb, planter (same); for £53 NC money sold 80 ac on E side of Long Cr between Arthr. Bourdeaux & James Portevint; border: begins at a pine by the swamp of the creek, joins James Portevint; granted Feb. 3, 1754 to Peter Lamb who sold to John Williams who sold to Mr. Swann who sold to Bourdeaux who sold to Baker Bowden who sold to Thomas Beesly who sold to Jacob Moore. (signed) Jacob Moore's mark "+~"; (witness) W Sharples & John Rivenbark; wit. oath Nov. 1793 by Wm Sharples; Nov. 30, 1793 recorded; book K p. 449.

2979. Dec. 8, 1792 John Willkings to Marshall Robert Wilkings; for £120 sold a Negro girl Hannah. (signed) John Willkings; (witness) Sam J Thurston [only one witness]; wit. oath Nov. 1793 by Saml Thurston; Nov. 30, 1793 recorded; book K p. 450.

2980. Jul. 6, 1793 James Moore & wife Margaret Moore, alias Lloyd (Wilmington, New Hanover Co) to John Allen, master builder (same); for $116 in silver sold part of lot #31 in Wilmington on "Princes" Street; border: 35 feet in front & 66 feet back, & joins part of lot owned by Col. John Ashe deceased; sold by William Grainger to Margaret Lloyd recorded in book H p. 758 [sic, 715]. (signed) James Moore & "Mgt" Moore; (witness) Ed Jones & John Macauslan; [note at end indicates Allen paid Moore $116 2/3 of full consideration Jul. 6, 1793]; dower renounced Jul. 6, 1793 by Mrs. Margaret Moore before Mar. R

Willkings, JP; wit. oath Aug. 1793 by Ed Jones; Nov. 30, 1793 recorded; book K p. 451.

2981. Nov. 20, 1793 William Campbell, merchant (New Hanover Co) to William Davis, gentleman (same); for £450 sold 220 ac on W side of NE Cape Fear R; border: begins at Walter Ross' lower corner stake & water oak on the river & joins William Campbell; being upper part of survey owned by William Campbell known as White Marsh survey "taken up" Nov. 1, 1729 by Maurice Moore before arrival of Lords Proprietor's orders forbidding sale of their land and sold Jul. 2, 1778 by Thomas Jones & wife Mary to William Campbell recorded in book G p. 518 [sic, 324 & 326]. (signed) Wm Campbell; (witness) Danl Heartwell & Thomas Moore; [note at end indicates Campbell received £450]; wit. oath Nov. 1793 by Thomas Moore; Nov. 30, 1793 recorded; book K p. 453.

2982. Aug. 20, 1789 William Davis esq (Brunswick Co, NC) first part, Margaret Moore, spinster one of daughters of Sarah Moore (New Hanover Co) second part, & John Baptist Moore esq & Thomas Moore esq (both of New Hanover Co) third part; Margaret owns in her own right "considerable" personal estate of Negroes & other effects; a marriage is intended shortly between Margaret Moore & William Davis; this deed is to secure the Negroes to Margaret or people she appoints during joint lives of William & Margaret; Negroes are: Will, Frank, Abigail, Elsy, Rhina, Josey, Hector, Moses, Chloe, Sylvia, Belinda, Walter, Sapphoe, Luna, Lucy, Priscilla, Polly, Henly, Primus, Stephen, Soloman, & Hannah; William agrees with J B Moore & T Moore that Negroes to remain for Margaret's separate use & not in power or disposal of William or liable for William's debts; during joint lives of William & Margaret, profits from Negroes' labor goes to better maintenance of William & Margaret; when Margaret dies, Negroes & their increase go to anyone Margaret wants to give them to during her life or in her will; if Margaret doesn't dispose of the Negroes, then they go to her issue; if Margaret survives William, then Negroes & increase to be in her estate and can be employed at her direction; William agrees to allow Margaret to make an oral or written will devising her separate estate to any one; William agrees that person who receives Negroes from Margaret is to have peaceable possession of the Negroes. (signed) Wm Davis, Jno B Moore, & Thomas Moore; (witness) Fredk. Jones jr & Maurice Jones; wit. oath Mar. 31, 1790 by Frederick Jones before Sam Ashe, JSC; Dec. 26, 1793 recorded; book K p. 455.